"These kids I teach do not read and they really don't read out loud in front of their peers. Since this book has been in circulation, the kids who have never had a positive experience with reading are asking for time in class to read."

- Polly Whiting
English Teacher/Intensive Reading Assistance
Lely High School

"When Travis tells a bunch of teenagers that it all starts out as fun, and the next thing you know, you're getting assaulted in prison, a hush falls over the crowd. He lets them know the reality of drugs – you're either going to end up in jail or dead."

- Chris Walsh, Owner
Inspirations Teen Rehab
Ft. Lauderdale, Florida

"*The Westcoast Kid* is a great read for anyone who really needs to buckle down in life. The book is sure to keep you on your toes while educating you about the dangers of a risky lifestyle. My students, along with myself, felt it throughout the whole book. This story shows you the consequences you will face when you make the wrong choices. It helps you to foresee a future you don't want to live. Good book!"

- Darren Watson
Leadership Facilitator
Youth Co-Op, Inc.
Miami, Florida

Lely 85 #33

The WESTC🍁AST Kid

My Redemption

Travis D. Waters

To Karen - thanks for
your support. Hope you
enjoy the book.

Travis D. Waters

MASCOT BOOKS

Mascot Books
560 Herndon Parkway #120
Herndon, VA 20170
info@mascotbooks.com

Library of Congress Control Number: 2010916413

ISBN-10: 1620861046
ISBN-13: 9781620861042
CPSIA Code: PRT1112A

Book design by Brad Vinson

Printed in the United States

www.mascotbooks.com

I dedicate this book to my beautiful mother, Nancy. If it weren't for her always being there by my side through the good and the bad, I might not be here today. And to my stepdad, O.D., for giving my mom and all of us a better life while growing up.

To my wife, Michele, for helping me get through the difficult parts of writing this book.

To our beautiful children: Travis Jr., Olivia, and Nicholas.

Finally, I want to dedicate this book to my mentor, the legendary Coach Don Stewart. I thank you for always believing in me.

Foreword

I have registered hundreds of little boys and girls for my basketball camps over the years, but this one was different. As I looked down and scrolled through the names, I spotted Travis Waters Jr. My mind immediately raced back more than twenty years to 1983–84, my first year at Lely High School in Naples, Florida. Travis Waters, who I soon found out was the boy's father, was a young man I had coached from 1983 to 1985, and I hadn't really seen much of him since then. I had come to Lely High School from southeast Michigan to become the new boys basketball coach while also coaching football. The football part went very well as football in Florida is a way of life. The basketball? That took a little more time and a lot more effort.

When I interviewed for the job, I was absolutely committed to giving Lely High School one of the premier basketball programs in southwest Florida. Basketball in Michigan is big time. They are very passionate about basketball in Michigan. We wanted to do that for southwest Florida. We made steady progress at Lely, and by my third season, we had turned things around. We had won twenty games, won the district, and hosted St. Petersburg Boca Ciega for the regional championship in front of an overflow crowd at Lely High School. This quick turnaround of basketball fortunes was because of young men like Travis. To be honest, he was the key, a long-legged, tall, skinny kid who I convinced help me make basketball at Lely High School something the whole community could be proud of. It didn't take much convincing. Travis, like a lot of young people in southwest Florida, was born someplace else. North Carolina was his home state and he brought the same enthusiasm for basketball that other Tar Heels share.

Travis was a talented high school basketball player who showed lots of promise. As our team improved, so did the recognition. Travis was an all-county, all-conference, and all-southwest Florida selection. He was voted our team MVP in 1984 and 1985 after leading the team in points and rebounds, and he still holds the record at Lely High School for most rebounds in one game: twenty-seven. He was a very talented high school basketball player along with being the school's first great player.

There was another side to Travis' life, however, that I didn't know about; the one they called the Westcoast Kid. I never knew the Westcoast Kid. The young man I knew was full of promise, had a great passion for basketball, and could have certainly played at the next level.

This book is the story of Travis' life and the mistakes that cost him the chance of living his dreams. It is a warning to others not to make the same mistakes.

The bond between Travis and I, player and coach, is stronger than ever. Most young people—and this is universal—do not appreciate everything their parents, teachers, and coaches try to do for them until later in life. I have recently retired from coaching after twenty-six seasons at Lely High School and a total of thirty-eight years of coaching. Travis and his wonderful wife, Michele, planned a great retirement party for me. All of the players from my first year at Lely came to the party. Some came in from other states. Michele put together a scrapbook to capture all the special moments. Travis sent a basketball all across the United States to have all of my coaching colleagues and special players, such as Deion Sanders, sign it. There is no doubt that Travis, Michele, and Travis Jr. have truly blessed me.

As I mentioned in the opening paragraph, this reunion started with young Travis coming to my camp. He and his parents came to practically every game in my final year. Young Travis always shook my hand and got a hug right before tip-off. We won another district championship, and Travis, Michele, and Travis Jr. were there to share it with us.

I know one of the reasons Travis wrote *The Westcoast Kid* was to educate other young athletes about the dangers of drugs. Travis shares his experiences. His series of bad choices destroyed his dream of going to college and playing basketball. Every young person needs to understand that successful futures are rooted in right choices. This book shares Travis' story about opportunity lost, but I know that Travis' reunion with his old coach one year ago has also led him to think about redemption.

Travis is now coaching Travis Jr. in the youth basketball leagues in Naples. Travis Jr. is very fortunate to have Dad as his coach. I hope everyone realizes that this is a special time and a special relationship. It goes by so quickly, but it is one that we will always remember.

We all make mistakes. We fall down, we get up. We pass on to the next generation the values that sustain us. You are not a winner or a loser; you are a chooser. Choose wisely. I hope this book serves as a warning to those who like to "live on the edge," but also as an inspiration to realize that our mistakes do not have to define who we are and what we can become.

God bless you.

Don Stewart
Head Coach, Lely High School

Chapter 1

January 22, 1967: The youngest of three, I was born on one of the coldest days ever felt in Lenoir, North Carolina. My father, Harold, and my Aunt Ruby were on their way to the Lenoir hospital and had a flat tire. The snow was so bad my father had no choice but to get out and change the flat. Back in those days cell phones didn't exist, plus living in a rural area with not a lot of traffic was a huge factor. As my mother, Nancy, was in the hospital giving birth to me, she couldn't help but wonder where my father and Aunt Ruby were.

My first home was located on Prison Camp Road, named for the chain-gang prison about a mile up the road. The prison is still there. One night, my dad had been out drinking, came home, fell asleep with a lit cigarette, and set the house on fire. My mother, thankfully, got all of us out safely. The house burned to the ground. After this incident, we migrated to Florida.

I have an aunt and uncle who were in the furniture business and they would make deliveries to Naples, Florida, quite a bit. Every time they came back to Lenoir, they would tell my mother that it would be a great place for us to move to. There was a lot of business and it would be a good place to raise the kids. My Aunt Callie and Uncle Larry were thinking of moving to Naples too.

We arrived in Naples in September 1967. My mom's parents, Grandma and Papa, made the move with us. My mom got a job as a waitress at Kelly's Fish House, which was the first and longest-running seafood restaurant in the area where the fish and crab arrived daily from the Gulf of Mexico. My father and Papa worked on Marco Island, building seawalls for the canals that were cut into the land to make room for the northerners who liked to flock to the area to soak up the Florida sunshine and enjoy warm winters.

Our first house in Naples was in a trailer park, now known as Riverwood Estates. It was located on the way to Marco Island, off State Route 951. When I was two years old, we moved into our second home located on Palmetto Court off Kelly Road. This part of town was known as East Naples, and there weren't a lot of fancy homes there. There were a total of sixteen homes on Palmetto Court at the time. The neighborhood was multicultural with Cubans, Mexicans, Puerto Ricans and Caucasians. Our house was an old wood-frame home built in the 1950s with two bedrooms and one bathroom. It was painted dark brown with white trim and the challis windows had ripped screens. Our lawn consisted of sugar sand, dirt, and sand spurs. Those things didn't feel great on your bare feet. Behind our house were two manmade lakes, which were dug for fill dirt. We neighborhood kids simply named these lakes, Lake Number One and Lake Number Two. My grandma and Papa lived on the other side of Palmetto Court. Their house, like ours, was built in the 1950s with three bedrooms and one bathroom. It was small like ours but had a flat roof. It was painted lime green with white trim. They also had landscape made of sugar sand, dirt, and sand spurs.

A favorite spot of mine near my home was Bayview Park. This park was about two miles west of Palmetto Court. Bayview Park was a place to beat the hot southwest Florida sun. It had seawalls, two boat ramps, lots of fishing, a small playground, and public bathrooms. There were chickee huts with picnic tables underneath, so we could sit and enjoy cookouts with family and friends. There wasn't much landscaping nor was the park maintained very well. Grassy pathways were considered to be sidewalks in this area. Looking across the bay at the park, I would see big, beautiful mansions with their large boats tied up to the private docks. I found out that this area, known as Port Royal, was where the rich lived. It was two miles west of our neighborhood. I would often wonder what it would be like to have that kind of money and lifestyle. I could only dream of having a life like that.

There was a convenience store called Del's Wholesale, one mile east of Palmetto Court. Dale, the owner, was 6-foot-6 and weighed 275 pounds. He had broad shoulders, white hair, and wore glasses. He played professional football as an offensive lineman for the Chicago Bears. When he was injured, he retired, came to Naples, and opened up Del's Wholesale which was located directly on the corner of Kelly Road and Thomasson Drive and was open twenty-four hours a day, seven days a week. Dale worked hard trying to provide convenience and supplies in a low-income area where everyone lived from paycheck to paycheck. He was a good man and treated everyone the same. He was also known to help out a lot of struggling families. That was just how he was. Today, Del's Wholesale is in the Guinness Book of World Records for never closing in forty years. Not even during hurricanes.

On Thomasson Drive across from Palmetto Court, a developer built two-story apartments for low-income families. They were painted yellow with tan trim and the roofs were made of brown shingles. The apartment complex had pools and beautiful landscaping as well. It was really nice to look at when you left our street.

To the west of the apartments and across the street from Palmetto Court was a road of lime rock, running north and south. This was an area where the neighborhood kids would hang out. In this area there were homes that were built in the 1940s and 1950s that had metal roofs. The adjacent areas in the neighborhood were covered in dense woods, pine trees, cabbage palms, and palmetto bushes.

My first friends on Palmetto Court were Mike and John. They were what you would call rough necks. We were all the same age. These brothers would always be in trouble with the law. You name it. They did it. They would get caught for stealing, grand theft, or for dealing in drugs.

The family that lived directly in front of my house and across the street was Cuban. They came to the States in the 1960s. Ruben and Rosa were the parents of Jorge, Ruben Jr., and Rufino. Ruben Sr. was of average size, 6-foot-1, and he had black hair. Rosa was of medium build, about 5-foot-4, and she also had black hair. Jorge, Ruben Jr., and Rufino were a reflection of their parents in their looks. Rufino was the same age as me and Jorge and Ruben Jr. were older. I remember Ruben Sr. and Rosa making some of the best Cuban food that anyone could ever imagine. Ruben Sr. would cook pigs in barbecue pits that he constructed. He owned a sod business located off Old Kelly Road.

Across the street and on the south side of where Rufino's family lived was another Cuban family. Chichi was about 5-foot-8 and had black hair and dark skin. He was three years older than me. He liked sports, especially baseball. Chichi's father was a heavyset man, dark skinned with black hair. He was a commercial fisherman and crabber. He would build and stack crab traps behind his house.

Bobby was another friend who lived across the street and on the north side of Rufino's house. He was about 5-foot-10 with big broad shoulders and black hair, and he weighed 250 pounds. Since he was Mexican, we gave him the nickname, El Zappo. Bobby's mom was a heavyset woman, about 5-foot-3. She had black hair, was light-skinned, and wore glasses. She would make, what I thought was some of the best Mexican food in Naples. Bobby was related to the Osceola family.

Jesus and Jorgé and their family came over from Cuba when Jesus was a baby. He and his family lived up the street, directly across from my grandpa's house. We would always stay at each other's houses when we were kids. I liked his mother's cooking and all my friends of Cuban descent liked my mother's cooking. So we would eat at each other's houses all the time.

Titico, another Cuban, was a tall man with a lean build. He was 6-foot-2 with black curly hair. He was about three years older than me. His older brother, Carlos, was a fat man and 5-foot-11. In my neighborhood there were plenty of homes where I could get all of my favorite food, which was truly was homemade Cuban food.

Chapter 2

My first memory of my father's abusive behavior goes back to when I was four years old. My dad came home drunk. Apparently I was making too much noise in the house, and he got angry and threw me up against the wall so hard that I passed out. As I came to, I felt these burning pains stinging my back, buttocks, and legs. I faintly remember seeing something that was long and black flying in the air with a popping noise that I certainly will never forget. That long black thing was my father's belt. He was beating me with it. I suddenly heard the front door shut and there stood my mom, in shock as she saw me with no shirt on and red welts covering me from my neck to my ankles. She looked at my dad and screamed that she was going to kill him. I got scared. I told her to stop or my dad would start beating on her, which he eventually did. We were the only ones in the house at the time. My two sisters happened to be playing at my grandma's house. My father started to beat my mother. I tried to do all that I could at the age of four to get my father to stop hurting my mom. I saw my mom's face turn blue because he was choking her. I ran out the front door as fast as I could up the road to my grandmother's house to get help. I will never forget the sight of my mother lying there on the floor, crying and gasping for breath.

My dad continued with his drinking and the abusive beatings. He was a violent drunk, and he took everything out on us. He was a miserable man. When I was about five years old, my dad lifted me up by the arm and beat me from head to toe. He attacked me because I was trying to get him to stop hitting my mother. I was so tired of his doing this to her that I would try to hit him with anything I could get my hands on—bottles, furniture. You name it. I tried it. As time went on, he became more violent and even angrier.

Even though I had a turbulent life at home, I tried to act normally, especially around my friends.

My first experience of being away from my mom for long periods of time was when I started kindergarten. On my first day of school I boarded the bus with all the other kids, but before the driver could close the doors, I jumped up, ran off the bus, down the street, and into the woods. I went to my grandma's house to hide under the bed. I was a really shy kid. My kindergarten school was uptown, a long way from home. Uptown was known for being where the rich people by the beach lived. They dressed and talked better than I did and I felt that I didn't fit in with their kids. My mom would walk me to the bus stop early in the morning before the sun came up. She wore sunglasses to hide her black eyes. All my friends would ask me why my mother wore sunglasses when it was still dark outside, and I would just look at them and say I didn't know why.

There were times when my sisters, grandmother, and I couldn't leave my mother alone with our father. We would be scared that something terrible would happen to her. I couldn't stand seeing everyone suffer at the hands of my father. I then realized it would only be a matter of time before my dad would kill my mom. I needed to free everyone from this horrible nightmare.

I can remember when I would be having fun hanging out with my friends, and as it was time to go home, I would begin to wonder how many beers my dad had drank, or when he would start beating mom. The abuse never seemed to stop.

I hated him.

I was watching a movie on television with my sister, Gay. It showed a man electrocuting someone in a tub by throwing a radio in it. This sparked my idea for ending all the abuse. I thought out a plan. My grandmother had a radio on the top of her dresser, which she said I could borrow anytime. The next time my dad took a bath, I would throw this radio into the tub and electrocute him. But before going through with this plan, I had to ask myself, could I really go through with it? What would happen if my dad didn't die? Would I go to jail and be taken away from my mother and sisters? What would my friends think of me? These thoughts were always on my mind. I had a lot of sleepless nights thinking about all of this, plus wondering if I could actually kill my own father. I came to the conclusion that it was either him or my mother, and if I didn't have my mom any longer, I didn't want to live anymore, so it had to be him.

One Saturday morning, after a night of drinking, my dad decided to take a bath. I went into the bathroom and asked him if he wanted to listen to some music. He said yes.

This was my chance to end the nightmare.

I went into my bedroom and got the radio my grandma had let me borrow. I stood there with it shaking in my hands. I decided to sit on my bed. I felt like throwing up, but instead, I started to cry. I couldn't do it. I couldn't go through with it, no matter how much I hated my dad. I put the radio back on the dresser, went outside, and got on my bike. I rode to the wooded area, to a fort that I had made out of old plywood boards I had rounded up from the neighborhood. I went inside and cried. I felt scared and helpless that I couldn't protect my family, especially my mother, from our miserable father. I thought maybe I could muster up the courage to go through with it another day, just not today.

The beatings continued. The local sheriff happened to be a friend of the family. He was well aware of the abuse that my mother was going through over the years. The sheriff told her, the next time my dad went into one of his drunken rages, she should shoot him. She wouldn't get convicted because the shooting would be in self-defense.

I was six years old and the beatings continued. One Friday night, Gay, who was eight years old, and I were at home. Gay was of thin build with brown hair and freckles. Our grandfather would call her Gay Baby because she cried a lot when she was younger. Our cousin, Tana, was with us at the house too. She was the daughter of my Aunt Seretta, who was my mother's younger sister.

I remember my grandmother coming over and getting us. She took us down to her house. We didn't understand what was going on, so we asked. My grandma warned us my dad had been drinking again and he was at my mom's work, Kelly's Fish House. He was trying to scare her and threatening to kill her. He believed that she was running around with someone behind his back. So he wanted to beat and kill her.

My mother left work early and came down to our grandma's house to make sure that we were doing okay, and then all of a sudden we heard a loud banging on the front door. My dad screamed at my mom to come outside. He said she was cheating on him with a customer at Kelly's Fish House. We were all scared. My grandfather happened to be at home as well, and he told my grandmother to take us to the back bedroom. Now, keep in mind my grandfather was 6-foot-2 and weighed 220 pounds. He instructed my mother to get her purse. He looked at her and said, "Now you know what you have to do."

Before my grandmother had a chance to shut the bedroom door, I saw my mother pull something black out of her purse. We were all too scared to cry or even say anything to each other. Grandma, Grandpa, and my mother had a plan. My mother's nightmare was going to finally end, once and for all, at the advice of the local sheriff. He was the reason why my mother is alive today.

There was nothing but total silence, kind of like when you go outside right after a snowstorm and there is snow everywhere and you can't hear anything for miles around. I looked up and there sat the radio that I was going to use to kill my father earlier. I wished I'd had the courage to do it, to stop the abuse a long time before.

I heard my mother screaming at my dad, telling him how much she hated him and was going to kill him. She stood in the front doorway, and my dad stood in the driveway about ten feet from the door. The screaming stopped, and we all looked at each other. It was so quiet that we could hear ourselves breathe. I looked over at the radio again, and I heard my dad say to my mom, "Don't you shoot me, Freck." Freck was a nickname my grandfather gave my mom when she was young because she had a lot of freckles on her face.

The first shot rang out. I thought that my grandpa and dad were fighting. I envisioned my grandfather's head slamming down on the concrete. A second and third shot rang through the air. That wasn't my grandpa's head hitting the concrete outside. The sounds I was hearing were shots from Mom's gun. Grandma tried to keep me in the bedroom, but I pushed my way out and started running down the hallway toward the front door. I was scared and crying, and then I heard the fourth and fifth shots ring out.

I made it to the front door and saw my mother standing there with a smoking gun in her hand. It was a sight and smell that I would never forget. A sixth shot rang out. The sound came from the barrel of a .22 long pistol. It was frightening as hell to see. My mother's gun held six bullets. I walked out the front door to see if my dad was still alive. As I looked at him, I realized I was in total shock. My father lay in the driveway, wearing his cowboy boots, blue jeans, and a blood-soaked T-shirt. I noticed that he was still breathing. It was getting dark and all the neighbors were coming out of their homes. In the distance I could hear police sirens and an ambulance. I looked over at my mom and saw her standing there with the smoking gun. She was crying, telling me that it was finally over.

It was like a scene out of a movie. My dad was put on a stretcher and into an ambulance while my mother was handcuffed and put into the back of a police car. After everyone had gone to the hospital and the police station, I just stood there watching the police wash my dad's blood off the driveway. I didn't want to stay at my grandma's house that night. I wanted to stay at home. I began to wonder if my father was going to survive and if my mother would be able to come home to us. I started crying and didn't stop all night. I couldn't get the night's events out of my head.

When I woke up the next morning I discovered that all the neighborhood kids who had played in the road and in their yards and who were my friends before any of this had happened now wouldn't talk to me. They left the street and their yards and went inside their homes. It looked like a ghost town. My mom was still in police custody and didn't have any bond until the investigation was finished. My grandma's driveway was stained with my dad's blood from the night before. It was a reminder of what had happened.

My grandmother told us my dad had suffered gunshot wounds to his chest, stomach, head, leg, and arm. He had been shot six times and had lost a lot of blood but had survived. After three days, my mother was released from jail. It was ruled as self-defense. The court ordered my dad to move out of the state, so he headed back to North Carolina. A part of me was sad that it had to end this way, but he deserved what he got. For years all of us worried he would come back to Naples to try and kill my mom.

I still have nightmares. It's something I'll never get over, no matter how much I try.

Chapter 3

After everything my family had gone through, time helped us to get better and to move on with everyday life. My mom continued to work at Kelly's Fish House, and I started first grade at Avalon Elementary, which was only two miles from my home. I could either ride my bike or walk to school. I really liked school a lot. The kids who went to this school were from the surrounding neighborhoods, and I felt I was fitting in. During recess I would play marbles with my friends, and we would play for keeps and money. It wasn't much, just twenty-five or fifty cents. I would lose all the time, so I started to practice with my older friends at home after school. I wanted to be like the rest of the kids at school. We would go to Del's Wholesale after school and buy sodas, Big John sausages, pickled eggs, and chips and play video games. I started getting better at playing marbles, so I won money to hang out with the kid's at Del's after school.

A couple of years went by. I was in the third grade when my mom started to date a man I didn't like or trust. Because of what had happened with my dad, I didn't trust men at all. His name was O.D. and in the 1970s he started his own lumber company, Naples Lumber and Supply Company. My Uncle Gary, my mom's brother, knew him when they worked at a local lumber yard called Trail Builders Supply. After some time, my mom and O.D. broke up, and Gary wanted them to continue dating. So one day, Gary took my mom over to O.D.'s company to look for some paneling for our home. While she was there looking at the samples, she told O.D. the only way she would marry him or even date him again was if he were to become a millionaire. He looked at her and said that if she married him, it would be while he was making his money. My uncle said she was a damn fool. O.D. was a good man and she should continue to date him, regardless of what he had. One day he just might become a self-made millionaire and he would be able to take care of her and her kids. My mom told Gary that she didn't like O.D. The next thing I knew, I was meeting O.D. for the first time at our house. He was in his early forties, 5-foot-9, with gray hair and glasses. My mom and O.D. were soon married. He moved in and remodeled our home, and for the first time in my mother's life, she was happy. We had new furniture, vehicles, and even went on vacations.

I began to play youth sports in baseball, basketball, and football. My stepdad bought me the best sports equipment, all the things we couldn't afford before. I finally had a positive male figure in my life. I got really involved in sports and loved every minute of it. I had dreamed of playing pro ball, especially college basketball, for the North Carolina Tar Heels.

At the annual, third-grade, school field day, I had my first experience of hearing people clapping, cheering, and yelling out my name. I had been too shy and scared to enter events before. I entered the softball throw, high jump, fifty-yard dash, and the hundred-yard dash, and won all four events. I ran faster, threw farther, and jumped higher than the older kids. The teacher would present my first-place blue ribbons to me at the front of the classroom so everyone could see me, and that would make me so nervous, but I knew right then and there that's what I wanted to do: play sports. Sports made me feel I had done something special. It would help to take my mind off the nightmares that I was having. It seemed that the nightmares weren't going away and I hated reliving all the graphic details of the beatings and the shooting. Some nights, I would just stay awake all night long so I wouldn't have to deal with the past. There were times I would be so sleepy that I would doze off and wake up punching, screaming, and kicking. I found relief when I'd grab my football, basketball, or baseball and start to throw the ball up to the ceiling while lying on my bed. I would play catch until the sun came up. I didn't want my friends to think that I was weird or crazy if they found out that I was afraid to spend the night at their houses. They might not spend the night or be my friends anymore. I had already gone through, losing friends after the shooting, and I didn't want to lose my friends again, so I kept everything to myself and dealt with it the best way that I knew how.

At age ten, I had my first experience of what drug smuggling was all about. Early one Saturday morning I was down at Bayview Park with my mom. I was fishing off the sea wall, and I had seen a couple of mullet skiff boats being towed in by the local sheriff's boats.

A mullet skiff boat is a flat-bottom boat with the outboard motor mounted in a hole cut out of the hull. A shaft and prop stick down through that cut-out hole so that the prop is in the water. The motors on these boats are mounted that way so that the nets used to catch mullet in shallow water don't get caught in the props and torn apart.

These boats were ideal for smuggling because they could run in shallow, brackish waters. Heavy V-hull boats that the sheriffs used to patrol the waters couldn't run in these shallow areas.

Aboard the sheriff's boat were two smugglers in handcuffs. They sat in the front of the boat while their skiff boats were towed by another sheriff's boat. The skiff boats contained bales of marijuana wrapped in burlap, which had a strong odor to it. As I watched, my mother explained that the men were drug smugglers, and if I did something like this and got caught, I would go to jail. That's where all the mean people were, she said, so I had better stay away from drugs.

I lived two miles east of Bayview Park, next to which were "spots," also known as "holes." These were places where boats and trucks could meet secretly. The smugglers would become familiar with these areas and use them if they needed to hide from the US Coast Guard, US Customs, DEA, or local authorities. These holes were also used as stash areas. Growing up down by the water, I saw my share of drug smugglers being chased because of a busted load. I soon learned that marijuana was imported to the Florida coast by way of freighters, shrimp boats, and twin-engine motor boats. Once the emptied twin-engine boats pulled into Bayview Park, they would be loaded up on the trailers and brought to the empty house next to my house. These boats belonged to my friend, Ralph, and a cousin.

They asked me to clean their boats and would pay me really good money to do this for them. First, I would sweep up any loose pieces and seeds of marijuana that had broken loose from the bales. Then, I would wash and scrub the boats and finally bleach them. As a bonus (I thought), I got to keep everything that I swept up off the boat. If a cop were to find a seed on your boat's deck, your boat could be confiscated, you could get a smuggling charge and do prison time.

At fourteen, I had my first experience with marijuana. A shipment of 20,000 pounds of marijuana arrived before dawn at Bayview Park. The bales were wrapped in burlap, taken off the boat, and put into a rented box truck to be transported to the east coast.

Since I was familiar with the area, having grown up there, I was often asked to help find more holes that were hidden in the backwaters. I knew all of the shorelines because I used to camp and ride my ATVs there. I had lots of secret fishing holes. The area was dense with trees and mangroves. Only an ATV could get through it. To be able to maneuver a boat through a mangrove channel with shallow water, you had to use a machete or axe. Any gas-powered piece of equipment was noisy and would draw too much attention to the hole.

After the smugglers went out in the Gulf of Mexico to pick up their shipment of marijuana from the shrimp boats, they had to head back through Gordon's Pass with their boats filled with bales of pot. On occasion there would be someone out fishing at night who would call the authorities to report suspicious activity. Soon, the sheriff's boat would appear and start chasing the smugglers, and they would pull off into these holes, either to stash the bales of marijuana and come back another day to retrieve them or wait it out until the heat was off.

When the sun came up, all activity came to a halt. It was like working with vampires. There would be no movement on the loaded boats, and all transport trucks waiting at the holes were told to leave. All activity would continue the following night if permitted. The smugglers would try not to leave the stashed bales of marijuana in these holes for too long, fearing that the bales would be spotted from planes or boats that were hiding in the mangroves. Another risk was that a local fisherman might stumble across the stash and report his findings to the cops. Too much work had been invested to have it all thrown away. The load had come a long way, not to mention the mad Cubans or Colombians you'd have to answer to if their shipment wasn't delivered to Miami as expected, especially after the load had made it to shore.

Chapter 4

It was my first day back at school as a junior. I was excited. Just two more years and I'd be off to college. I was finally moved up to full-time with the varsity basketball team. I pulled into the school parking lot in my light-green Caprice Classic. My stepdad had bought my mom a new car, so she had given me her old one. As I walked up to the school, I checked out who had turned sixteen and started driving over the summer, and I caught up with friends I hadn't seen since the previous year of school.

I went through the front entrance of the school, and as I walked toward the cafeteria, a friend of mine, Billy, told me the new basketball coach was looking for me. I remembered that our old coach was being transferred to Barron Collier High School. While I played for my old coach, I felt that he didn't really believe in me as a player, especially during my freshman year. When I made the freshman squad, all I did was practice, especially at home. My stepdad had built a basketball goal at the back of the house for me. I would play pickup games with older friends who lived on my street. I found that playing against older and better players helped me become a better player.

There were times when I was shooting around by myself and dreamed of being the best player in high school. I would fantasize about walking out on the court with the fans cheering for me. I wanted to be the best player ever.

I ran into another friend, named Frankie. He said the new basketball coach was looking for me and wanted to meet with me before school. Frankie said he saw me coming into the school and told the coach I was there. I was wondering what he looked like when there he was in the cafeteria. Coach saw me, approached me, and introduced himself. He was a young man, about six feet tall, athletic, with a mustache and sandy-blond hair that was parted to the side.

"Hi, I'm your new basketball coach, Don Stewart."

"Hello, I'm Travis Waters. I understand that you were looking for me?"

He asked where I was from originally. When I told him North Carolina, he commented that a lot of talented basketball players come from there. I agreed with him and asked him where he came from, and he said he came from Michigan. We started chatting for a while about his move to Naples and I asked if he liked it down there compared to Michigan. He said it was different, but he would eventually get used to it. He had heard that I was a good ball player and he wanted me to become a part of his basketball program. He also wanted to turn the Lely High basketball team into a winning program and couldn't wait to get started. The bell for first-period class soon rang and I had to go. The new coach's parting words to me that day were, "Travis, I want Lely to compete for championships. Now you go on to class before you're late. I will catch up with you later. We have a lot to talk about and a lot of work to do."

As I walked away from him to my first class that morning, I thought about what my former coach's replacement would be like. I had thought about this all summer long. My mom reassured me that I would find out when I went back to school. After meeting our new coach, I realized how nice and sincere he was. He really made me feel important, and I couldn't wait to tell my mother about meeting him. I had a good feeling about our conversation, and I was excited about our first basketball practice. I remembered when I had dreamed of playing for the North Carolina Tar Heels. I wanted to walk out on the court wearing the Tar Heels uniform and playing for Head Coach Dean Smith. Sitting beside him and getting instructions from before I went back in the game—I dreamed about that often.

The first day of school went as well as any. We were given our class schedule, met teachers, and learned what they expected of us for the school year. We got to catch up with old friends and see how some had changed. The last bell rang. School was out for the day and I was on my way home. I walked into my house. My mom was there. She asked how my first day of school had gone.

I said, "I met the new basketball coach and he's from Michigan. He wants to build a winning basketball program. He wants our team to start winning championships."

My mom asked, "What do you think of him?"

"I think that the new coach is special." She wanted to know why I felt this way about him after meeting him for the first time.

I said, "He makes you feel really special, like you belong and you matter. He was very sincere." Mom reminded me that over the years of playing sports, I had a lot of other coaches who had made me feel the same way too. When I was eleven years old and playing football, my coach informed me that I was the number-one-rated quarterback in the state because of the numbers I was putting up in the middle of the season. Mom reminded me that I hadn't played football since then. I reminded her that she didn't want me to get hurt and wanted me to play either baseball or basketball. My conversation ended with my mom telling me that I had better listen to my coach. I might be able to get a scholarship to play for the North Carolina Tar Heels, which I had always dreamed about.

She asked, "Is he an older or younger man?"

I said, "I think he's in his thirties. He looks like he just got out of college."

At our first practice, we got to know a little about our coach's background. He had played guard in basketball and quarterback in football at Eastern Michigan. He had played basketball with George Girvan. Coach seemed to always wear black or orange shorts with a white shirt and a whistle around his neck, and he wasn't afraid to blow it and raise his voice at you if you weren't where you were supposed to be in the plays he was running. Being a religious man, he didn't curse. When he got upset about the way we were running a play, he would say "Jezz O Petes" all the time and blow his whistle. "We practice that play every day," he said. "When will some of you understand, it's the same play every day." I would hear him yell, "Richie. No! No!" "Travis put your hands up, Jezz O Petes." "Dennis what are you doing?" "Frankie passes the ball inside. Travis is open." "Rebound the ball, Travis. Get back on defense." I heard it in my sleep.

We started having two-a-day practices, one in the morning and one in the evening, but I wasn't a morning person. Coach would call me at home at 6 a.m. and ask me why I wasn't at practice. I would say I had overslept and I wasn't a morning person. He warned that I'd better become a morning person while he was the coach at Lely or I'd be running laps during the evening practice and sitting on the bench when the season started. I didn't want to miss anymore morning practices. That was for sure. Coach said I had a lot of talent and not to waste it. The other guys on the team didn't like the morning practices either, but we all wanted to win.

We played our first game in the *Naples Daily News* Classic Tournament. It was against Everglades City High School. I'd heard that a couple players from Everglades were the ones to watch. Coach Stewart would give us players a scouting report on each team and which players we needed to try and stop, or slow down if we couldn't stop them. The players that concerned us were named Robby and Darrin. They both grew up in the Everglades. There wasn't a whole lot to do there except fish, crab, play sports, or smuggle drugs.

The game was about to start and I was nervous. We had one guy on our team named Lloyd. He was a senior and played guard. Coach would get upset with Lloyd when he had the ball on top of the key. He continued dribbling it between his legs instead of hitting the open man down low or just driving to the hoop and scoring when the lane opened. I was 6-foot-2 and could jump pretty well. The tallest players on the team were John and Richie. They both were 6-foot-3.

The refs blew their whistles and it was game time. I was at the center of the court waiting for the ref to throw the ball in the air. I got the jump ball. It was not only about jumping ability and timing, and the fact that the fastest jumper to the ball won the jump. I was getting double- and triple-teamed every time I touched the ball, but I was still scoring and rebounding.

We were down and Coach wasn't happy. I was doing everything I could to keep us in the game. I especially wanted to win our first game of the season to impress our new coach. I ended up being the high scorer for the game with twenty-three points and twelve boards, but it wasn't enough. We lost the game 62–73 to the Everglades crew. That loss hurt. We should have won. We were a better team, but they outhustled us.

We continued with the two-a-day practices but ended that season with a record of four wins and sixteen losses. I averaged sixteen points and ten rebounds a game. Walter Sutton from Riverdale and I were tied for the Class Three, a South Florida scoring title. I started to receive letters from small, division two schools after my junior year of high school.

All summer long we played basketball and practiced with Coach. I couldn't wait for my senior year of high school. It would be my last year and I'd be off to college to play basketball. I hoped we'd have a winning season my senior year. Coach's youngest son, Scott, was our water boy. He was in seventh grade and when the balls were brought out for practice, he would end up with one in his hand. He would play pickup games with us after practice and was already better than some of the ninth- and tenth-graders. He always wanted to be on my team. I was Bird and he was Magic.

My beautiful girlfriend, Pietra, was a year older than me, so she was at college. Pietra was valedictorian her senior year. She had goals that she set for herself. She had her life together. We had been dating for almost two years. Pietra attended the University of South Florida so she was only a few hours away. This allowed us to see each other on the weekends and she could come to some of my games. I missed her a lot. Pietra was a special girl. She and her family lived on Marco Island. Her father's name was Vito, and he could cook the best Italian food. I missed his cooking. That was for sure.

It was the first game of the season and I was pumped and ready to play. It was against Immokalee on a Tuesday night. Pietra wouldn't be at this game because it was on a weekday. Coach's oldest son, Stacey, a sophomore, was on our team. He played guard. Some players had moved up from Junior Varsity or had been transferred from other schools. Greg, Albert, and I had played on teams together when we were younger. We played in the Youth Basketball League. Coach Stewart's assistants were Coach Hill and Coach Kerlek. Coach Kerlek also was my history teacher. He was an older guy and definitely old school. He had played ball in his younger days. I owe a lot of my high school career to Coach Kerlek. Before the game and after everyone left the locker room, he would get me pumped up for the game by pushing me up against the lockers and telling me, "You, Travis Waters, you own the boards and don't let any of the black guys intimidate you. You dominate the boards. Show them all what a white kid can do on the basketball court." Then he would look at me through his glasses and say, "Get out there and make me proud and get mean. Everyone in this school is counting on you!"

The refs blew their whistles and it was game time. I looked up and nodded at my mom and stepdad in the stands. Immokalee was an all-black team. I knew if we were going to have a chance at winning this game, I had to dominate the boards. I was 6-foot-3 and weighed 190 pounds. I had conditioned myself over the summer. I was ready.

I won the jump ball and we ran our first play, me down low, moving up to the foul line. The ball was passed to me. I did my turnaround shot. Swish! I was feeling it this game. I scored four of our first five baskets and I controlled the boards. We were out to a 10–2 lead, and on my next shot I drove to the basket and turned my ankle. It hurt like hell and I was pissed. I left the court and went back to the locker room to immediately put ice on it. I sat there thinking "Why now?" This was the first game of the season and I wanted us to win. My ankle was already swelling up, and Coach Kerlek congratulated me on dominating the game at both ends of the court. He taped up my ankle up, and I went back in at the beginning of the second quarter. I scored four more points in a minute and seven seconds, but the pain was too much. Coach didn't want me to injure my ankle anymore, so I sat on the bench for the remainder of the game. We won our first game of the season. The headlines in the paper the next day read, "Winning Trojans Don't Dry Up Without Waters" (Tom Rife, sports writer, *Naples Daily News*).

Immokalee Coach Jack Hyatt's comment was, "I'd like to have that first four minutes back."

After that we played them even. Coach Stewart commented, "Travis is our leading scorer and rebounder. I don't plan on playing any games this year without him in there. Imagine that: Travis had twelve points and he only played five minutes. Think about if he had played the whole game. He would have had forty points." I ended up as the high scorer of the game, but I would have to sit out the following week's game against Key West and that sucked.

My ankle started healing up, and I was back by the third game. I wasn't feeling 100 percent, but I wanted to be the South Florida Class Three AAA scoring leader and go to college.

We were winning games that season, and I put up some big numbers, but my ankle still hurt sometimes, especially if I turned it a little. During the season I read and heard a lot about this guy from North Ft. Myers named Deion Sanders. He was a three-sport star who had the speed and talent required to excel in all three. I knew if I could compete with Deion, I could play with anyone in South Florida.

We played North Ft. Myers at home. I thought about this game all week and especially about Deion. It was to be our first meeting. Coach Kerlek was in the locker room taping up my ankle as he did every game. He said to me, "Here's your chance to show everyone in South Florida you can play on the court with anyone."

He asked me if I was nervous about playing against Deion. I said, "Yes, I am." Coach pumped me up for the game as usual with his speech and pushing me up against the lockers. As I dashed out of the locker room, Coach Stewart looked at me and said, "We are counting on you, Travis. For us to win this game, you have to step your game up and you can play with these guys."

I said, "Okay, Coach." I joined the team, warming up on the court. Looking down the court, I saw Deion with his jerry-curl hair and his red shoes. I heard he had dunked over the 6-foot-7 Danny who played for Naples High. Some guys said he wanted to dunk on me. I shook Deion's hand along with the rest of the players and the refs blew their whistles. It was time for the jump ball.

I won the ball, and we went down the court and missed the shot. Deion grabbed the ball off the back board and went to the other end for the easy lay-up.

This guy was the real deal. I'd have to play my best game of the year to compete with him.

My butterflies went away and I started scoring on Deion. This guy brought the best out of me. I wasn't going to be outplayed once I saw I could play with him. As the game went on, we pulled ahead and were leading by nine, but the run and gun of North Ft. Myers and Deion pulled the game back even, and we ended up losing 69–64. The headlines in the *Naples Daily News* read, "Sanders Saddles Trojan Boys." Sports writer Tom Rife wrote, "Lely's loss put a damper on the 26 point performance of Travis Waters." I wanted to beat North Ft. Myers and I did all I could against Deion, but he also scored twenty-six points. I was happy the way I had played against him. I told myself if I could compete with the best, I could play with anyone. There was no doubt he was the best athlete I'd ever stepped on the court against. He proved that to me during the game. Everything I had heard and read about him was true, but I knew one thing: he didn't dunk on me and I matched him point for point. That was all I could ask of myself."

Being the star of my high school team was the best time of my life. It was everything I had dreamed about growing up. I had a beautiful girlfriend. I was on the local news and in the newspapers every week during basketball season, and I was in the running for the Class Three AAA South Florida scoring title.

May 14, 1985: the Senior All-Star Game was the last time I would ever lace up a pair of sneakers and compete on a high school level, and thank God, I got to play my last game under Coach Stewart. I walked up to the gym doors leading into the Edison College Gym and there was Deion, talking to a couple girls. I looked at him and he stared back at me. We nodded at each other as if to say "hi." Deion was the star on the North team, and I would face off against him one last time. I played as well as I could. My left knee needed to be operated on. It was worn out from all the games and practices, so my doctor gave me a Velcro strap to wear under my left knee cap to help with the pain when I jumped off my left leg. I scored fifteen points, but Deion played really well in that game. I enjoyed watching him play when I was on the bench. After the game, he and I shook hands and said, "Good game." As I look back I now, know that was where my dream of basketball ended—on the hardwood. Before school had ended, I was chosen to be one out of twelve all-stars to play on the Junior Olympic team, representing South Florida and traveling around the country playing other teams. I started practicing with the Junior Olympic team at Riverdale High School in Lee County. What an honor.

* * * *

It was a beautiful Tuesday morning and I was at Bayview Park, sitting at the dock in my boat, waiting for a couple friends to join me. We were going out to Key Waden Island to spend the day. My mom showed up at the dock and said the school had called. I had missed too many days of school and would have to go to summer school to graduate. This meant I wouldn't get my scholarship to play college basketball. I couldn't believe what I was hearing. I had let my basketball success go to my head. I didn't want to go to summer school. That was when I decided to fuck everything I had dreamed of doing my whole life. I told myself I was going to have money one way or the other, no matter what I did.

Chapter 5

In March 1986 I found myself climbing up the ladder in the drug world. I decided it was time for me to move up faster, which meant working outside my local area. I wanted to move more products and make more profit.

While I was up in North Carolina on vacation, visiting my family and friends, I asked them about the drug situation. I learned that an ounce of cocaine was worth $1,500 and a pound of marijuana (Colombian commercial brown), was worth $900 to $1,000. I was surprised. These were better prices than I could get in my area. I started seeing dollar signs. Money, money, money! Doing the math in my head, I quickly realized that this was where the big profits were. Up north was where I would take my next step up the ladder.

Back home in Florida, I started experimenting with hiding places in vehicles. I would take the panels off the doors, remove seats, consoles, spare tires, you name it, looking for hiding spots. I would spend hours in the garage trying to find that perfect hiding place. I knew there was always the threat of police checkpoints, especially on I-95 on the east coast of Florida. If I were to be pulled over by suspicious cops, I would have the

K-9 unit to deal with. It was really hard to conceal the smell from the dogs. Cocaine was smaller and easier to conceal. Hiding marijuana took a lot of thought and even more ingenuity. For better or worse, I made my decision. I decided to conceal the marijuana in two suitcases on top of the car in a luggage rack, and I hid the cocaine in the right-side door under the panel, triple packaged, which somewhat camouflaged the smell.

I then set up a timeframe for my first drug deal up north. The plan was to use pay phones to arrange drug drop-offs and money pickups. At that time—in the 1980s—if you called the number listed on the pay phone, it would ring. We then chose certain pay phone locations and set a schedule of the days and times to take and make calls from those phones. I also wanted to make sure that the drop-off and pickup were done on the same trip.

I could buy a pound of the Colombian commercial brown marijuana for about $450 and a single ounce of cocaine for $700 to $800. I could get the cocaine cheaper if I bought more than five ounces at a time, and I could get the marijuana cheaper if I bought ten pounds at a time. So I bought ten pounds of the marijuana and ten ounces of the cocaine. The cocaine was in the form of a solid brick and looked like a mirror on either side. When you broke a piece off to see what it looked like, it was soft in the middle and pure all the way through. It was 99 percent pure cocaine. I got it from a Cuban childhood friend I could trust. It came right off the boat.

I had everything in place. It was time to reach for that next rung.

I had my bags packed ready to make my first drug trip up north. I said good-bye to my mom and told her I loved her. She wanted to know where I was going. I said I was going out of town for about a week and for her not to worry. She reminded me that I was throwing my life away watching my cousin, Greg, and friend, Ralph, making lots of money from smuggling drugs, and she suggested that I go to summer school so I could graduate from high school, attend college, and play basketball. I might even be able to play professional basketball and make my fortune that way. Mom wanted me to quit running around with the wrong people. I reminded her it was my fault I had lost my scholarship and wasn't going to summer school.

She said that my girlfriend, Pietra, had chosen to attend college in Florida to be closer to me, and I had let her down. She didn't want any part of me and my drug business and had left. "Pietra is the smart one here," Mom insisted. "She went to college to make something of herself. You should've stayed with her."

I didn't have any job skills, and I wasn't going to work for someone else 8 to 5, five days a week, for $400. I wanted to be my own boss. I said good-bye and walked out the door. She was crying when I left.

I headed north on I-75, and I never looked back. I was worried about not making it out of the state of Florida. Though my chances of getting pulled over were greater in the other states I had to go through. I was alone, eighteen years old, and had Florida tags. I was not on a family vacation. The rules were to maintain the speed limit and never drive at night. The sun went down; you were up for the night in a hotel.

I reached Asheville, North Carolina, and decided to stay for the night before I moved on to my final destination, a town called Hickory. It was located just outside my hometown of Lenoir. I woke up in Asheville and it was a beautiful morning. I decided to get breakfast at a little country diner. They always seemed to have the best food. After breakfast I got back on the I-40 and headed to Hickory. I stopped to get a room at the Holiday Inn. I then went to the pay phone just outside my hotel to make my scheduled call. My friend let me know that he would be there in thirty minutes for pickup. I sat in my hotel room, waiting, and I started to reminisce about what I would have been doing if I hadn't started selling drugs. What would my life have been like if I had been raised in North Carolina? Would I have been playing basketball for the Tar Heels? I had always dreamed of being able to walk out onto that basketball court. I still wanted to know what it would be like to be on that court. I had never thought I'd be sitting in a hotel room waiting to make my first drug deal.

I heard a knock at the door. It was the friend I'd been waiting for. I showed him the cocaine, and he couldn't believe what I had. He'd never seen it so good. I kept the marijuana wrapped. It had a strong odor to it. I didn't want the hotel cleaning lady to smell it and then call the cops on me. I wanted $1,500 an ounce for the cocaine and $950 for each pound of pot. He said he would have no problem selling it and I shouldn't worry. I handed him the two suitcases filled with the cocaine and marijuana. I told him that there were a few instructions to follow. "No speeding; check your turn signals and brake lights; check your rearview mirror and switch lanes; pull into a store or parking lot if you notice a cop behind you. Don't ever keep them behind you, which will give them a reason to pull you over. Good luck. I'll be waiting here for your return with the money." He reassured me that everything would be fine and left. For the rest of the day and night I went crazy with worry, hoping that everything had gone smoothly.

The next morning, my friend showed up at my hotel door, smiling, and holding my suitcase full of money. I let him in and he dumped $24,500 in cash onto my bed. I couldn't believe it. He looked at me and asked, "What do you think, Travis? Looks like you've never seen that much money before."

I said, "I've seen more than this before. It's just that this was my deal that I had put together all by myself and had been wondering for months if it would work." All of this money in front of me was mine to keep. It was an awesome feeling. My friend said his customers wanted more because it was the best cocaine they'd ever seen He asked me if we were in business, and I said yes. I thought that if I were going to do this, I'd need to do some fine-tuning. I needed to start by hiding the drugs in a better way, especially the pot.

Before I left, I set up another scheduled payphone call within a week to organize another delivery. After my friend left the room, a million thoughts ran through my head. This was too easy. I had just doubled my money. What would come of this, and how long would it last? I had a lot of work to do when I returned to Naples. I decided that I would need to drive but must hire someone I could trust to go with me the next few times to make sure that everything was done right and to introduce him to my connection. I had come too far just to hand this responsibility over to someone else. I wrapped the stacks of cash tightly together with rubber bands and then put the cash in a zip-lock bag. The cash was mostly in large bills, which made it easier to hide, less bulky.

I checked out of the hotel and headed out of Hickory on I-40. As I drove, I started to think of a good place to hide the money in my car. I didn't want to get pulled over for speeding and have a cop find the money. It would have been very hard to explain why I was driving with $24,500 in cash. I found a rest area and stopped. I acted as if I were on vacation so that I would fit in with the others. I got out of the car and went inside to use the restroom. As I walked back to my car, I thought of a suitable hiding place for the money. I decided to stash the money underneath the dashboard of my car. I drove straight through and made it back to Naples without any complications. I couldn't believe how easy this trip to North Carolina had been.

I walked into my bedroom, locked the door, and sat down. The money that I had just made was spread out on my bed. I counted it in total disbelief. I had done it. My mom came to the door and asked why I was back so soon. I lied and said I'd been bored and hadn't had any fun. I'd decided to come back early. I started to think about my trip, and found myself feeling excited and scared at the same time. It was thrilling knowing that I had gotten away with this deal. I found myself getting hooked on the money as well.

I decide to call a friend of Ralph's. He went by the name of Snapper because of the way he looked. He was six feet tall, weighed 350 pounds, and had light-colored skin and red hair. Snapper ran around with Ralph and my cousin Greg. We needed to go to his house to talk in private.

Snapper had a two-story house on five acres of land out in Golden Gate Estates. Inside it was decorated with granite and marble throughout.

I remember his bathroom in the downstairs area having black marble with gold-plated fixtures. He took me outside to a building behind the house where he kept his "toys." He had a Harley Davidson Fat Boy, ATVs, boats, jet skis, go-carts, motocross bikes, cars, and trucks. It was obvious to me that he was well connected and doing very well for himself. As he showed me all of his "toys," he sat on his Harley, and it hit me—Hog Daddy. From that moment on, he was known as Hog Daddy to me.

After showing me his toys, Hog Daddy wanted to know why I needed to talk to him. I said that I was in need of someone I could rely on every month for a supply of cocaine and marijuana. He asked me if I had someone that I could trust to give the drugs to. I said yes and told him about the connection I had up north and how I got paid for the ten ounces of cocaine and the ten pounds of pot in one day.

He then asked me if I cut the cocaine. I looked at him and said, "I don't know what you mean." He said, "Hang out with me and I'll show you how to do this. Besides, I need some help with cutting my own supply." The only stipulation was if I told anyone about it, he would never sell any drugs or show me the ins and outs of the drug business. I gave him my word. He instructed me to stay in the garage and he'd be right back. He had to get something out of his house. I sat there waiting. The garage door opened suddenly. It was Hog Daddy with a green duffel bag. He set it down, unzipped it, and removed these square-shaped objects that were wrapped with tape. They looked like wax. He removed a triple-beam scale, plastic bottles that had a white powder in them, four boxes of gallon-sized, zip-lock bags, and three large Tupperware bowls. I asked what the yellow square things were. He called them footballs. They didn't look like any football I had ever seen or played with. He laughed and said they were a kilo each of pure cocaine. We called them footballs. They just came off the boat, and now we were going to cut them so we would have more.

I counted out ten kilos of cocaine.

Damn! I'm only eighteen years old, and I've never seen one kilo let alone ten kilos.

Hog Daddy said to snap out of it and start busting the kilos open and while I was at it, to chop some up for us to snort. I was nervous about breaking open my first football. I asked him how much it weighed and he said, "Two point two pounds."

I exclaimed, "Wow! There's over twenty pounds of pure cocaine here in this garage. How much is each football worth?"

"On the street, about twenty-five grand." Casting a curious glance my way he asked, "What's the most you've ever seen?"

I didn't brag. I told him the truth. "The ten ounces of coke I just sold up north."

The cocaine that I chopped up for us looked like pieces of a broken mirror. I laid out four lines for us to snort. I then broke open two footballs and put one in each Tupperware bowl. Hog Daddy used an electric mixer to blend the coke and this white powder called Inositol. It's a dietary supplement that can be bought at any health-food store. The preferred ratio of the mix was two footballs and a half kilo of the Inositol powder. Once this mixture was blended well, it was weighed out into a kilo and poured into a zip-lock bag. The plastic bag was labeled with a black marker, indicating that it weighed one kilo. As we prepared the drugs, we snorted the pure cocaine. That made it no work at all. After we finished cutting the last two kilos, Hog Daddy ended up with a total of twelve and a half kilos of cocaine. I passed and graduated from Hog Daddy's coke-cutting class while I was high on coke.

Now there were almost twenty-seven pounds of about 75 percent pure cocaine that would be broken down into ounces, quarter kilos, half kilos, three-quarter kilos, and kilos. These would be sold locally and to Hog Daddy's connections up north. This was my first big cocaine buy and I never looked back.

I was Hog Daddy's first sale of the day. I bought my first pound of cocaine at $10,400. It averaged $650 per ounce. He gave me four ounces of Inositol to cut the sixteen ounces of cocaine. I put them both into a mixing bowl and mixed everything together with the electric mixer. Hog Daddy showed me how to press the powdered cocaine into the form of a brick, its original shape. He said it was more presentable to the customer, plus you couldn't tell it had been cut. Hog Daddy weighed eight ounces of cocaine and poured it into a gallon-size, zip-lock, freezer bag. He then double- and triple-bagged the original bag for protection. He twisted the bag tightly so that the cocaine moved down to the corner of the bag. Finally, he placed it in between two steel plates, a quarter-of-an-inch thick and 8-by-8 feet square, on the concrete floor of his garage in front of his truck tire. He instructed me to drive his front tire on top of the steel plate and leave it there. I did as he asked, and then I got out of the truck to observe the result. I thought it was a brilliant way to make more of a profit. The process took a couple of hours, so Hog Daddy suggested that we go into the house and snort some more coke to pass the time.

A couple of hours later, we were back at the garage. I backed the truck off the steel plates and removed the wrapping from the finished product. It was a solid brick, the original shape that we had started out with. It was amazing!

Chapter 6

On January 22, 1987, I turned twenty years old. My drug business up north was doing well. I purchased my drugs either in Naples or Miami, wherever I could find the best prices, though my main connection was Hog Daddy in Naples. He seemed to have the best cocaine and pot, at the best prices.

I wanted to keep my drug business up north on an on-the-side basis. It usually took care of itself. There were occasions when I would lose some of the drugs due to someone getting busted up north with product on him and/or that person cheating me of an ounce or two.

I would hide the drugs in my vehicle and then I would give my driver specific instructions as to where the drop-off point was, and every four to six weeks I would receive $50,000 to $75,000 from two states.

After mastering the art of selling both cocaine and pot in two states, my thoughts turned to expansion. I wanted more money. Growing up, I remembered some of my family members and their friends smuggling drugs into the country and it looked like fun to me. So I decided to talk to my Cuban friend Ralph, who had been smuggling for years. Since he had known me practically my whole life, he could trust me. Plus, I was an

American. So he agreed to bring me into his circle. He had already offered me a job in smuggling. He wanted me to get some experience on the water and learn the business. He also wanted me to see how it worked from the bottom up. He advised me that to make the big money, I needed to be more than just an off-loader, someone who brings the bales of pot off one boat to load onto another.

I went with Ralph to Miami to meet with some Cubans and Colombians. This was my first lesson in how to negotiate, not only in bringing a load into the country, but how much to charge for the service. At the end of the meeting it was decided that I would escort the Colombians as soon as they arrived in the States and drive them wherever they wanted to go. Everything was set.

For my first job, I was instructed to unload 10,000 pounds of pot, twenty-five miles off the coast of nearby Marco Island. There were a total of four boats. I would be working with Cubans from Miami. Our boat was a T-craft with a center console. It had twin Evinrude 235-HP motors and was less than thirty feet long with a wide beam. This type of boat could run in shallow water.

Around nine that night, we left Bayview Park with fishing poles and bait as a cover. The three other boats involved set out from different locations so they wouldn't draw attention from law enforcement. I shared one of them with a Cuban named Reuben. He was a cousin of the man from Miami who had helped to arrange this job with Ralph. Ralph wanted Reuben to be on the boat with me because he wasn't familiar with our local waters. He was also there to watch the off-loading crew and to make sure no one stole any of the 10,000 pounds of weed that was being off-loaded from the shrimp boat onto ours.

We traveled through Gordon's Pass to get to the Gulf of Mexico and we punched in our location numbers on the GPS. The shrimp boat had the same GPS numbers so we could meet at the same location. Reuben got a map and a hand-held radio—an Icom—out of his bag. He looked at his watch. It was 10:00 p.m. We were five miles off the coast. Reuben told me to turn the motors and lights off so that he could make contact with the other three boats. They were supposed to be sitting five miles out in the Gulf of Mexico off the coast of Marco Island, with their motors and lights off, waiting for his call, which he made in Spanish. Each boat responded. The other boats were ready to go and everyone was in place. So, we headed out twenty more miles. The lights were still off and we met the shrimper at 12:00 a.m. Reuben told me to stop the boat about twenty-three miles off the coast. He got his duffel bag and grabbed two pairs of infrared night-vision goggles and two ski masks, and he asked me if I had ever used night-vision goggles before. I had. My friend Ralph had three pairs of them, but I'd never used them on a job. He turned the goggles on and showed me how to adjust the vision.

He said, "Put your mask on so no one else on the other boats sees your face, especially the captains on the shrimp boat."

Reuben said, "I don't know some of the guys on the other boats or the captain on the shrimp boat. The conspiracy laws are a pain in my ass."

Conspiracy law means it only takes two people to say you were at the crime scene and you're busted. That's if they get caught and point you out as being at the same crime scene.

I was on my first load. I wore a mask. The black night became a bright vision of green.

Reuben tapped me on the shoulder and said, "Welcome to your first load, green goat. What do you think?"

I said, "This is exciting. I'm hooked on smuggling."

I saw the shrimper in the distance. It was still heading, with its lights off, to the secret location to the south. I also saw the three other boats moving to the same location with their running lights off.

We had to make the exchange fast. We pulled up to the shrimper. They were also wearing masks and goggles, and so were the other guys on their twin-engine boats. The guy on the shrimp boat said, "You guys are right on time," and he threw a line down to us so we could tie up. The other boats did the same all around the shrimp boat. Reuben opened up the hatch on a storage box built into the deck and grabbed a large duffel bag and two green canvas tarps. I helped him spread it out across the entire deck of the boat. Another guy walked out of the wheelhouse of the shrimp boat and asked which boat had the money on it.

Reuben told the captain, "I have the money."

Per Reuben's instructions I grabbed the bag. It was heavy and there was a lot of cash in it. I showed it to the guy on the shrimp boat. I guessed he was the captain. His men to started off-loading the weed. There were a total of four guys on the shrimp boat. One of the guys from each of the twin-engine boats tied up to the shrimper and helped bring the bales up from the bottom where ice and the shrimp they caught were usually stored. One guy stayed on each of the twin-engine boats to stack the bales on the deck. Reuben counted the bales coming out of the bottom of the shrimp boat. The captain of the shrimp boat was the lookout man for any boats moving in our direction. It was obvious these guys had done this before. They had a well-organized system for getting the pot off the shrimp boat as fast as humanly possible. Boats tied up together in the middle of the Gulf of Mexico don't look good on radar screens or to law enforcement boats looking for suspicious activity. I was hoping I could stack those bales right and fast. Reuben explained on the way how to do it. "Start stacking from the back and leave us a walking area and room to drive the boat."

Each boat was loaded at the same time. Guys on the shrimp boat were appointed by the skipper to help load each twin-engine boat. The bales of commercial-grade pot came from Colombia. The pot had a strong, fresh odor. It was brown and had seeds in it. This was why the green canvas was laid on the boat deck to try to keep as little pot and seeds as possible from getting on the deck because bales sometimes would be dropped and busted open in the transportation and off-loading process.

Here came my first bale. It was heavy; the bales on this load weighed eighty pounds. I started stacking from the back and counting each bale that went on our boat. I noticed the corners of some of the bales had a white tag. Some tags on the burlap the pot was wrapped in looked like manufacturers' tags. Everyone else was doing what I was doing. On my sixteenth bale I began to get tired and I was sweating like hell in the muggy summer night. The ski mask made it worse. I tripped and almost dropped the bale. One of the guys on the shrimp boat said, "Hurry the fuck up. We don't have all night." I ended up with twenty-five bales on my boat; exactly what Reuben said to put on the boat.

I told the guy bringing me the bales, "I have twenty-five. That's it. Put them on the other boats."

I sat down for a second, and the captain yelled at me, "Get off your ass and get on the shrimp boat and help with the other boats! We don't have all fucking night. Nobody here wants to go to prison."

The other guys laughed. I was tall, so I was put in the storage hold of the boat. I started handing the bales up to the guys on deck. It was hot down there with no breeze, and I couldn't wait to get the ski mask off my head. That job down there in the hull of that boat was hard, and you couldn't rest. Finally the last bale was lifted out of the hull. The captain said, "Where's my money?"

Reuben instructed me to get in our boat and bring the money to the shrimper. Then he ordered the other three boats to start heading back slowly. He said that we would catch up. Reuben, the captain, and I were in the galley of the shrimp boat, still wearing our ski masks. I dumped the money on the table, and the captain said, "Is it all there?"

Reuben started explaining how much money was in each bundle.

The captain said, "It's $450,000. That was the agreement. Good luck with the rest of the trip. I have to get the deckhands to scrub and bleach this boat. We're headed back to shore."

I was glad to be able to rip my ski mask off. The hard part of this operation was getting these loaded boats safely to the secret hole while the pot was visible on the deck.

I told Reuben, "I'm more worried about this drug agency called the Blue Thunder Strike Force than the DEA, the US Customs, or the coast guard."

Reuben and I caught up to the other loaded boats with our ski masks back on but no goggles. I'd seen my share of boats coming loaded through the pass, and I'd always wondered what it felt like. It was exciting. Adrenaline pumped through my body. Sneaking these drugs into the country all the way from Colombia was addictive. There were two boats. One was stationed in the pass, back in from the gulf. A couple of men on it appeared to be fishing. They were our lookouts. They would let us know on the hand-held radio if it was safe to come into the pass. The pass the other two men were stationed at was the one that ran north and south through Gordon's pass alongside Bayview Park. We were headed to a secret hole south of Bayview. It was three o' clock in the morning. Reuben and I came into the pass first. The other three boats came in behind us, but we were about a quarter-mile apart. The second set of men stationed in the Bayview Park pass, said to come on in. It was safe. Reuben took the hand-held radio and called the truck driver to make sure he was in place at the secret hole. A lot of people were involved in these operations and we didn't know everyone who was working the load. We didn't know who was trying to rip the load off or pretending they were cops so they could bust the load and steal it when everybody threw the bales overboard. Some of the guys working the load could be informants or cops standing right next to you, handing you a bale of pot or a duffel bag of footballs.

We entered the hole. I was driving the boat since I knew where the hole was located. We put our night-vision goggles back on and headed into the mangroves. It was dark and we couldn't use lights. The water was shallow. Because we were ahead of schedule, we were also ahead of the tide, which would come in once we were deep inside the mangroves where we would be safe. We could wait for the tide to come in and lift our boats up.

Reuben said, "Can you handle it?"

I said, "Do you want to drive?"

"I don't know where I'm going."

"Alright then, sit back and let me concentrate. I grew up in these mangroves, and I know where the deeper holes are. Radio the other boats and tell them to follow my exact path."

I told Reuben to stay at the front and start stacking some of the bales up on the very front of the boat. This would put more weight on the bow, lifting the back and motors up so I could keep moving. Reuben radioed the other boats and had them do the same thing. Some of the other boats had thirty-plus bales on their deck.

When we finally made it to the hole, Reuben patted me on the back and said, "Good job, kid. You got our load in. I'm going to tell my cousin if wasn't for you, we would've been stuck in the mangroves and the sun would have come up and a plane could have spotted us."

Reuben emptied some pot out of a busted bale on the tarp, and I said, "What are you doing? That's a lot of wasted pot."

He said nothing. We loaded the bales in the box truck and started wrapping up the tarps and hiding them in the mangroves. Reuben told me to keep all the excess weed, and go back in a couple days to get it. He said, "That's your bonus for getting the load to the truck."

That explained why Reuben put that extra pot on the tarp. I was paid $30,000 in cash for the load and was given a total of forty pounds of pot. I sold it for $500 a pound in Naples for a quick sale. I could have sold it for a lot more if I had taken it up north. I made a total of $50,000 for one night's work. I was hooked.

Chapter 7

———————— /// ————————

I got a call a few weeks later from Reuben. His cousin Juan wanted to meet me and my friend. We went to Miami where we met Reuben in a parking lot. We sat in his four-door, all-black Mercedes with tinted windows and drove out into the country on the outskirts of Miami. *This should be interesting*, I thought.

We pulled up to a gate that was about eight feet high. Beyond it we could see a big mansion. A camera rotated on top of the fence. Reuben punched in a couple numbers on the keypad. The gate swung open and we drove up this long, winding, cobblestone driveway. Mexicans were working in the beautifully landscaped grounds. Three cameras on the front corners of the house and one at the front door were all moving, scanning the property. Reuben rang the doorbell and spoke in Spanish into a speaker in the wall. The huge door opened up and a Colombian lady let us in. The ceilings soared at least fifteen to twenty feet. The floors were white marble and there were huge black-marble columns throughout the house. Beautiful chandeliers hung from the ceiling and the granite counter tops were the most beautiful I'd ever seen. The furniture, Reuben advised, was handmade and came from all over the world. This was the nicest house I'd ever been in. I noticed there were cameras inside the house, scanning the rooms with infrared beams that beeped when we passed through a doorway. We approached the back of the house, and I could hear the sound of music, which seemed to be coming from a party. We were led into Juan's office and control room. Video monitors lined the wall, showing everything that was going on outside and inside the house.

He was a big, fat Cuban, sitting behind this large, beautiful desk, talking on the phone. I looked over at one of the video monitors to see eight or ten smoking-hot girls wearing bikinis with no tops, playing in a pool. I tapped my partner on the shoulder and pointed to the monitor. He looked at me and smiled. We both smiled, and I realized that the pool party had to be the noise I had heard out back.

Juan hung up the phone and said to Reuben, "That fucking Colombian, Pablo Escobar, is a pain in my ass. He wants me to work for nothing … Sorry, guys. I was on an important call overseas with the fucking Colombians."

He got up and hugged my friend Ralph. They exchanged words in Spanish. He looked at me and said, "You must be the kid from the West Coast. Reuben told me a lot about you. I hear that was the first load you brought in, and you're the one that kept the boats from getting stuck and got the load to the truck before the sun came up. The Colombians asked me to thank you. I want you and Ralph to work for me. I want you to bring in more loads for me and the cartel in Colombia."

He walked over to a door at the back of his office, and we all walked into the room there. It was like walking into a bank vault. Juan told us it was a fireproof room. He pointed to a large table and asked me, "Do you know where all that money came from?"

I said, "I guess drugs."

He laughed and said, "Of course drugs. That's my most profitable business. It's the money from the load you helped bring in." He asked me how much I was paid.

I told him with weed and $50,000 in cash. He grabbed a stack of hundred-dollar bills and threw them at me.

He said, "Here's some more money for getting the load to the truck for me."

"I can't take this. I was already paid. You can make it up on the next load."

Juan said, "That means you agree to work for me?"

"Yes, I will."

"Kid, how old are you?'

I said, "I'm nineteen years old."

"You are a kid. Your new code name, when I talk to the Colombians overseas and on the phone here in the States, will be the Westcoast Kid.

"Okay, whatever you want."

Juan pointed at the table and asked, "What do you think of that pile of money on the table?"

"That's a lot of fucking money."

Juan asked me if that was the most cash I'd ever seen.

I said, "Yes. If you don't mind me asking, how much is there on the table?"

"No, I don't mind. It's six million dollars."

I said, "Is that all yours?"

Juan laughed and said, "I ship over half of this money to my partners in Colombia and the rest is mine."

I said, "All right."

Juan wanted Reuban and I to drive the money to a warehouse by a shipping yard in Fort Lauderdale because I was an American and would therefore draw less attention. Juan also said his partners in Colombia would try to kill him if he lost the money.

I said, "Okay, Juan, I will do it."

Juan said, "Enough talk about business. Let's celebrate. I have a surprise for you guys. Since you wouldn't take more money for the load, maybe you will take this next gift from me."

He led us out of his office through some more hallways and rooms to the back of the house where he opened a large, sliding, glass door. I thought this was a dream. The girls stopped playing and Juan said, "Girls, I have a couple friends from out of town. Say hello to my old friend, Ralph, and my new friend, the Westcoast Kid. I want these men to have whatever they want. Is that clear, girls?"

They said, "Anything you want us to do we will, Juan."

I thought I had died and gone to heaven. There were Cuban, Colombian, and American Chinese girls. On a scale of one to ten, every one of these girls was a twelve. The pool lanai was all Key stone with marble columns supporting the overhanging lanai roof. At each end of the pool were large lion statues and tropical landscaping. Underneath the waterfall was a bar. You swam through the fall and through a large hot-tub pool. Juan had placed at least a pound of pure Peruvian cocaine on silver serving trays with gold-plated coke spoons and gold-plated double tubes for both nostrils. A smoking-hot-ass, topless girl walked around with the tray of coke. Whenever you wanted a line, you just waved at the girl. Another hot-ass, topless girl walked around with a couple bottles of Dom Perignon and full champagne glasses. If you didn't want champagne, you could walk up to the lanai bar and order whatever you wanted. I knew I wasn't leaving anytime soon. There were ten girls, me, and Ralph. Reuben and Juan didn't join us. They went into town to run some errands.

I snorted my first line of cocaine, jumped in the pool, and swam under the waterfall to the bar, where there were two smoking blondes with hair down to their asses. One was lying on her back on the bar and the other was licking her pussy. At least two pounds of coke sat on the counter on another silver tray.

Juan had just become my best friend.

Now there are twelve girls. I snorted some more coke and the two blondes wanted me to snort coke off their ass, tits, and stomach, and they asked me to rub it on their pussies. So that's what I did, and thirty minutes later, there were six girls in the waterfall bar with me and six girls with Ralph inside the pool lanai cabana. After I was sexed out, I sat at the bar and snorted more coke and watched the girls snort coke off each other. This really aroused the girls, who had sex with each other all night. I joined in whenever I could until the next day. I stayed at Juan's mansion for three days, partying with the girls for two days. Juan had Ralph flown back to Naples in one of his twin-engine planes. I needed one day to recover from the all-you-can-snort-cocaine-and-girl buffet. Juan knew how to throw a party and entertain his crew. That was for damn sure.

Reuben and I were in the home vault when I noticed there was more money in the vault. We counted out $6,250,000 more dollars. The money was from a 250-kilo drop that had come from Colombia through the Bahamas. It was air-dropped off Marathon Key in the Florida Keys. We counted this money all day, using money machines. We had to separate all the bills, wrap stacks of each denomination together, and label them with the total amount of money in each bundle. I never thought I would tire of counting money in my short life, but if I had not seen another bundle of cash for a while it wouldn't have upset me. Reuben had a pile of coke on the table and had been snorting it all day while we were counting the money. I didn't want to see another line of coke or a girl right at that moment either.

Juan returned home and walked in to see Reuben all coked out. He yelled at Reuben in Spanish, pulled out his gun, and stuck the barrel to Reuben's head. "I don't give a fuck that you're my cousin," he said in English. "I'm the one that brought you into this business. You were a fucking nobody when you came over from Cuba."

Holy shit! I hope he doesn't shoot Reuben in front of me. I don't want to see that.

Juan said, "We don't mix business with pleasure. You know that, Reuben."

Juan whispered something in Reuben's ear in Spanish and Reuben's eyes opened up real big. He looked at me, but I wasn't saying anything. I had just met this guy.

Juan pulled the trigger. The barrel was still stuck to Reuben's head. I jumped a little bit, and Reuben also flinched when the gun clicked. Juan told me to grab the plate of coke, which weighed at least a pound. He said something in Spanish to Reuben, jumped up, and told me to wait a minute because he'd be right back. Then he left the room. I'm now sitting looking at $12,250,000 in cash that I had been putting in stereo boxes with electronic equipment on top to hide it, ready to ship overseas in shipping containers. It was destined for the Colombian cartel and a guy named Pablo whom Juan referred to as a fucking asshole. I heard a gunshot go off and I jumped. It scared me and I wondered if Juan had just shot Reuben. Would I be next if he had? I wondered if I should get up and leave or sit there.

Juan returned and said, "Hey, kid, did you snort any of that coke today?"

I said, "No, but Reuben offered me some. I've snorted enough coke the last couple of days and I don't want to be high when I count all that money." I wanted to make sure the money added up the amount it was supposed to be in each bundle.

Juan said, "Kid, I need more guys like you working for me. Grab that plate of coke and follow me to the pool."

"Okay."

I wondered if I would see Reuben floating dead in the pool, but he was alive and tearing open a kilo of cocaine that he dumped in the pool. After he had dumped two more kilos in the pool, Juan told me to hand the plate of coke to Reuben. Reuben dumped the coke in the pool and Juan pulled out his gun. He fired three more shots into the pool and said to Reuben, "The next round of bullets is going to be in your head if you disrespect me again."

Almost a $100,000 worth of cocaine—its street value—lay in the pool.

Juan said, "Reuben, the coke you poured in the pool is coming out of your pay on the next load. I'm hungry, but I'm sure you're not hungry, Reuben, since you've been snorting coke all day."

Juan turned to me. "Hey, kid, you like Cuban food?"

I looked at him and said, "I love Cuban food."

So Juan and I went out to this large garage with ten roll-up doors. Three of the roll-up doors are thirty feet high. There were rotating cameras on each corner of the building. Juan typed in some numbers on a keypad and we walked in the door. He turned on the lights.

"Come on, kid. I'll show you my toys."

Wow!

A Ferrari, a Porsche, a Rolls Royce, a Mercedes, a Lamborghini, and two stretch limos were in the first seven stalls. The other three stalls contained his offshore racing boats. He raced as a hobby.

"Kid, which one do you want to drive first?" he asked.

I said, "I'm not driving one of these cars. I might get in a wreck and total the car."

"If you total it, I'll buy a new one."

"You drive. I don't know my way around this area."

"Okay, kid. Which car do you want to take?"

I said, "Let's take the Lamborghini. I've never ridden in one." It was blue; it was beautiful. "How much did you pay for the car?"

He said it was a gift from "that fucking asshole Pablo in Colombia."

I asked, "How much is it worth?"

"It's customized, so it's about $400,000."

"No shit."

I noticed we were going 140 miles an hour. Juan looked at me and said, "Welcome to my world, kid."

I said, "I think you need to slow down. I think I just saw a cop back there on the side of the road, hiding."

He gave the car more gas and said, "The cop won't catch us."

We were in the city of Miami, driving on I-95 at the speed limit. Juan said the next month he would have 500 kilos dropped out of a plane fifty miles off the coast of Fort Lauderdale. "The coke is coming from a friend of mine who works out of the Bahamas."

I told Juan that Reuben said the 250 kilos had come from Juan's friend in the Bahamas. Juan looked at me and said, "Reuben told you that?"

I said, "Yes, he did."

The boat picking up the coke belonged to a commercial fisherman who ran charter fishing trips out of Lauderdale. Juan said he'd never had this charter captain bring in a load for him before and he didn't trust him. The captain had been recommended to him by a friend and had guaranteed the load would make it to shore. Juan wanted me in the water with Reuben to watch the coke being dropped out of the plane and loaded on the captain's boat. He wanted us to escort the fishing boat back to the marina because the captain didn't know where the drop would be. Reuben and I were the only ones on the water who would have the GPS numbers and we would be the only ones talking to the pilot dropping the coke. The kilos would be stacked in coolers. A company fishing truck would be parked at the marina. It would have fishing logos on it so we wouldn't be stopped. Juan wanted me to follow Reuben to a warehouse in Miami and break the load down for the buyers.

I said, "Will there be any coke on our boat?"

He said, "No, that's all taken care of."

Juan offered me $50,000 to do the job and I accepted.

Juan also said, "You and Reuben can split the left-over coke that breaks open in the coolers from the impact of the water."

I hoped some of the footballs would break open. That could turn into a lot of money for Reuben and me.

After lunch I took a call from my up-north drug connection. I informed Juan I needed a pay phone to speak to my drug connection up north. I didn't want to use Juan's car phone in case I got this kingpin mixed up with my small drug business. I used the phone and I was not very happy when I got off.

Juan asked me, "What's wrong?"

I said, "One of my loads in Tennessee was just busted along with $40,000 in cash."

Juan asked me, "Can they connect you with the drugs and cash?" He said, if the drug dealer could connect me to the drugs, he would send a couple of his guys up north. No one would testify against me when his hit men were done with them.

Juan said, "Kid, I don't need you going to prison. I need you here working for me. You don't need that drug business up north. You work for me now."

I said, "I know. I'm not going to prison, so you don't need to kill anyone. I'm not about to let you kill someone on my behalf. I don't want any part of murder."

I was only moving drugs to one state now. I'd lost income with the up-north job, but then again, I was riding in a Lamborghini with this international, multimillionaire kingpin, and I had looked at more than twelve million dollars a couple hours before. So I couldn't be that upset over losing $40,000 and a connection. I had just made the biggest connection of my life.

Reuben and I packed eight million dollars in cash and loaded it into a white van with business logos on it. These guys were good. We left Juan his cut of the coke load and the 10,000 pounds of pot I got to shore for him and his Colombian buddies. It left Juan with $4,250,000. I jumped in the driver's seat and Reuben, carrying his pistol, jumped in with me. A car escorted us to the warehouse in case someone tried to rip us off and another car went ahead to look out for cops. As we drew closer to the warehouse, Reuben told me to pull over in a parking lot. He radioed the two cars escorting us. In Spanish, he advised them to go back to Juan's house and that we would take the boxes the rest of the way by ourselves. Reuben handed me a black hood. I put it over my head and laid down in the back of the van. The guys in the other two cars and I weren't allowed to find out where the shipping warehouse was located. The van stopped and the back and side doors opened up. I noticed Reuben wasn't wearing a ski mask. I got out of the van and saw six guys standing guard. They carried machine guns and wore ski masks. I counted eight cameras in all scanning the warehouse. Reuben told me to grab a pallet, place it by the van, and start stacking the boxes of money on the pallet. Reuben was busy talking to the armed guards while I looked around the warehouse and saw more pallets loaded with the same type of box I was unloading from the van. I wondered if the boxes all contained money.

Reuben jumped on the forklift and put the pallet I had just loaded next to the other pallets lined up against the wall. There were at least ten to twelve pallets stacked five feet high.

I asked, "Is that all money?"

He laughed and said, "Yes. Those boxes don't have the electronic equipment on top of the money yet and they haven't been sealed. Look inside them."

I started looking in the boxes on the pallets, and each box I looked in had cash stacked almost to the top. There was just enough room in the box for electronic equipment to hide the money.

I said, "Reuben, how much money is here?"

He said, "Usually $80,000,000 to $125,000,000. Other drug smugglers also bring their money here to be shipped out once a month. The money only sits here for two to three days before being shipped to the cartels overseas. You have a timeline to get what money you want shipped overseas, or you will have to wait until the following month. It's the safest way to send the cash overseas."

Just when I thought I'd seen the most cash I'd ever seen at one time, the amount kept getting larger and larger, and I kept getting in deeper and deeper. These guys were tied to one of largest drug-smuggling and money-distribution networks in the world. I'd just seen it with my own eyes. I was convinced that I knew too much and all this could get me killed. I was in their life and world now.

Back in the van I lay in the back with my hood on, waiting to leave the warehouse and thinking about all the money I'd just seen. Until you've seen it in person, it's hard to explain. You wonder if there really is that much cash floating around on our streets. You begin to ask yourself these things to try and understand the magnitude of the operation and to convince yourself that, yes; there is that much cash out there. It's all real.

I'd been given the okay to get back in the passenger seat and Reuben drove. I didn't say much and Reuben asked, "What's wrong, kid?"

I said, "I guess I'm in shock from all the money I've just seen."

Reuben knew how I felt. He said he couldn't believe it either, the first time he had entered that warehouse. "It kind of gives you an understanding of how big the drug trade is and how serious this business is," he said.

I said, "Yes. This is all happening really fast for me. I just helped you guys bring in a 10,000-pound load a couple weeks ago and now all of this. It's hard to comprehend."

"Don't try to understand it all, Travis, because you never will. This thing is bigger than all of us here in the States. It's worldwide."

"Yes, it is. I just saw how big in the warehouse."

Reuben dropped me off at my truck in the parking lot so I could head back to Naples. He gave me the date I had to be at Naples Airport so Juan's pilot could pick me up to fly me over to Miami to help out with the 500-kilo load.

Chapter 8

On my drive back home to Naples I had second thoughts about what I had just experienced the previous four days. Should I just forget about those Cubans in Miami and stick with my drug business up north? I still had one connection I could work with while I tried to get some more connections up north. The more I thought about it, the more I didn't want to go to the airport where Juan's pilot would pick me up.

I called my mom at home to let her know I was okay. She worried about me and said if I were in college, playing basketball instead of running around with all the wrong people, she would be able to sleep better at night. I said, "I know, Mom. Right now I wish I was playing college ball too." If I had told my mom what I had experienced during the previous four days, she would have said she might as well kill herself because she couldn't take it any longer. She'd said it before.

I didn't call my connection in Tennessee to find out more about the drug bust, or to find out if my drugs actually got busted. I could have been ripped off. Who knows? But if my drugs had been busted, I was not going to call to be sure. The cops could have been listening in on the phone if my connection had already snitched me out. It was their word against mine.

The cops didn't have shit. It would take more than one person to tie me to the crime and no one had been there when I handed the cocaine to him in the hotel room. Only he and I knew about the conspiracy law. I had learned about it from Reuben when I had helped him bring in my first load of pot. I would take the $40,000 loss. Eventually I would make that money back with my other connection in North Carolina and now my new connection in Miami, if I decided to work for Juan.

I started thinking about what Hog Daddy had taught me about cutting the coke and pressing it back into its original shape of a brick. I wanted to make the cocaine brick squarer and harder. I grabbed a piece of paper and stayed up most of the night drawing out a design for a new way to press the cocaine into bricks using a twenty-ton hydraulic jack. I came up with a design using quarter-inch steel plates welded into the shape of a kilo box, measuring 7-by-8 inches, with four-inch sides. The four sides and the bottom were welded together. The half-inch top plate was not welded to the box but would fit freely in the box down to the bottom, so I could determine how many ounce bricks I wanted to make. Some kilos were two bricks and some were three bricks. I thought the Colombians in the middle of the Colombian jungle used these same principles to turn the powdered cocaine after it had been processed and pressed into two- and three-brick kilos.

This was my theory. If it worked, I could cut the pure cocaine, wrap the bricks up in plastic, find a tape similar to the type the Colombians used, and cut a small V-shaped window to sample the kilo when I sold it. I would write a cartel name on the kilo so it would look just like the ones we bought right off the boat. The box had to be strong enough to withstand the pressure of a twenty-ton jack. The stand was made with half-inch steel legs, braced together with a one-inch thick, 12-by-12 inch steel plate that was welded to the top of the legs like a table.

The welder, at the company I gave my design to, asked me, "What the hell are you making?"

I planned to use the contraption to straighten out steel lawn-tractor blades that were bent. I had all of it put together. It cost $450, and I couldn't wait to try it out because the design worked in my head and on paper. I rented a storage bay because I didn't want anyone to know what I was doing. The same people I would sell coke to could copy my design.

I lined the inside of the box with three layers of thick plastic. I broke up a pure, twelve-ounce, cocaine brick, added six ounces of cut, and mixed it up in a bowl with an electric mixer to a semi-fine powder. Then I poured twelve ounces of the now-cut cocaine into the box. I put the one-inch-thick top plate on top of the cocaine, and then I put the jack up against the bottom plate of the stand. I jacked it up so the piston in the jack pushed the top plate into the box and pressed it against the cut cocaine. I continued jacking it up until it was tight and the jack handle won't go up any more. I left it for about three hours under tons of pressure. It seemed to be working, but I wouldn't know until I saw the finished product, but I was excited and hoped it worked.

I return to my storage bay and couldn't wait to release the pressure on the jack. I removed the top plate and looked in the box. The coke was completely flat on top but not really shiny. I would have to experiment with getting the bricks to look more like a mirror. I removed the coke from the box. It was completely square and hard just like the kilo brick. That part of the test was perfect, and I counted money in my head. I couldn't believe it. I cut out a line of coke to celebrate what I had just discovered, snorted it, and started my next experiment on how to make the outside and the inside of the brick shinier and more presentable.

I didn't break the pure coke in the next batch down to a fine powder. I left pure chunks the size of marbles and added the same ratio of cut to the twelve ounces of pure cocaine. I put the mix in the box and tightened it down as much as I could. I left it in the box for five hours this time. When I unwrapped the coke, it was harder, better for shipping in tight places. The bricks wouldn't break apart as much and it would sell better as one brick. The top and bottom of the brick had a lot more shine than the previous brick. I rubbed my finger along the brick's surface and noticed the shiny, pure, cocaine flakes had spread out on the surface and become a lot shinier. I was on to something. I ran up to the store and bought a pack of Bic razors. I took the razor and dragged it along the surface. It started lifting the pure chunks of cocaine and giving the brick the mirror shine I was after. But I didn't know if it would work perfectly. I did my final test. I broke a piece of the brick open to see what the inside looked like, and there they were, pure, shiny chunks of cocaine, hiding the white, dull cut that we used to make more profit. I couldn't believe I had just pulled this off. I was now going to start buying pure kilos to break down to make more kilos, which meant more money. That was what this was all about. I cut out another line and snorted it. I'd have to keep this as my secret.

I decided that it would be in my best interest to go to the airport and have Juan's pilot pick me up so I could go to work on my first 500-kilo air drop in the Atlantic Ocean. Drug smuggling had become an addiction for me. The thrill of getting the drugs into our country from Colombia and the secrecy of sneaking them into the States gave me a rush I can't explain. I boarded the twin-engine plane, and Juan sent me a present so I wouldn't be alone flying back to Miami.

In the plane were two smoking-hot Colombian girls with long, dark hair, beautiful dark skin, and some pure cocaine. Juan had given it to the girls to give to me. The girls whispered in my ear that they couldn't wait to land the plane because Juan had his limo waiting for us. They wanted me to rub the coke all over them when we were in the limo. I thought this was part of my addiction to drug smuggling—all these great benefits. These girls loved to have the coke rubbed on them. Apparently it numbed them and made their orgasms three times more intense. It got in their blood stream and made them as high as if they had snorted the coke.

In the limo the driver rolled up the privacy window. These two smoking-hot chicks stripped their clothes off and started making out with each other. They wanted me to get the coke and rub it on them. I could get used to this. One of the girls pulled out her bag of toys. I said, "Wow! This is going to be interesting." They wanted me to watch before I joined in.

The driver told me through the radio system to pick up the phone. Juan was on the other end. He said, "Are you enjoying the show, Westcoast Kid?"

I said, "Absolutely."

He said, "These girls are special. I flew them in from Colombia."

"Yes, they are special."

Juan informed me the job was delayed for a couple days and that he wanted me to enjoy myself and party with the girls. He said that he was sending me to his house in Coconut Grove because his mom was visiting at the ranch house. Reuben would be there to hang out with me until it was time to go to work. He said that he would send some more girls over to keep me entertained.

I said, "More girls?"

He wanted to keep me happy.

I said, "You're doing a good job at keeping me happy."

We pulled up at the house in Coconut Grove and it was just what I had expected: beautiful. It was smaller than his ranch house but just as nice. The usual cameras were everywhere, along with granite, marble—the works. This fucking guy had got it going on. Every time I saw those guys, it seemed as if they had more money, mansions, toys … The power and the money this guy had was mind-boggling, and to be a part of it all was unbelievable.

Reuben said the load of coke was delayed because Juan had been having issues with Pablo over the price of the kilos and some guy who flew coke out of the Bahamas. We rang the doorbell and five smoking-hot girls appeared. These girls were strippers from the Solid Gold strip club. They looked like solid gold.

Reuben explained that these girls and the Colombian girls would be staying with us for a couple days and partying. I couldn't believe this was happening to me. This was what boys and men dreamed about their whole lives. My dream kept coming true every time I was around these guys. I had another of Juan's all-you-can-snort-cocaine-and-all-you-can-fuck buffet for a couple days. Reuben came into my room. The Solid Gold girls were gone, but I couldn't seem to let go of the two Colombian girls for some reason. I went into the bathroom and found myself staring in the mirror and wondering what had happened to me. I realized then that I was out of control.

Reuben said we had to go. Juan was waiting for us at his ranch house. The limo driver was waiting for us out in the driveway. Reuben told me to say bye to the girls and that I would see them again. I kissed them both good-bye. I left them in bed, naked, and holding each other. We pulled up at Juan's ranch house, and I met his mom and dad. Juan's mom had made paella for us.

It's a seafood dish with lobster, shrimp, clams, oysters, octopus and scallops. What goes in the dish depends on the cook. Everything is mixed together with yellow rice. When we finished eating, I thanked Juan's mom for the food and told her it was delicious.

After dinner, Juan, Reuben, and I sat in Juan's office. We looked at a map and went over instructions, checking our hand-held radios and night-vision goggles. Juan gave us the GPS numbers for the location of the air drop, and said something in Spanish to Reuben about the pilot who was flying the coke in. We jumped into Juan's Chevy truck and headed to Fort Lauderdale. The boat we would use was already in the water. It was about eight o'clock in the evening when we boarded the thirty-four-foot scarab with triple 225-HP Mercury motors. When we headed out of the marina, the commercial fishing boat was already out in the Atlantic waiting for our call to meet it at the drop zone. We were forty miles out when Reuben called the fishing boat's captain. He gave him our GPS coordinates and we waited for a while with our lights off. We wore our night-vision goggles to be able to see the fishing boat. We spotted it heading toward us. Reuben was instructed to have the fishing boat follow us the last ten miles of the trip, staying a couple of miles behind us because Juan didn't want the fishing boat to know where the drop zone was. For that reason, we weren't wearing our ski masks.

It was almost midnight and we were fifty miles out in the Atlantic.

Reuben radioed the plane to make sure it was on schedule and to let the pilot know we were at our location. The pilot radioed back, "ETA is in fifteen minutes; stand by."

We could hear and see the twin-engine plane with its lights off. It started its descent, flying 200 feet off the water. It slowed down. Reuben flipped the running lights on the boat on and off a couple of times, signaling the plane that it was clear to drop the load. The plane door opened and a guy threw out the first duffel bag of coke. It crashed down, skidding and tumbling across the top of the water. The second, third, fourth, and fifth bags all came crashing down in the water. It was an awesome sight to see through the night-vision goggles. Each bag had a green glow stick attached to it so it could be located in the water without the use of a spot light. We watched the captain pick up the duffel bags before we headed back to shore, all in a matter of minutes. Cocaine worth $12,500,000 at $25,000 a kilo had hit our waters and would be on our streets in a matter of days.

We pulled into the marina where the truck sat already loaded with the cocaine. I jumped in. The keys were in the ignition. Reuben drove the dually, and I followed him to one of Juan's warehouses in Miami. There was more than 1,000 pounds of pure Colombian cocaine in the back of that truck. What had I gotten myself into? I looked in the driver's side mirror as I drove south on I-95 and wondered what had happened to me. Was this really me? What had happened to the kid who grew up on Palmetto Court in East Naples and dreamed of playing ball in college? I was addicted to drug smuggling. I could never turn back. I'd have to put sports behind me and live for the present. No one had made me drive this truck but me. I pulled inside the warehouse and stepped out of the truck. Reuben and I started unloading the coolers full of footballs. He hoped some of the kilos were broken open. If none had been, he would break some open because Juan had said we could keep the open kilos.

I said, "What if Juan finds out you did this?"

Reuben looked at me and said, "Are you going to tell Juan?"

"I guess not."

Reuben said, "Do you know how much money Juan makes off each load?"

"No, but I'm sure it's a lot."

"It's millions he makes off each load after he splits it with the Colombian cartels. Besides, I have to pay for the kilos of coke Juan made me break open and dump in the pool. Do you remember that, kid?"

"Oh yeah, I remember. It was about a $100,000 worth."

"That's right, but I'm fixing to get that money back with this load."

We took the kilos out of the coolers and laid them all out on the warehouse floor.

We start counting them, and Reuben asked me if this was the most cocaine I'd ever seen.

"Yes, and this is the first time I know the meaning of the coke just getting off the boat."

We count out 502 kilos. Reuben looked at me. "You and I just got two kilos."

He grabbed three more kilos that had busted open and said, "Now we have five kilos to split."

I started thinking about the press I had made and how much money I was fixing to make when I got back to my storage bay. The kilos, wrapped with white tape on the outside, were marked to identify the cartel this coke belonged to.

Reuben and I spent the rest of the night filling out a buyer sheet, showing the exact number of kilos ordered by each buyer in each duffel bag. I was learning this business firsthand from these guys. One of the biggest buyers ordered 150 kilos. Reuben said this guy always paid cash up front for each load and he was well connected in Miami. His brother was a cop in Miami and cops were on his payroll. His name was Frankie. Another big buyer ordered 100 kilos. Reuben told me he was from Tampa and his uncle was a federal judge there.

We loaded the coke back in the truck and turned the alarm on in the warehouse.

In the morning, Reuben and I headed back to Juan's house with our five kilos. We were tired. Juan met us at the door and advised him that everything had gone as planned and the commercial fisherman hadn't ripped off any of the kilos. We told him the load weighed 502 kilos, three of which had busted open. He said that was our bonus.

I said, "Thanks."

Juan wanted me and Ralph to meet with him and a couple Colombians the following month. He had a 30,000-pound load of weed he wanted us to bring in on the West Coast. Ralph and I would be totally responsible for this load. I would be in charge of hiring the shrimp-boat captain and the off-loading crew. I mentioned that it was a lot of responsibility and I didn't know if I was ready. "You're the Westcoast Kid," Juan said. "You can do it. I will give you and Ralph three million dollars to get that load to shore and in the truck."

I said, "Out of the three million dollars we will have to pay the shrimp-boat captain at least $500,000. For a load that size we will need at least seven to eight off-loading boats with two guys on each boat. They have to be paid at least $40,000 to $50,000 each; three radio men, $5,000 each; and the truck driver, at least $30,000 to drive the truck loaded with 30,000 pounds of pot to Miami. We'll need two escort vehicles at $5,000 each to lead and follow the truck to Miami. When all these numbers are added up, I don't know if the money left to be split between me and Ralph will be worth it all. I'll go over the numbers with Ralph when I get to Naples. I'll tell Ralph what we are being offered and see what he says. He will be the one hiring the shrimp-boat captain and the off-loading crew."

Juan took me into his vault. More than four million dollars representing his cut sat on the table. The rest of the money had been sent overseas. Juan told me to get a $100,000 out of the pile of money and give Reuben $50,000. He said he would be in Naples the next month with a couple of Colombian friends. He would bring them to Naples to meet me and Ralph. I was to get a hotel room for the meeting. I agreed and said I would tell Ralph about the meeting. Juan's limo driver took me to the airport so I could fly back to Naples.

On my flight back with the cash and the two and a half kilos of almost pure cocaine in my suitcase, I pulled out my calculator and calculated it would cost at least $1,300,000—maybe a little more—to get the 30,000-pound load to Miami. That would leave me and Ralph about $1,700,000 to split between us. That was a lot of money, but was it worth the stress of all that responsibility?

Chapter 9

I got home and took out my cash and hid it in the AC vent with the rest of my money. I also put money in zip-lock bags and hid them in my mom's old sewing machine. I thought these were the safest places in my house. My cousin gave me money to hold and hide for him. He was connected with another drug-smuggling ring.

I took the coke I got from Juan to the storage bay, and I broke it down, just one kilo, and I ended up adding twelve ounces of cut, turning those thirty-five ounces from the kilo into forty-seven ounces. I planned to send the forty-seven ounces up north where I'd be paid $1,400 an ounce. That would be a total of $65,800, but I'd have to pay my driver $3,500 out of that money. I would hide the coke under the bed liner in the back of my truck. The bricks of cocaine were only two inches high and wrapped separately. I placed them under the bed liner throughout the truck bed. I packed them that way so they were not too thick when two or three bricks were piled on top of each other. That way someone could walk in the back of the truck and not even know he was stepping on bricks of cocaine. I knew the hiding spot worked because I had been pulled over once. The cop searched my truck but didn't find the coke under the bed liner.

I bought a two-story house up north near Asheville, North Carolina. I had Juan set the deal up for me through his real-estate company. We used a fake name to conceal my identity. I paid him $200,000 for the house. I only went there once. I bought the house as an investment. I also had to buy a house in Naples. My drug business was developing really fast and I needed my own garage to make my own kilos instead of running back and forth to storage. The owner of the storage unit asked me why I spent so much time in the storage bay. I knew he was getting suspicious, and I didn't want him cutting my lock off to see what was really going on there. I told my mom because I was going on twenty years old and needed privacy, I was going to buy a house and move out. She started crying because she didn't want me to leave home. I didn't want her and my stepdad to be around the drug business anymore. It was too much of a risk for them. I was going to buy a house in town on the water, but I needed something out of town where I had more privacy. I couldn't have nosey neighbors watching me all the time. I decided to buy a house in Golden Gate estates. I remodeled the whole house, and that's where I ran my cocaine and smuggling business.

After I settled into my new home, I started throwing all-you-can-snort cocaine parties. I'd bust open a football of coke and put the whole thing into an ice bucket. I placed it in my bar so when you wanted to have a snort of coke, you could take the tongs, grab a rock, and chop it up for yourself. At the parties I would either have someone watch the ice bucket or turn on my infrared beams, which would beep when someone walked from room to room. Many came to these parties and became my friends, and the one rule I abided by was no guests could leave my home with coke on them. Aside from throwing coke parties, I hit the nightclub scene in Naples and Miami as well. At the time, I wasn't of legal drinking age, but in Naples, luckily for me, my cousin and I had a friend who owned a club. He was in the drug business too. I started hanging out at his club on the weekends since it was always packed with people and I never needed an ID to get in. Eventually I made more drug connections and ran around to other clubs as well. Through these clubs I met others who smuggled drugs out of Miami. We all became friends and ran in the same circles.

Smuggling in the seventies and eighties seemed to be the norm. Everyone was doing it or trying to. Naples was a quiet little ocean-side town where everyone knew each other. There were a lot of waterways in the back country that were accessible before the building boom started. High-rises and homes started filling in our coastline and waterways. Along with the construction boom came more people relocating to the Naples and Marco area. The Everglades was a smuggler's paradise and that's why the business thrived in those days in South Florida.

I took my boat out, looking for some new holes, and checked on some old ones for Ralph. I knew Juan was counting on me and Ralph to bring in his 30,000-pound load. He was already set up with the Colombians. Ralph also worked with other drug circles in Miami, and I was getting new connections and wanted to bring in some smaller loads myself. Ralph and I still hadn't committed to bringing in Juan's load. I spent most of the day south of Marco, around Cape Romano. I worked my way back north, winding through the back country around the Isles of Capri and Key Waden Island. I brought in a small kilo job at La Peninsula, condos on the point of Marco Pass. I unloaded the coke on the docks and drove out of the condo complex as if I lived there. I ended back at Bayview Park, loaded up my boat, called Ralph, and said I was on my way to his house to report what I had found out and which holes needed to be cut back for the boats to get through the mangroves.

When I arrived at Ralph's house, he was partying as usual. He had a large plate of coke on his pool lanai bar. He asked me about some old smuggling holes he had used in the past. I told him they were all overgrown and whichever hole we used, it would take two, maybe three, days of cutting back to get the boats through to the hole. He asked me which ones I preferred, and I said, "If we bring in the 30,000-pound load for Juan, we'll have to bring it through Cape Romano. You'll have to get someone in the Everglades we can trust to off-load the weed and put it in the truck.

Your crew and I don't know the back waters in the Everglades. It's too risky to send our guys to that area and get the boats stuck. We'd lose the load, and Juan and the Colombians won't be happy with us. It's a big load. Plus, a load that size will take more boats and Cape Romano is isolated since there are no houses or high-rises. Juan has three more back-to-back, 30,000-pound loads he wants us to bring in plus this one. He doesn't want to contract these loads to anyone else. He told me he trusted us and wanted us to do the job. He also told me to tell you, Pablo, in Colombia, is having some kind of problem with the cartels and is in trouble. That's why he's sending these loads back-to-back to get as much money as he can right now. Juan wants me to be responsible for the load with you and he wants to pay us three million dollars. I did the numbers on the load on the plane back from Miami and it will cost us at least one point three million and maybe more to get that load to a warehouse in Miami. Juan wants you to split the profit with me."

Ralph said, "Juan is my connection."

"I'm not being responsible for this load if I'm only getting paid $50,000," I said. "I make that much and more every month with my cocaine business up north, or I can help Reuben bring in coke loads on the east coast. I made $50,000 with two and a half kilos of coke, and I wasn't held responsible for anything. I also have some new connections here in Naples I made with other drug circles that want me to do loads for them. I've been the one setting up these loads with the Cubans in Miami, and Juan wants me to work for him. I'm the one who drives the Colombians around when they fly in. I'm the one that counts and drives around the millions of dollars for you and Juan and drop the money off to other smugglers after the load is brought in. I'm the American that drives the millions of dollars to the money warehouse on the east coast to be shipped over to the cartels. I see the armed guards carrying machine guns while you are sitting over here snorting hootie and enjoying the money, like you're doing right now."

Ralph asked me how much money I wanted to help him bring in the first load and share part of the responsibility.

I said, "If I'm going to be part responsible for this load and the next three loads, I want $500,000 for the first load and for the next three loads I want $700,000 on each load. All four of these loads are coming to shore in one year."

"Okay, I'll give you that but only if Juan agrees to give us three and a half million for each of the four loads."

I said, "At three and half million dollars you will still make $1,500,000 on each load after every one is paid."

Ralph said to get a hotel room at the Comfort Inn on the south corner of Goodlette Road and Route 41 across from Tin City.

"Why? Did Juan call you already?"

He said, "Yes. We have a meeting with some Colombians that were sent here. I guess it's the same cartel Juan works with."

"The guy Juan calls Pablo—that group of guys."

He said, "I guess so. That's what Juan told me."

I said, "Why here at the Comfort Inn and not on the beach?"

"The Colombians like to eat and walk around Tin City. They also like to eat at Kelly's Fish House."

I said, "Is Juan coming to the meeting?"

"Yes. He has to introduce us to them. I don't know them. These are Juan's guys. They are coming from Colombia by boat. They don't have passports and aren't allowed in the United States. When they get into Miami, Juan is having them flown in one of his planes to meet us here in Naples. He doesn't want them driving in the car from Miami to Naples. They might get pulled over by the cops and could be taken to jail because they don't have passports."

I said, "I guess I will be picking them up at Naples Airport."

"Yes, you are, and I will meet all of you at the room."

I picked Juan and the two Colombians up at the Naples airport. Juan introduced me as the Westcoast Kid. One Colombian said his name was José. He said, "Juan told me you were the one that got our 10,000-pound load to shore." He was glad to be able to thank me personally for that job.

I said, "Thanks. No problem."

The other Colombian was in his late fifties. He had a pockmarked face and a lean build with grayish black hair and a mustache. He said his name was Jesus. "I'm glad to meet you."

José was in his forties, heavyset with black hair and a mustache. He asked me how long I had been in Naples and if I had kids and a family.

"No, I don't have any kids, but I do have family living here. I've lived in Naples all my life."

José said, "You won't be too hard to find if someone was looking for you."

"No, I guess not."

José asked me if I wanted a line of coke he had brought over from Colombia. He had hand-picked the cocaine himself right out of the lab in the jungle where the drug was processed. I said no thanks, and he asked me why I didn't want a line.

I said, "Because I'm driving some undocumented Colombians around in my home town, and I don't need to start getting high. We have a meeting to go to."

Juan laughed and said, "That's why the Westcoast Kid doesn't want a line of cocaine?"

I said, "Maybe later."

We were in the room now—Ralph, Juan, Jesus, José and I. All three men were introduced to each other and started talking in Spanish. All of them were doing cocaine and so was Juan. José asked me again if I wanted a line.

I said, "Not right now."

He jumped up, grabbed a gun out of his waistband, and pushed me up against the wall. He pointed the gun at me and asked if I worked for the DEA or the US Customs. Then he started searching me for a wire. Juan and Ralph yelled at him in Spanish and he backed off me and put his gun back in his pants. Ralph said to go down to his truck and get his map out and bring it back to the room. On the way to the truck I realized these were the whacked-out mother fuckers we were going to be bringing loads in for.

I returned to the room with the map. José wanted to search me again to make sure that when I had gone to the truck, I hadn't put a wire on to record our conversation.

We all looked at the map of our coast and Ralph and I pointed out where the loads would come to shore. We explained to the Colombians why it was the best place to bring in a load of that size. Ralph informed them we would use an off-loading crew in the Everglades, the reason being that those guys had grown up in the Everglades and knew the waterways better than our crews. Juan asked Ralph if we would have someone on the water we could trust so we didn't get ripped off.

Ralph said, "Yes. We will have someone watching the load go down. The two men in charge of the off-loading crew are friends of mine. One of them worked for me before, on another load, and I didn't have any problems with the guy."

José asked me again if I wanted a line.

I said, "Yeah, if you don't search me again."

They all laughed. Juan said he would send Reuben from Miami to be with Ralph and the Westcoast Kid to make sure everything went as planned when the load came to shore. They started talking in Spanish again, and Juan cursed about Pablo and money. Ralph and I sat there and stared.

Juan looked at me and said, "I told the Westcoast Kid three million dollars for this load, didn't I, Kid?"

Ralph spoke up. "We're not bringing this load in for three million dollars." They all shut up and looked at him.

He said, "It's three and a half million dollars or you have someone else do it."

I said, "Yes, you did, Juan," and they started arguing in Spanish again. They all looked at me.

"I'm with him," I said. "If you want this load brought to Miami, it's three and a half million."

They started arguing even louder. I said to keep it down, that they were getting too loud.

They stopped talking and asked us if we would guarantee the load.

Ralph said, "Yes, but we want some start-up money."

They asked how much and Ralph told them we wanted at least $250,000 and the balance was to be paid in full when the load arrived in Miami so we could pay the off-loaders, radio men, and the driver. Of this money, $150,000 would be a deposit on the shrimp boat bringing the pot back to the off-loaders. The shrimp-boat captain wouldn't do the job without the deposit. I had already talked to the shrimp-boat captain who wanted some of his money up front.

I got up to go to the bathroom. The toilet was stuffed up with the whole rolls of toilet paper and a couple of hotel towels. I walked out. Ralph looked at me and shook his head. The look on his face told me not to say anything about what I had just seen.

Juan and the Colombians came to the agreement that they would give us three and a half million on each load and the $250,000 up front on each load. We would be paid in full when the load was in the warehouse in Miami. Juan said the four loads were to be brought in within one year. The first load would be in two months and the other three loads would be every three months.

"Make sure the bales that have a red or white tag on the corner get loaded into the truck," he said.

The GPS numbers would be given to us one week before the shrimper was to meet the freighter in the Gulf of Mexico off the Yucatan Peninsula. Juan said Reuben would keep us posted on everything.

We all shook hands and snorted some more cocaine. José asked me if I wanted to bring in 500 kilos of coke. It would be dropped out of a plane just like the job I worked on with Reuben in Miami, wherever I wanted it to be dropped.

I asked, "When will the job be ready?"

José said, "Next month and I will pay you $1,000 a kilo and all you have to do is get the coke into shore and truck it to Miami to one of Juan's warehouses."

I said, "Why me? A couple hours ago you thought I worked with the feds."

José said, "Because I trust you now."

Ralph looked at me and said, "There you go. That can be your first load all by yourself."

I said, "I don't know. That's a lot of responsibility for me to have especially with these four loads we just contracted from you guys. I will have to think about it and I will let Juan know. Okay?"

José said, "You have a few weeks, or I will give the job to someone else."

"Okay."

Ralph and I left the hotel in Ralph's truck. Juan and the Colombians stayed in the room. I left them the car keys so Juan could drive the Colombians around town. I knew they had plenty of coke to snort because José had about three ounces in his plastic bag. I didn't know where they would use a bathroom because the Colombians had stuffed everything but the bathroom sink in the toilet.

Ralph said, "Did you notice when José walked in the hotel room, he went straight to the bathroom?"

"Yeah. I was wondering why he was in there so long."

Ralph said Colombians don't trust Americans. When José offered me a line of coke, I said no, and he thought I was an informant. That's why he stuffed up the toilet.

I said, "Yeah. He offered me a line of coke when I picked him up at the airport."

"José searched you for a recording device after he stuffed up the toilet in case you had one you wanted to flush away."

I said I would rather work for Juan and not the Colombians. They were too unpredictable.

Ralph said, "Where do you think the drugs come from? Not Cuba where Juan and I are from. We have to work for the Colombians. They grow all the drugs we smuggle. That's how Juan makes all his money—through the Colombians."

"José offered you a coke drop. Are you going to do it? It's $500,000 you can make."

I said, "Yeah, and it's worth over twelve million dollars of coke on the streets, and the Colombians sit in Colombia and collect all the money while we take all the risk here in the States."

Chapter 10

Ralph introduced me to his personal pilot in Naples. I started renting planes to fly over to Miami, buying footballs, and going to the strip clubs. I didn't have an ID. When I entered the strip club, the door man would ask for my ID. I would pull out a stack of hundreds and hand each bill to him until he said, "Okay come on in."

I had my own private section and asked the manager to bring the hottest girls to my table for the night. I spent $15,000 to $25,000 a weekend on friends, girls, planes, limos, and hotels. I was a kid and having fun.

After the weekend was over, I would meet Reuben at the airport, load the kilos on the plane, and fly back to Naples. I didn't have to worry about being pulled over on US 41 by the cops. It was a safe way to transport the kilos.

The first of the four, back-to-back, 30,000-pound loads was ready to be brought in. I was going to make $500,000 on the first. Ralph and I loaded up the night-vision goggles and the ski masks for the captain and his crew on the shrimp boat. I counted out $150,000 for the deposit on the shrimp boat.

Ralph and I met the captain and his first mate at their house. We gave them both the final details on the load. The captain's name was Johnny. He was fat and wore a beard. He looked as if he had been a shrimper all his life. The first mate's name was Skitter. I guess that was his nickname. He was skin and bones and wore a mustache. He smelled of alcohol first thing in the morning. I wondered if the first mate was strong enough to even lift a bale of pot, or if he was able to survive the trip. We handed over the money to the captain. We would still owe him $350,000 when the load was delivered to the off-loaders. Ralph explained to the captain the Everglades crew would make the pickup forty-five miles west of Cape Romano, and the shrimper would meet up with the freighter 200 miles out in the gulf. We gave them the time of the meet, the GPS numbers, and the radio channel. We would be on a different radio channel from the off-loading crew, coordinating the off-loading crew when the shrimp boat was in the drop-off location. We told the captain all the Cubans ordered was 30,000 pounds, and that's what Ralph and I had contracted. That was it.

Ralph told the captain, "Don't make radio contact with us until you are a few hours away from the drop-off location."

Ralph and I took the captain and the first mate to the grocery store to buy supplies for the trip. All Skitter worried about was having enough beer. That was all he cared about. I told Skitter he might need to eat some food. He laughed and said he didn't eat much food. That was obvious, and I wasn't too happy having this drunk on the boat when I was bringing back 30,000 pounds of pot I was partly responsible for.

We were now headed to a marina in Fort Myers, Florida, where the shrimpers docked their boats. Ralph and I helped load the groceries on the boat, which was so old I wondered if it could make the trip. I didn't want the boat breaking down on the way back with our load on it. The captain assured me the boat would make it back with our load.

It was ten o'clock at night. We're sitting together in a house in Everglades City—Reuben, Ralph, Robert, the guy Ralph had hired to take charge of the off-loading crew, and I. He was a weather-beaten, medium-build, gray-haired, older man who had been raised in the Everglades and looked it. The house was a run-down, stilt home with a wooden frame. The exterior needed new paint, but inside, the house looked like a new model home with marble floors, granite counter tops, and the works. I guess the Everglades boys hid their money pretty well. Robert told me and Reuben not to worry about the load. Robert's partner, the one on the water with the crew, had brought in lots of loads with a good crew. Reuben snorted coke and so did Ralph. I was in charge of monitoring the radio and waiting for the call from the shrimp-boat captain.

It was eleven o'clock. A call came over the radio. It was the captain letting us know the weather was beautiful. That was the code to tell us he was right on schedule. He was three hours away from meeting the off-loaders forty miles off Cape Romano. I radioed the captain back to let him know the weather was also beautiful where I was—no rain in the sky. That was the code to tell him the off loaders were on their way to the pickup location and everything was clear on the coast. Reuben made a call to Juan in Miami to let him know the load would soon arrive and to stand by. Reuben and Ralph continued to snort coke. The pot coming to shore in a matter of hours had a street value of fifteen to eighteen million dollars and they both should stop snorting coke and be alert. I advised them if Juan had been there, he would have been pissed at both of them. They told me to shut the fuck up and warned me not tell Juan they were snorting coke.

Another couple of hours went by. Ralph and Reuben were coked out and had started to become paranoid. They took out their guns, looked out the windows, and hid in the bedrooms, believing the cops were outside watching the house. I could only think about how fucking dumb they had been to get coked out in view of the responsibility we had. Now I was on my fucking own. Those two coked-out assholes were no good to me.

I got a call on the hand-held radio from the guy who was on the water and in charge of the off-loading crew. He said the job had been busted. I said, "What do you mean, the load is busted?" He told me the US Customs, DEA, and Blue Thunder were everywhere and the cops were chasing the off-loading crew. I sent Robert down to the water to find out if the bust was real, or the load was actually being ripped off. I went into the bedroom where Ralph and Reuben were hiding and still snorting coke. I told them I thought the load was busted, and I had sent Robert down to the water to make sure. Reuben needed to ask Juan to call the Colombians and let them know what was going on.

Reuben said, "I'm too coked out to call Juan."

I said, "I'll wait until Robert comes back to the house with an update from the radio men on the water."

Robert came back with the report that the load has been busted and the DEA, US Customs, and the Blue Thunder strike force were out on the water chasing and boarding the off-loaders' boats.

I said, "Fuck, you have to be kidding me. Did any of the loads make it to shore?"

Robert said he didn't know and he didn't want to go out on a boat to see for himself what was going on if the DEA, US Customs, and Blue Thunder were all over the water. There was no way he could be on the water with two coked-out Cubans at three o'clock in the morning. He knew he would surely be boarded and taken into custody. I told Reuben, "I have to report to Juan and tell him the load is busted."

I called Juan and gave him the bad news. He flipped out on me and said, "Ralph said he would have someone on the water watching the load to make sure it wouldn't get busted."

"Let me talk to Reuben."

I said, "He can't talk right now."

Juan asked, "What's wrong with him?" He was getting suspicious and had started thinking I might be busted and recording the phone call.

"No, Juan, Reuben, and Ralph are too blowed out to talk. They were partying the whole time we were waiting for the job to make it to shore."

He started yelling in Spanish and told me to watch the news on TV and get the newspaper so we'd have proof for his friends overseas the job was busted. He'd head to Naples in the morning to deal with the bullshit and asked me to flush the shit down the toilet; he would deal with Reuben and Ralph when he arrived in Naples. I told him we would be at Ralph's house. He instructed me to pick him up at Naples Airport at eleven o' clock the next morning.

I tried calling the captain several times on the radio, but there was no answer. I figured he and the crew were also busted. I didn't know anything. All I knew was that I was in deep shit, and I was responsible for fifteen to eighteen million dollars' worth of busted or missing pot. I went to the bedroom and grabbed the plate of coke. Reuben asked me what I was doing.

"Juan told me to flush it down the toilet."

Reuben asked me if I had told Juan he had been snorting coke and I said yes. Juan was pissed at him and Ralph. Reuben pulled his gun on me and said, "If you flush the coke down the toilet, I will shoot you."

"Go ahead, Reuben, shoot me because right now, I'm in a lot more trouble than getting shot. We are all in deep shit. Juan has called the Colombians. Some of them are flying over to see proof the load had indeed been busted and hasn't been ripped off because Ralph and I were responsible for that fucking load. I hope like hell it has been busted. Juan is flying here to Naples in the morning at eleven o'clock to see what the hell is going on. He is pissed at you and Ralph. So, you might want to save some bullets and get some sleep before Juan gets here."

I dropped them both off at Ralph's house. I told Ralph to throw out any drugs he had lying around in case the cops came by. I went home and cleaned my house too. I couldn't sleep. I kept thinking we should have been on the water watching the load go down. We didn't know the off-loaders, and we could have seen what happened.

I got out of bed and turned on the morning news, hoping to see the load busted on TV. I turned to the other local news channels and there was nothing on the news about a busted load. The bust couldn't have been in the newspaper because the load supposedly got busted early in the morning. I would have to wait until the following day's paper. I could still watch the noon and the evening news in hopes the load got busted.

I dressed and picked Juan up at the Airport. He had one of his bodyguards with him, a 6-foot-4, 290-pound body builder. Juan got in my truck and said, "I haven't seen anything on the news."

I said, "Not yet. I haven't heard anything from the shrimp-boat captain either. I've tried calling their cell phones and there's no answer."

Juan told me to take him to Ralph's house. We got there to find Reuben still sleeping. Juan woke him up by yelling at him in Spanish. Ralph heard all the commotion and came out of the bathroom. The bodyguard stood there watching as Juan yelled at Reuben, who got out of bed. We were all sitting at the dining room table discussing what we knew about what had happened the night before. The noon news was on and there still wasn't anything about our busted load. Juan said one of us should have been out on the water watching the off-loaders and making sure there was no bullshit going down instead of getting high on cocaine, waiting at a house in the Everglades, trusting the off-loaders to bring our load in. The Colombians were on their way to see proof the load was busted. Juan called his pilot at Naples Airport and sent me there to have the pilot fly me to some of the marinas where the DEA and the US Customs took confiscated boats. He wanted me to see if I could spot the shrimper that was supposed to bring our load in.

We flew to the marinas between Marathon and Fort Myers but couldn't find the shrimper. We were in deep shit and the Colombians were going to think Ralph and I were in on the missing load that we were responsible for.

We landed back at Naples Airport. I called Juan and told him I couldn't find any sign of the shrimper. Juan said there wasn't anything on the evening news either. I drove back to Ralph's house and tried calling the captain on his cell phone. Still no answer. Juan was pissed. We couldn't even get in touch with the captain Ralph hired. Juan and Ralph started arguing in Spanish and the bodyguard stood up beside Juan. Reuben calmed Juan and Ralph down. Juan wanted me to monitor the newspaper and watch the local news so we could show the Colombians where their load was in case it had been busted. Juan said he had to head back to

Miami to meet the Colombians when they arrived. He told me to keep calling the captain of the shrimp boat to find out where the fuck he was.

Four or five more days passed before I received a call from the shrimp-boat captain, who asked me to pick him and Skitter up at Naples Airport at 11:30 a.m. I called Juan and Ralph to let them both know I was on my way to pick up the captain. Juan asked me to bring him and the first mate to Miami. I said okay. I called Ralph. "Are you going to Miami with me so we can meet Juan and the Colombians with the captain?"

"He's pissed," Ralph said. "No. I better stay here."

"You want me to go by myself?"

"Yes, you will be okay."

The captain and the first mate got in my truck and acted as if nothing were wrong.

"Where the fuck have you two been and where is the fucking load?"

The captain said the leader of the off-loading crew took the whole crew off the shrimper down to Marathon to a hotel for a few days.

"It's been almost a week and you left the whole fucking load and the boat with the off-loading crew leader? Why the fuck didn't you call me or Ralph? It's our fucking load. The load doesn't belong to the off-loaders. The load is missing, you mother fucker."

The captain then told me a Colombian on the freighter had said someone in the States had ordered another 10,000 pounds of weed to be put on the boat, no matter what. We hadn't ordered 10,000 extra pounds. The captain said the Colombian told him the order came from the Cubans and the Westcoast Kid. They had put the extra weed in the sleeping quarters, and filled up the galley and everywhere on the boat they could find to hide the extra pot. An unmarked gray plane had buzzed the shrimp boat twice at a low altitude on the way back to the Florida coast.

I realized there was something not right. The load was missing 10,000 extra pounds, and an unmarked plane had buzzed a shrimper full of weed. It had to be the feds, and someone was an informant for the DEA or the US Customs. Someone on that fucking freighter from Colombia was also an informant or an agent.

The captain said he knew nothing.

I said, "Okay, you can tell what you know to some of the guys who own part of that load in Miami."

The captain asked where we were going.

"I'm taking you both to Miami to meet the Cubans and the Colombians."

I called Juan, who wanted to meet us at a restaurant. When I pulled into the parking lot, Juan, Reuben, three body guards, and the two Colombians, José and Jesus, got out of Juan's van. I introduced the captain and the first mate to Juan, and we all went inside to eat. The captain and the first mate told Juan they wanted some coke and some girls as if nothing were wrong. Juan and the Colombians were getting pissed. Juan told me to give my truck keys to Reuben. I gave my keys to Reuben and he left the restaurant for about twenty minutes in my truck. A million thoughts went through my mind. Were they putting a bomb in my truck? Why would Reuben take my truck down the road? I didn't like that and the fact these two mother fuckers were still talking to Juan about partying and girls while fifteen to eighteen million dollars' worth of pot were missing.

Reuben returned to the restaurant and handed me my keys. Juan said, "I want you guys to follow us to a hotel."

I agreed, threw the truck keys to the captain, and told him to crank up the truck because I had to go to the bathroom. I wasn't going to crank up that fucking truck in case they had put a bomb in it. Outside, Juan told me to ride in the van with him. He said the captain and the first mate knew what had happened to the load and I would find out what they knew.

"Juan, I don't know what's going on. All I know is the captain told me the leader of the off-loading crew ordered the captain and his crew off the shrimp boat, and they were taken to a hotel in Marathon. The captain told me a Colombian on the freighter told him the Cubans in Miami and the Westcoast Kid had ordered another 10,000 pounds of pot on top of the 30,000 pounds.

Juan said, "I didn't order that, and the two Colombians in the van,

Jesus and José, said they didn't order the extra pot either. The shrimp boat was buzzed twice from a low-flying, unmarked, gray plane as it was coming back to Florida with our load."

I asked Juan why Reuben had taken my truck. He said Reuben had gone through the captain's and first mate's luggage to search for recording devices and to remove the bullets from their guns. We got to the room where two of the body guards now had weight-lifting belts on. Juan took me in the bathroom and said the Colombians thought Ralph and I were in on the missing load because we were both responsible for it and neither one of us knew where the hell it was. Juan said it didn't look good for Ralph and me. He told me, the captain, and the first mate to act as if nothing was wrong and all they wanted to do was party. He said he was going to send a message to Ralph in Naples. Ralph should have been at the meeting and the Colombians were pissed at him. Juan was going to have his bodyguard break the captain's leg in front of me and the first mate to let us know the Colombians weren't playing games with us, and they wanted their fucking load back. I told Juan I didn't want to see the bodyguard break the captain's leg, and I'd leave the room. Juan pulled out his gun and stuck the barrel to my head and said, "No. I think you will stay and watch the body guard break his leg."

"I think you're right, Juan. I will stay."

He lowered the gun and said he knew I had nothing to do with the off-loading going badly, or I wouldn't be there in the hotel with him and the Colombians.

I said, "If you break the captain's leg, he will go straight to the cops and that will jeopardize all of us."

"You're right, Kid. It's too early for violence."

Juan told me to get back to Naples and tell Ralph what had just happened and the Colombians were pissed at him and me. He couldn't hold the Colombians off much longer before they took matters into their own hands.

"Alright, Juan, I will still monitor the news and the newspapers."

"Stay in touch with me on any updates, try to get the captain to talk, and find out who the off-loading crew leader is."

"Okay."

I headed back to Naples to tell the captain the bodyguards were going to break his leg, but I had talked Juan out of it.

The captain said he would have pulled out his gun and shot the body guard.

I said, "What were you going to shoot the body guard with?"

The captain pulled out his gun from his pants waist and said, "My .38 pistol."

"Yeah, well, how the hell are you going to shoot the bodyguard with no bullets in your gun?"

The captain said, "I have bullets in my gun." He opened up the chamber and said, "What the hell happened to my bullets?"

"Remember when Reuben took my truck?"

The captain nodded.

I said, "Reuben took the bullets out of your guns because he was going to break your leg. You'd better come clean and tell the Cubans and the Colombians what you know about this load because I'm not taking the fall by myself and getting killed for something I didn't steal. I saved your ass once. I will not do it again. I will bring the Cubans and the Colombians straight to your house and let them deal with you and get the answers they are looking for out of both of you."

I dropped the captain and the first mate off at his house and the captain said, "When can I get the rest of my money for the load?"

I said, "You're kidding, right?"

He said, "No."

"You will get the rest of your money when you tell us what you know about the load. Then you might get lucky and Juan might let you live, but I have no control over what Juan is going to do to you. Good luck and enjoy what life you have left."

Chapter 11

I drove straight over to Ralph's house. He was partying as usual. I told him, "The Colombians think you and I are in on the missing load. Juan was going to have the bodyguards break the captain's leg—he wanted me to watch—to send you a message the Colombians aren't playing games with us anymore. They said it's our responsibility to find the load. We are the ones that hired the off-loaders, and we better find out who stole the load."

Ralph started yelling in Spanish and cursing Juan out.

I said, "The Colombians think you have something to hide because you weren't at the meeting today."

Ralph said, "You and I didn't steal the load."

"You and I know that, Ralph, but the Colombians don't know that. The Colombians want to know what we are doing to get the load back."

I explained to Ralph what the captain had said, about him being taken off the shrimp boat to a hotel in Marathon and about the 10,000 extra pounds. The Colombians and Juan hadn't ordered the extra weed either, and an unmarked, gray plane had buzzed the shrimp boat twice as it headed back to Florida. Juan and I thought an informant or an undercover

DEA or US Customs agent was working the load, someone with ties in Colombia. That was who was in on the extra 10,000 pounds. Juan wanted to know why the crew leader had removed the captain and the crew from the shrimp boat and the captain of the shrimp boat had told me, Juan, and the Colombians in the hotel room the off-loading crew didn't want the shrimp-boat crew to see their faces. That excuse didn't make sense because they all wore ski masks to hide their faces.

I asked Ralph, "Have you talked to the two crew leaders you hired to run the off-loading crew?"

Ralph said, "The only one I have talked to so far is Robert, the one at the house with us in the Everglades the night the load came into shore. Robert says he doesn't know where his off-loading partner is."

"Ralph, something's wrong. The load is ripped off and hidden, and you and I are getting the blame for it because it is our load."

Ralph said, "I know, and I don't want us to get killed for something we didn't do. We have to start carrying guns until we solve this mess."

I said, "I don't want to carry a gun."

"Do you want to get killed for something you didn't steal?"

I said, "Hell, no!"

Ralph said, "You better carry a gun, then."

A few days went by. There was still nothing on the local news channel or in the newspaper. Ralph couldn't locate the other off-loading-crew leader and Juan and the Colombians weren't calling Ralph and me as much as they had before. When the Cubans and Colombians cut off all communication, Ralph and I knew that was not good. Juan didn't answer his phone either when Ralph and I called him.

After picking up a few things for dinner at the grocery store, I walked out to my truck in the parking lot. A van door opened up beside my truck and three huge men jumped out, grabbed me, and threw me into a van and put a hood over my head. I was so fucking scared, I couldn't breathe. I ended up at Naples Airport. I was put on a plane with the three bodyguards and a Colombian I hadn't seen before. We flew at about 4,000 feet in a twin-engine plane over the Gulf of Mexico. A phone rang in the seat behind me and a man spoke in Spanish. I thought I was going to puke when one of the men said, "Someone wants to talk to you." I'd seen a couple of these men already. They were Juan's bodyguards. The man handed me the phone. A man's voice asked, "Am I talking to the Westcoast Kid?"

"Yes."

The man said, "This is Pablo Escobar from Colombia. Do you know who I am?"

I said, "No, but I heard Juan mention your name a few times."

The man on the phone said he and his cartel partners owned the load I had stolen with Ralph, and they wanted their fucking load back, or he would have me tortured and both of us killed. The phone went dead. The plane door opened, and one of the bodyguards pointed a gun at me and told me to stand by the open door.

The Colombian said, "Tell me where the load is, or you're going swimming."

The body guard said, "Stick your legs out of the plane, or I will put a bullet in the back of your head."

I was now sitting with my legs hanging out of the plane and looking at the water, scared to death.

The Colombian said, "I'm going to ask you one more time: Where is our load?"

I panicked and said, "I know where it's at, and I know who has it."

The plane door shut, we landed back at Naples Airport, and I was back in the van. The hood went back over my head and I started to puke. I asked one of the guys to take the hood off my head because I couldn't breathe and I was starting to puke. The hood came off, and the van pulled over on US 41 so I could puke on the side of the road. I got back in the van, shaking at this point. I knew I was on my way to Miami. A million thoughts ran through my head: my mom, family, my coach, and college ball. Were they going to torture me and kill me and then go after Ralph?

No one knew. I was in this van, just me and the guys who had kidnapped me from the parking lot. I hadn't seen this coming. The van had been parked right beside my truck. I had been pulled in the van in a matter of seconds with guns pointed at me.

The hood went back over my head, and we continued driving for a while. I knew we were somewhere in Miami now because I could hear other cars blowing their horns. The van stopped and started repeatedly. When it came to a final stop, I was escorted out with my hands handcuffed behind my back. I was put into a chair, and all I could hear were footsteps walking around me. In the distance the footsteps stopped. It was silent. I shook and wanted to puke. Again the hood came off and it was dark. All I could see were red laser lights pointed at me and flashing all around my body. At first I thought I was in a night club or something. A light came on and I saw these same three men pointing machine guns with laser lights at me. I was in a warehouse. An oriental guy stood at a table. He wore a white lab coat with a clear shield over his face. He had rubber gloves on up to his elbows and the table had tools on it that looked like doctor's tools. I started shaking and asked one of the body guards if Juan was there and what they were going to do to me. They wouldn't speak. The oriental guy came over to me, carrying some kind of tool in his hand. He smiled at me, got closer, and stuck that tool on me. I screamed and fell out of my chair onto the floor, flopping like a fish. He was giving me electric shocks. He stopped and I thought my heart had stopped. He shocked me again, this time longer, while I was still lying on the floor. He stopped again and waited a couple of minutes for me to regain my composure. He walked back over to the table of tools and grabbed another one. He was coming back over to me when the door opened and in came the two Colombians, Jesus and José.

José said, "I see you met our oriental friend already."

"Yeah, he just shocked the shit out of me."

José said, "That's nothing compared to what he's fixing to do to you for stealing our load."

I said, "I didn't steal your fucking load. I told the guys on the plane I can get it back. I said the off-loaders stole it. José motioned to the oriental guy to come over to where I was still lying on the floor. He had a tool that looked like a drill a dentist would use. José asked me if I knew what the oriental was holding in his hand. I said no. José told me it was a drill to put holes through my finger nails. José asked me if I would like the oriental to show me how it works.

I said, "Do I have a choice? You are asking me to give you a load I don't have."

José told the body guard to grab and hold my arm. Two bodyguards grabbed me and one held my hand out behind my back. The oriental turned the drill on and walked closer to me. The door opened again and Juan walked in. He told the bodyguards to let go of me, put me back in the chair, and turn that fucking drill off. He asked me what they had done to me.

They had put me on the phone with Pablo Escobar and had made me hang my legs out of the plane, fixing to push me out over the Gulf of Mexico, and I had ended up there asking for him. I thought my heart had stopped. I felt as if I were in a deep sleep. They had given me shocks even while I was still lying on the floor.

Juan yelled at the Colombians in Spanish and they yelled back at him. They pulled out their guns and pointed them at Juan. Juan's body guards pointed their guns at the Colombians. I sat in the chair even more scared, if that were possible. Thinking there was going to be a shootout, and we all were going to end up dead, I yelled at them, "Wait a minute. We can get the load back. Don't start shooting each other. Put your fucking guns down, and we can talk. Everyone put your guns down. We can recoup some of the lost load. We can start kidnapping the off-loaders one by one, and they can lead us to the stolen pot."

Juan apologized to me and said, "The Colombians in Colombia ordered you to be kidnapped to find out what you know about the missing load. Pablo is the main guy in the cartel in Colombia. He ordered all this, and José and Jesus followed Pablo's orders."

I said, "Yeah, José and Jesus had your bodyguards throw me in the van."

Juan said, "I know. One of my bodyguards called me behind José's back to tell me they were going to torture you. That's why I came here to the warehouse. You have my bodyguard to thank for saving your ass from the oriental. That guy is brutal. Kid, this missing load is getting out of my hands. You and Ralph have to start rounding up the off-loaders to prove you didn't steal the load. It's a lot of money that's missing and the Colombians are pissed. They think you and Ralph are in on the rip-off."

"Juan, thanks for saving my ass. I know what Ralph and I need to do. I don't want to die or especially be tortured for something I didn't steal."

Juan had his pilot fly me back to Naples and his bodyguard escort me to the airport. On the flight back I hoped this body guard wouldn't throw me out of the plane because at that point I didn't trust anyone. I wanted out of the smuggling business while I was still alive.

I drove to Ralph's house and told him I had been kidnapped. José and Jesus were going to throw me out of a plane, and then they were going to torture me while he was sitting in Naples. I didn't say anything to him about getting electrocuted. I didn't want another argument to start between Juan and Ralph.

"I'm tired of fucking around with the off-loaders. I told Juan we will start kidnapping them one by one, and they will lead us to the pot."

I told Ralph we had no choice. The orders were coming from Colombia and Juan said it was out of his hands. "We better get some of the lost load back and prove to the Colombians we aren't in on the rip-off."

Ralph said okay. He called a Cuban friend in Miami and hired a couple of guys to be our enforcers. We set up a meeting between the two men we had just hired in Miami. One was an American; about 6-foot-2 with a beard, shoulder-length hair, and a muscular build. He said he was in the Special Forces. His name was Shane. The other guy was a short Cuban with an attitude. He was an older man with a beard and scarred up face.

We called him Shorty. We explained to them what our problem was and what we wanted to do.

They said, "Just show us the people you want kidnapped and we'll take care of it and get your weed back."

We told them, "We're not killing anyone. Is that understood?"

Shorty said, "What about torture?"

I said, "That won't be necessary. Once these guys are secured, they will talk. I know from experience."

Ralph and I had a warehouse set up where the off-loaders could be brought for questioning. Ralph showed the enforcers where one of the off-loaders lived. Three hours later we got a call from Shane telling us he had a visitor who wanted to talk to us.

Ralph and I drove to the warehouse. We walked in and there sat a young guy from the Everglades with his hands tied behind his back. He was crying and his lip was bleeding. I told him to quit crying, and I had Shane untie his hands.

I said, "We're not going to kill you. Here are your options. You tell us what you know and what we want to hear. It's weed or bleed. It's your choice."

He was hired to help off-load the pot. When he got to the shrimp boat, the crew had gone, and the off-loaders were taking the weed off the boat.

I said, "How much weed do you have?"

He had 400 pounds and had already sold 150 pounds. He still had most of the cash.

I said, "We want the weed and the cash back. How much cash is it?'

He said, "About $75,000."

"We want the names—who was with you? And we want to know how much weed they have, and who else you know that was working that load."

He said, "Okay, whatever you guys want. Just don't hurt me."

I said, "You will ride with me in my truck and take us to where the weed and cash is, and I will drive you around and you can tell me where the other off-loaders live."

The next guy we kidnapped had 800 pounds of weed and $150,000 in cash. Ralph and I kept the cash we collected. Each guy we kidnapped led us to another. It was simple.

We told each guy we kidnapped, "Weed or bleed, that's your only option."

Once the word got out to the off-loaders we were kidnapping them, they all started going out of town and hiding, or going to the cops for protection.

We collected about 8,000 pounds of weed and more than a million dollars in cash, and I gave it all to the Colombians, but they were still pissed. We owed them another 22,000 pounds. I found out why Juan had told Ralph and me to make sure we loaded the bales that had a red or white tag on the corner. Those bales had kilos of coke hidden in the middle of the bale. The Cubans and the Colombians had hidden their cocaine in the bales of pot and had only paid us for smuggling the pot. They were not stupid. That was for sure. With the 10,000 extra pounds of pot was put on the shrimp boat, some of the other off-loaders, informants, and agents walked away with 32,000 pounds of pot. It had a street value (depending on what the stolen weed was sold for and what else the pot was used for) of $19,200,000 if sold for $600 a pound.

The Colombians wanted Ralph and me to make up the difference on 22,000 pounds. The Colombians thought they were still owed. They wanted us to work out the difference on the next three loads. I told Ralph I was done working for that circle. "They're fucking crazy and someone is an informant or agent building a case on us. I'm sure they already have us under surveillance and know who we are because that load was set up from the beginning. We were used by the government to get whatever it is the government was after. All I know, Ralph, is 32,000 pounds of pot disappeared along with the shrimp boat."

Chapter 12

I continued running my drug business up north, and tried to get over the nightmare of the load that had gone bad. I was still trying to figure out what had happened. Ralph continued bringing in small loads when he got the chance.

Six months went by. I was out in front of my house. A car had stopped on the street and someone was taking pictures of me. I thought it might be the Colombians wanting to kidnap me again. I went in the house and called Ralph, who said the same thing had happened to him a few days earlier. We were scared and thought it might be the Colombians or the feds. A few days later, another guy stopped in my street and took pictures of me. I got in my truck with my pistol. I chased the car down my road. It was a dead end so the guy was cornered. I pulled up behind him so he couldn't turn his car around and leave. He stuck his hand out of the window and held up his badge.

I said to myself, "Shit. At least it's not the Colombians."

He got out of his car and said, "I'm DEA Special Agent Ryan of the narcotics unit."

"What the fuck are you taking pictures of me for?"

Ryan said I was under surveillance for narcotics trafficking and the importation of narcotics into the United States.

I said, "Who told you this?"

He said he was not allowed to tell me that. It was confidential information. He gave me his card and advised me I was on the top of his list and US Customs also wanted to talk to me.

I said, "I don't have anything to say."

The agent said, "Can you move your truck so I can leave?"

I called Ralph and told him it was not the Colombians looking for us.

"Who was it?" he asked.

"It was the DEA and the US Customs. He told me I was under surveillance and I asked him what it was for and he said I was on the top of his list."

"What list?"

"I don't know. Probably the same list you're on, I would guess. The agent wants to talk to me."

"What did you tell the agent?"

"I told the agent I didn't have anything to say. He said the agents are on to us. It's about that fucking load that went bad."

Ralph said, "Yes. That's what it's all about."

A couple more days goes by. I was in my bedroom and I heard something on my audio-video monitor. I looked at the monitor and saw a cop car and a couple of undercover agents pull in behind the cop in my driveway.

Holy shit! I had two kilos of coke in my garage and a lot of money I hadn't buried yet.

They knocked on the door. I answered. There were three agents. One of them was Agent Ryan who had taken the pictures of me. The other agent said he was the lead US Customs agent from Miami, and he wanted to ask me questions about some Cubans in Miami and Colombians. The agents had some pictures of Juan, Reuben, José, Jesus, and some of Juan's bodyguards. The lead detective's name was Agent Smith. He knew Ralph and I were tied to the drug smuggling operation that was responsible for importing tons of marijuana and cocaine from Colombia for the cartels. The agents asked me if I were willing to cooperate in exchange for a lighter sentence. If I didn't cooperate, they would personally make sure I'd never get out of prison and would die in there.

I told them, "I don't have anything to say to you guys."

Agent Smith said, "When you're ready to talk, here's my card and by the way you might want this picture." He handed me a photo of me, Juan, and Reuben getting on one of Juan's planes in Miami with the Colombians. The agent said there were more pictures of me, Juan, and the Colombians. He asked me if I wanted to see the rest of the pictures. I shook my head. The agent said, "We heard about what happened to you in the warehouse with the Colombians in Miami and those are the same men you are trying to protect. You have my card and you have a nice day, Westcoast Kid. I will be waiting for your phone call."

The agents left and I drove over to Ralph's house to let him know what had just happened. I hadn't told them anything but the agents already knew about us. They had showed me pictures of us together and told me about the warehouse incident with the Colombians. The agents had us under surveillance the whole time. The pictures were from almost a year ago when I was boarding the plane in Miami, doing the coke drops for the Colombians.

"We're going down, Ralph. We're getting indicted. They told me if I don't cooperate, they will personally make sure I die in prison."

Ralph didn't say anything. He knew our life as we knew it was coming to an end, and there was nothing we could do about it. He snorted a big line of coke and said, "Travis, it's all over."

"Yes it is."

I left his house and went home. I lay in bed staring at the ceiling. Now it was only a matter of time before the indictments were handed down.

More months passed by and I continued my cocaine business. Why should I have stopped? I was going to prison. It was only a matter of time.

I set up a deal to buy one kilo of cocaine for a new connection I had up north. If the new connection liked the first kilo, he would buy five to ten kilos a month, and with my cocaine press, I could make some good money.

October 12, 1989. Hog Daddy didn't have any kilos so he hooked me up with a friend of his named Wayne. I gave my driver $20,000 to pick up the kilo. Wayne called to tell me the deal was taken care of and the Cubans were on their way back to Miami.

I said, "What deal? What are you talking about? Let me talk to my driver, Mike."

Wayne said, "Mike's in the store. I'll have Mike call you back."

I hung my phone up. I knew Mike was busted and Wayne was setting us up because Mike would have been the one calling me, not Wayne. The phone rang again. I picked it up. It was Wayne telling me I would like the football and Mike was on his way to my house.

I said, "I don't know what you are talking about. Let me talk to Mike."

Wayne said, "Mike is busy," and hung up the phone.

I cleaned the house and flushed ten ounces of coke down the toilet. I had all the money buried and only kept $2,000 in the house. I was in my bedroom looking at my monitor when I saw the SWAT team out front, jumping over my fence and hiding behind my trees, holding their rifles. The undercover agents drew closer to my house. One of my audio-video cameras was by the front door, so when the agent came closer to the front door, I pushed the audio button on the monitor and yelled into the monitor, "What the hell are you doing?"

The agents dropped down on the ground. They didn't know where that sound was coming from. They called out their police warnings. "We have a warrant for Travis Waters."

I said, "Put your guns down," through the camera. The agents said they couldn't do that and I should step outside with my hands behind my head. I told myself it was all over and opened the front door. The agents grabbed me and threw me on the ground, handcuffed my hands behind my back, and read me my rights. I was charged with trafficking in cocaine and conspiracy to traffic in cocaine. I told them to quit pointing the guns at me.

One of the cops said, "The feds are going to be glad we got your ass. The feds have been after you for a couple years and the state got you first."

They searched my house and found my safe. They wanted me to open it or they would blow it open.

I said, "Blow it open, and destroy the evidence. I don't care."

I opened the safe, and the agents' jaws dropped because there was nothing in it but some titles and paperwork. I was sitting there at home. They had nothing on me. They brought in a dog to search the house, and the dog found a couple of marijuana roaches and a couple of grams of pot in my night stand. They asked me where all the money and drugs were.

I said, "I don't know what you are talking about."

I was taken to jail, fingerprinted, photographed, and made to wear an orange jumpsuit. I was scared and didn't know what to expect. I was put in a separate cell block from my driver. I wondered what he was telling the cops since he had been caught at the scene buying the kilo with my money. I went in front of the judge the next day and my bond was set at $275,000. The lawyer I hired said he would have my bond lowered so I didn't have to waste more money. I stayed in the county jail for sixteen days, waiting for my bond reduction, and then I bonded out.

My bond was lowered to $75,000 because I wasn't a flight risk, or that was what my lawyer told the judge, anyway. The lawyer I hired was recommended by some friends of mine who represented them in drug cases. He wasn't cheap. I can tell you that much. The money I gave him up front was to go toward the trial and to fight the case. I ended up bonding out my driver and paying for his lawyer too, in hopes he wouldn't rat me out.

A couple of weeks went by. My lawyer set up a meeting with the local and state detectives, DEA, and US Customs officials. We met at the Collier County Courthouse. My lawyer, the detectives, and I sat around the table. The lead detective started the meeting by thanking me for coming and explained the purpose of the meeting was to offer me a deal to reduce my prison time because at that point I was facing a fifteen-year-minimum mandatory sentence in state prison for cocaine trafficking. The detective said I'd been very active in the drug business, and the US Customs and the DEA officials also had me under surveillance in Miami and in Naples. He understood I had a very profitable cocaine business up north. He wanted to charge me with interstate trafficking in cocaine. I was also under investigation by the state authorities in North Carolina. They were very interested in talking with me. I was in a lot of trouble and a lot more was on its way from other states and the federal government.

"We have you here today to offer you a deal so you won't end up in prison for the rest of your life," he said.

The DEA agent spoke up. "Travis, you know the man we want in Miami, and we can get him with your cooperation. Your partner, Ralph, was on the run and was captured. He's is in jail on a $1,500,000 cash bond."

The US Customs agent said, "We are here to help you, but you also have to help us. Everyone around you in your circle and other drug circles are already cooperating against you. That's how we know these things about you. We don't make these things up. Other guys that were arrested are already making deals behind your back right now. But we're not going to bullshit you, Travis. We also need your cooperation to get the big fish in Miami and Colombia. We have lots of pictures of you and the Miami gang. We've been trying to indict that gang for years and you can make it happen for us so we can close that operation down for good."

The US Customs agent, Smith, from Miami, asked everyone, even my lawyer, to leave the room. Just he and I sat there. He pulled out a file and told me it was all classified information from Washington. He showed me pictures, with the CIA stamp, of pot and coke loads being loaded onto planes and boats in Colombia. The agent made sure I saw the CIA stamp. He pointed it out and looked at me so I would know the agents weren't fucking around with me.

"Some of the loads were brought in through an island in the Bahamas here to you and Ralph in South Florida," he said. He showed me pictures of Juan, Reuben, and me getting on Juan's plane in Miami to fly back to Naples, and other pictures of Juan in Colombia standing next to José and Jesus and two other men. He said the guy next to Jesus was Pablo Escobar, and they were all part of the cartel in Colombia. This picture was taken over four years earlier. The agency finally figured out I was the Westcoast Kid from phone taps between Miami and Colombia. This group was an international drug ring responsible for bringing in hundreds of millions of dollars in cocaine and marijuana over the years. He went on about all the people who had been killed because of it. "You are probably wondering what happened to that load you and Ralph brought in through the Everglades," he said, "and how most of that load and boat disappeared."

I didn't say anything. I had to let all this information sink into my brain. This was all crazy. Was it for real or was it all a bad dream?

The agent looked at me and said, "You had no idea who these people were you and Ralph worked for, did you?"

I said, "No, not really. Besides the Colombians, Juan and Reuben, who else knows I'm called the Westcoast Kid? Do any of the guys cooperating against me here in South Florida know I'm the Westcoast Kid? I didn't want anyone to know it was actually me. I would tell the people we kidnapped I worked for the Westcoast Kid, it was his load, and I was just following orders given me by the Westcoast Kid."

Agent Smith said he could keep the Westcoast Kid identity confidential and no one would ever know it was me. I had his word on that.

"We will put in our file the Westcoast Kid was a fictitious name made up to protect a CIA informant."

He said that with the testimony of the people who were already cooperating against me, I was looking at four counts. Two counts carried sentences of zero to life, and the remaining two carried sentences of ten years minimum to life. Each count had a fine of up to four million dollars. He said that did not include the fifteen-year minimum mandatory state charge and the interstate trafficking charge that was also pending, not to mention some of the guys I had kidnapped in the Everglades were scared and had started to cooperate against me. That charge was pending in my file and would most likely also incur a life sentence because drugs and guns were involved in the kidnapping.

I asked, "How much more time could I possibly be looking at? It looks like if I don't cooperate, I will die in prison anyway, without all these other pending charges you're throwing at me."

"If you help us, I can make a lot of these charges disappear."

Yeah, just like you and the CIA made our load disappear and I almost was killed because of it by being thrown out of a plane, not to mention the oriental guy shocking me and wanting to drill holes in my finger nails.

I said, "What do you want me to do?"

"I want you to wear a wire."

"No fucking way. That's a death sentence." I remembered what José had done to me with the gun in the hotel in Naples and how he had clogged up the toilet.

"You just told me with my cooperation you could take down the guys in Miami."

"Yes, we can."

"Why do you want me to wear a wire? I haven't been around those guys in a while. What am I to do? Just call them up and tell them I want to meet with them about bringing in a make-up load to make everything better between us? No fucking way that is happening."

"You could wear a wire for the state and help take down some of the local and Miami coke dealers."

"No, I'm not doing that either. If you want me to testify and help you take down those guys in Miami, that's all I will do. But who will protect me from those guys in Miami? I'm not leaving my family and going into protective custody for the rest of my life. Testifying against those guys is a life sentence in itself."

The agent said, "No, it's not. Those guys in Miami will be locked up in prison."

I said, "They still have connections on the street."

The agent said, "Travis, that's the chance you have to take or stay in prison for the rest of your life. That's all I can offer you, plus no one will ever know you're the Westcoast Kid."

I had to think about it. It was a lot to comprehend all at once. Agent Smith said he understood and advised me to take my time.

I left the courthouse meeting confused and scared as hell about what to do and not to do. I was pissed that certain friends of mine and family members were snitching on me behind my back so they could get their deals from the government and the state. I'd better make a decision about my life before I was left out and ended up with a life sentence or three or four life sentences from what the agent was telling me about all the charges pending against me. I knew they needed me to testify with Ralph against Juan and Reuben because we were the main witnesses who could take the guys in Miami down. Ralph and I were the only ones other than Juan and Reuben who knew the two Colombians, Jesus and José. I knew the two Colombians all too well, and I hadn't forgotten what those two motherfuckers had done to me. I wondered what they did to other dealers and how many people they had killed.

July 1990: I heard a knock at my door. It was five thirty in the morning. I turned on the audio-video monitor by my bed and saw a blue and a red light over my fence, and a couple cars.

I said to myself, "Fuck, back to jail again." I opened the door and there stood Special Agent Ryan and two other detectives with the US Customs official and a uniformed cop, standing out by his police car. No guns were drawn.

Ryan said, "You know why we're here, Travis."

I said, "Yes, come on in. Where is Agent Smith? I thought he would be here for this."

Ryan said, "No, but he sent me to pick you up, and he still has his deal on the table for you."

"I bet he does."

Ryan read me my rights and informed me the United States of America had issued an indictment for my arrest for the importation of more than 1,000 kilos of marijuana into the United States of America. I said it was a lot more than 1,000 kilos of pot.

Ryan said, "I know, Travis. That's why the indictment says more than 1,000 kilos.

I said, "Let me go to the bathroom and get some clothes on."

One of the agents followed me to the bathroom and watched me use the bathroom and get dressed, and then I was told to put my hands behind my back and was driven to the federal courthouse in Fort Myers, Florida. I bonded out on a signature bond. Back at home I wondered what the hell I was going to do. The drug business was pretty much over with. A part of me was glad it was all over. I felt I could start a new life if I made it out of prison and didn't receive a couple of life sentences. If I cooperated, I'd always have to worry about the Colombians and the Cubans coming after me for the rest of my life. Or would they? But right now I didn't have a lot of choices did I? Ralph was also out of the county jail. He had his $1,500,000 cash bond reduced because of his cooperation, and I knew the only way Ralph got his bond reduced was because he had cooperated against Juan, Reuben, and the two Colombians, Jesus and José, and me.

Ralph showed up at my house a couple weeks later asking me if I had decided to cooperate with him so he wouldn't get a life sentence because it would take the cooperation of both of us to take the Cubans down in Miami. He asked me if I wanted him to go to prison for the rest of his life.

"No, Ralph, I don't want you to go to prison for the rest of your life."

He said, "I don't want you, Travis, going to prison the rest of your life either."

"Well, you should have thought about that before you cooperated against me."

"That's why I'm here talking to you now. If we don't both cooperate against the Miami Cubans and the Colombians, we will be going to prison for the rest of our lives. The feds also know about your cocaine business up north."

"Yeah, I know. Everyone is telling on me about that also. And what did you tell the feds and the state about my cocaine business, Ralph?"

Ralph looked at me and at first said nothing. Then he said, "You had better think about it and let me know what you are going to do."

I said, "What do you think Juan and the Colombians will do to us when we're in the federal courtroom pointing our fingers at them and describing the loads to the judge, the jurors, and the federal prosecutor."

Ralph looked at me and said, "Right now that's the only choice we have, and we can worry about what happens to us later like we always do."

After that meeting I really had no choice. I didn't want Ralph going to prison for the rest of his life. We needed each other. I didn't want to end up in prison for the rest of my life either. I called Agent Smith and told him I was ready to cooperate since I didn't have a choice. Everyone else was already cooperating against me and saving their own asses. I set up a meeting with the new federal lawyer I had hired for this case. In my first meeting we were to go over the so-called rules that apply to defendants who want to cut a deal for a lesser sentence. I had to tell the truth about everything I was asked and was supposed to divulge every drug transaction I was ever a part of, but mainly talk about the loads and the large amounts of money involved. If I were caught lying in a particular case, there would be no deal, and if I didn't tell the agents about all the loads I was a part of, or even the loads I knew about but was not involved in, there would be no deal. So basically I tried to tell the agents about everything I did and knew about. The agents got all the information they needed. Some of it might lead to more arrests or help start another case for the feds or the state. At any time they could say, "Thanks for all the information. You've been a big help, but you didn't tell us about that load in '86. Another codefendant told the feds about it. You forgot about that load and the ten ounces of cocaine you sold two years ago that someone else remembered you sold to them."

Those were the odds I was up against. So all I could do was hope for the best because it was the feds' rules and their game I was playing.

My second meeting was set up with the state authorities. I was questioned about the death of the informant who had worked on the load that we had brought into the Everglades, the load that had disappeared and I had been indicted on.

I asked the lead agent, "I thought the informant's death was ruled an accident."

"Yes, that's what's in the file for now."

This whole thing was a cover up.

I said, "All I know is John Doe was hired to be in charge of the off-loading crew to bring in our 30,000-pound load. John Doe was recommended to my partner through a smuggling friend and this John Doe would guarantee the load would make it to shore. He knew the back waters of the Everglades like the back of his hand. We had three more loads, back-to-back, at 30,000 pounds each. We were going to bring it in through the Everglades."

The agent asked me if the informant had known about the three back-to-back loads.

I said, "No. Only I and three others here in the States knew about it, and two in Colombia."

The agent asked me to give him the names of the other five who knew about the back-to-back loads.

I said, "I can't give you that information. That's confidential."

The agent got pissed at me. He stood up and started yelling and calling me a piece of shit, telling me I was already lying and there were no deals for me now. I stood up and started yelling at that mother fucker, telling him to go fuck himself. My state lawyer walked in.

I said, "The fucking feds told me not to tell the state. Who else knew about the back-to-back loads?"

The lead agent looked over at his partner and said, "The fucking feds are withholding information on us."

"The fucking federal case has nothing to do with my state cocaine case."

The agent apologized to me and said, "Please continue."

"What are you getting at here with these questions?"

The agent said, "We are trying to figure out who killed the informant because we don't think it was an accident."

The agent asked me if I had ever met John Doe.

I said, "Yes, I did at a warehouse here in Naples. All I know is John Doe was working both sides with the feds and the smugglers. He turned on the feds and started ripping off loads. I know he ripped off our load, and he is the reason why it disappeared. He and the feds are the ones with an informant in Colombia that ordered another 10,000 pounds of pot on top of the original 30,000 pounds of pot we contracted to bring in on the first of the back-to-back loads."

The agent looked at his partner and said, "Another 10,000 pounds?"

I said, "Yes."

The agent asked me, "Who ordered the extra pot?"

"It wasn't me, Ralph, or the Cuban in Miami, or the two Colombians. We were the only ones that had the authority to order the extra pot."

The agent looked at me and said, "We never knew there was extra pot. The feds never gave us that information."

The agent looked at me and asked me if I had killed John Doe or had him killed.

I said, "I'm not in the killing business, and no I didn't do it."

The agent asked me if it wasn't an accident, who did I think would benefit from John Doe's death?

"All I know is the Cubans or the Colombians wanted to kill me for the missing load."

The agent asked me, "What did the Colombians do to you?"

I said, "I can't tell you that. You will have to ask the feds. The Cubans and the Colombians figured out there was an informant on our load and another informant in Colombia who ordered the extra 10,000 pounds. The Colombians wanted to find them both and kill them so they would not lose any more loads. So that's one group I would say has a lot to benefit from killing the informants here in Florida and in Colombia so they could keep bringing in loads. The second would be the feds, I guess, because from what I know about the informant, he was making the feds look bad, going behind the feds' back, and jeopardizing the loads. The feds had both of the informants working on these loads. The informants were stealing most of the pot, like our load, and only turning in loads they could benefit the most from financially. The pot the feds kept or wanted, for whatever reason, also disappeared like the extra 10,000 pounds on our load. I don't know if the informant or the feds got that extra 10,000 pounds. All I know is there was a total of 32,000 pounds of pot missing on our load. Maybe the informant was out of control and knew too much about our drug circle. I'm sure there were other drug circles the feds had both informants working on and they didn't want all this information out on the streets. I'm not saying the feds or the Cubans or the Colombians killed John Doe, but this is who I think would have the most to gain from killing John Doe and the other informant in Colombia. I don't know if the Colombian informant is dead or in hiding. Last I heard, he disappeared. That's all I know."

The agent said, "Tell us about your cocaine business."

"I used to take cocaine and pot to northern states and would double and triple my profits."

"Who were you buying your cocaine and pot from?"

"From the Colombians and Cubans on the east coast and the guy who set me up with the kilo."

"Did you buy kilos from your friend Hog Daddy?"

"No, I didn't."

"The agent said, "You know your friend Hog Daddy is indicted for smuggling drugs into the country?"

"Yes, I know about that."

"What about your cocaine press you make kilos with when you pressed back the cut cocaine?"

I thought I knew who had told the agents about that. I said, "I thought the idea up in my head and on a piece of paper."

"We think it was ingenious plan. We understand you would then write a name on the newly pressed kilos and sell them as kilos right off the boat."

"Yes, I did."

"We want your kilo press for evidence and for our agents to look at for training purposes."

I said, "I don't have it. I threw it away since I was busted."

"We want you to take a polygraph test. If you pass the test, we will give you a five-year deal. If you fail, you will get the maximum fifteen-year sentence."

The agent hooked me up to the polygraph machine and started asking me questions. Some of the questions pissed me off because they were asked only of me and one other person I knew about.

The polygraph examiner asked me if I had hidden kilos of coke and hundreds of thousands of dollars at my mom's house."

"No."

"Did you ever hide kilos of coke at your brother's house?"

"No, I never did."

"Are you sure?"

I said, "Yes, I'm sure."

The examiner asked, "Did you ever sell kilos of coke to family members up north?"

"No."

"Did you ever sell kilos of coke to your cousin Greg up north?"

"No!"

The examiner asked me again, "Are you sure?"

"Yes, I'm sure. I was selling it to friends up north. I already told you that several times and you guys keep coming back to that question.

The examiner asked me if I ever injected steroids.

"What does that have to do with this case? I'm not going to answer that question."

The agent said, "Answer the question."

I said, "No."

"Did you ever bring in loads of pot?"

"Yes."

"Did you ever bring in loads of cocaine?"

"Yes."

"Did you ever count out millions of dollars in cash with the Cubans in Miami?'

"Yes."

"Did you ever park trucks full of drugs for the Cubans after a load came into Naples at the Florida Power and Light parking lot at the beginning of your street?"

"Yes."

"Did you have magnetic signs made with the Florida Power and Light logo, and did you place the signs on the truck loaded with drugs to make it look like it was a Florida Power and Light truck?"

I said, "What the hell does that question have to do with this case?"

The agent said, "Answer the question."

"Yes."

Last question was, "Did you kill or have the informant killed who worked on your load in the Everglades, the one that you were indicted on?"

I was wondering when this question would be asked.

"No."

The polygraph examiner gave me these same questions three times. I was unhooked from the machine and asked, "Tell me, Travis, did you hold millions of dollars in trash cans in your garage for the Cubans after a load was sold?"

I wondered why the agent had asked me that. I was not hooked up to the polygraph machine. I wasn't going to say yes.

I said, "No, I didn't."

The agents and their state examiner went to a room in private, came back in to where I was sitting, and said I had failed one question. I knew they were setting me up because I had lied on several questions, and I knew what the agents were after.

I asked, "Really? Which question did I fail?"

The agent said, "The one about your cousin. Are you sure you never had any drug transactions with your cousin Greg? You failed that question three times," the agent said. "I guess you have no deal."

"I guess I don't."

The agent said, "Why don't you go home and think about the question you failed and if you want to go to prison on a fifteen-year prison sentence or come clean about your cousin up north?"

The agent told me to come back to the office at ten o'clock in the morning and they would give me the polygraph test three more times.

I asked, "Are we going to use the same state examiner again?"

The agent said, "Yes, we are."

I left there pissed off, knowing what the fuck was going on. It was all a set-up. They already knew everything and wanted me to roll over on my family. That was not going to happen. The local cops and the cops up north had been after my cousin for years. He had been in prison in Naples for smuggling and was under indictment again in a federal case and cooperating. My cousin was bringing loads in with one of the biggest drug rings. He couldn't afford to have another felony charge against him. It would be his third and that was not good. Three strikes and you're out.

Chapter 13

‒‒‒///‒‒‒

It was 9:30 a.m., and I was on my way to fail the polygraph test three more times and to play the state's game of trying to scare me into talking, as if I didn't know what was up. It didn't take me long to figure that out. I was hooked up to the machine again with the same state examiner giving me the same round of questions. After the third test I was unhooked, and the agent and the examiner went into a private room. Now they were back with me again.

I acted stupid and said, "Did I pass it this time?'

The agent looked at me and said, "Travis, you failed the same question again."

"You have to be kidding me. How did I do on the other questions?"

"Oh, you passed those again," the agent said.

"But I only failed the one about my cousin?"

The agent said, "Yes. Do you want to talk to us and tell us why you failed the question about your cousin six times?"

"What do you want me to tell you?"

The agent said, "The truth."

I said, "I think you guys already know what the truth is and this is your way of trying to protect the ones that are telling you everything you want to hear. You guys want me to back up the snitch's story so you can take down my cousin and some more family members."

The agent said, "Is this how you feel?"

"Yes, it is, and I'm not snitching on my family."

"The deal's off," the agent said.

I got up and said, "See you later."

Two more months went by. I now sat in a conference room in the federal courthouse in Fort Myers, Florida, with Agent Smith, Agent Ryan, and another well-dressed agent who had not been introduced to me and didn't say too much. The meeting started out with my explaining everything I knew and had done with Ralph, Juan, Reuben, and the two Colombians, Jesus and José. Well, not everything. I didn't tell them about some of the loads and the warehouse where the money was shipped to the cartels overseas. One of the agents asked me how many times I had talked to Pablo Escobar and exactly what was said.

I said, "I talked to him twice. The first conversation was on the phone when a Colombian I had never seen before and a few of Juan's bodyguards threatened to push me out of the plane. Pablo asked me if I were the Westcoast Kid, and I said yes. He asked me if I knew who he was. I said no, but I had heard Juan mention his name. Pablo said he and his friends in Colombia wanted the fucking load back that Ralph and I had stolen, or he would have me tortured, and then he would have me and Ralph killed. Then the phone went dead."

"The second phone conversation with Pablo was at the warehouse where I was electrocuted and the oriental guy was going to drill holes in my fingernails. He asked me if I was getting the message, and he said Ralph and I'd better give his load back because he and his friends needed that money because he said he was having a lot of problems in Colombia. I said I would get it back because I didn't want to be tortured or killed for something I hadn't stolen. Pablo said Ralph and I were responsible for the load and to give it to Juan when I got it back. I said I would and then the phone went dead."

The well-dressed guy in the room looked at Agent Smith and nodded his head. I told the agent that Pablo didn't stay on the phone very long. The agent said Pablo knew the US and Colombian governments were trying to trace his calls. Agent Smith asked me how much pot we recovered when we kidnapped the off-loaders. I said, "About 8,000 pounds and we gave it to Juan."

"Tell me, how much money did you recover?"

I paused and said, "About $250,000."

The agent asked me if I had given it all to Juan and I said, "Yes, I did. All of it."

The agent asked, "Are you sure?"

"Yes."

"What did you tell the state about this case?"

"The state wanted to know who else knew about the back-to-back loads we were going to bring in through the Everglades."

The agents asked what the Colombians had done to me when I was kidnapped and taken to the warehouse in Miami. I got into a shouting match because I had told the state officials that, according to the feds, this was confidential information, so the state officials would have to ask the feds, not me, about it.

"The state told me you guys were withholding information from them."

"The state didn't know about the 10,000 extra pounds that was put on the shrimp boat?"

The agents looked at the well-dressed guy and said I shouldn't have told the state about that.

Agent Smith asked me, "Did you tell the state about the phone conversations between you and Pablo Escobar?"

I said, "No."

"Are you sure, Travis?"

"Yes, I'm sure."

The agent didn't care whom I told in the future about this overseas operation, but right now I was not allowed to tell any law enforcement agency in this country or any other country, and did I understand that? I nodded.

"What else did the state ask you?"

"The state asked me if I killed the federal informant and I said no. They also asked me who I thought would benefit the most from killing the informant."

The agent said, "What did you tell them?"

I said, "The Cubans in Miami and the Colombians would have a lot to benefit from killing the informant so they could keep their operation going and continue bringing loads into this country. We also know there is an informant in Colombia that the Colombians want dead."

Both agents looked over at the well-dressed guy again.

"I also told them the feds might benefit from killing the informant."

The agent said, "Why do you think that?"

"The informant was making you guys look bad because he was stealing the loads you guys had him working on. He had a lot of information you guys might not want out on the streets like what happened to our load."

Agent Smith said, "Tell us all in this room about your load disappearing."

"I was almost thrown out of a plane to my death and was about five minutes from getting my fingernails drilled out after I was shocked because you and your informant stole the load for whatever reason. /we didn't order the extra 10,000 pounds of pot your informant from Colombia ordered."

Agent Smith said, "How do you know all this?"

"We researched it. It was our load and none of us here in Florida or the two in Colombia ordered the pot, and we were the only ones that had the authority to order the extra pot. I flew in a plane to all the marinas on the East and West Coast where the confiscated drug boats were kept and there was no sign of our shrimp boat. We monitored the local news channels and the newspapers and there was nothing about the load being busted.

The captain of the shrimp boat said the guy in charge of the off-loading crew in the Everglades removed the shrimp-boat captain and his crew and took them to a hotel in Marathon, Florida. He also said a gray plane buzzed the shrimper at low altitude on the way back to the Florida coast. The Colombians wanted to kill me and Ralph because the load was missing and we had no proof the load was busted. Why don't you guys tell me what happened to the load?"

The well-dressed guy spoke up, "This case here is bigger than all of us. The operation was ordered out of Washington. This drug circle you and Ralph started working for is an international drug cartel that I and Washington have been gathering information on for years. This group of drug runners is responsible for bringing into the United States hundreds of millions of dollars in cocaine and pot. We have agents and informants working on some of these loads you and Ralph brought into the United States."

"Who are you?"

"I can't tell you who I am or who I work for."

He continued telling me I was right about the informant in Florida and the one in Colombia.

I asked, "Where is the missing 32,000 pounds of pot?"

"Don't worry about that. You, Travis, will get on that witness stand and help me bring down the Miami connection so these guys will lead me to the cartels in Colombia. You are the main witness, Travis. I noticed you didn't tell these agents here about the 500-kilo load you and Reuben were in charge of watching that was air-dropped fifty miles off the coast of Ft. Lauderdale and loaded onto a charter fishing boat."

I remembered when Juan and I were in the Lamborghini going to lunch in Miami, he had said he didn't trust the charter-boat captain. The agent had said the charter-boat captain was an informant.

"These sneaky mother fuckers," I said. "What? Is there another case pending against me now?"

The well-dressed guy said, "No, but if we need you to testify in that case, you will." He understood Agent Smith had told me in a previous meeting if I didn't cooperate with the government, I'd spend the rest of my life in prison.

"Do you remember that meeting, Travis?"

"Yes, I do."

"You already figured out way too much in this operation and if you tell other agencies or anyone about this case and jeopardize all these years of hard work until it's all over with, I will personally see to it that you won't have to worry about dying in prison. Do you understand exactly what I'm talking about?"

"Yes, I do. I already know you don't give a fuck about me because of the way you guys play your game. It almost cost me my life. No matter who dies here in the States as long as you get the big fish in Colombia."

Agent Smith spoke up, "Travis, you have no idea who these guys are in Miami that you started getting involved with. Well, now you know what the war on drugs is about and what the magnitude of this operation is."

Agent Smith told me not to wear my Rolex on the stand and to wear casual clothes.

I said, "Okay."

He said, "Is there anything else you want to say before the trial starts?"

"Yes. Why is this drug ring in Miami the one you guys are so adamant about taking down?"

"I can't tell you everything, Travis, but they are well connected with the cartels in Colombia and this circle is our best chance right now to start trying to take some of the leaders down in Colombia. You and Ralph just happen to be the ones that started working for Juan at the right time. When we finally started getting guys inside their operation, unfortunately for you and Ralph, you ended up here with a federal indictment."

I asked if he was going to keep the Westcoast Kid name confidential.

"Yes, Travis, that has already been taken care of."

I said, "Right now I don't trust anyone. I don't know who's a snitch, an informant, or who's even working for what agency anymore with all this bullshit going on."

Agent Smith said, "I know it's all confusing, isn't it?"

"Yes."

"Travis, why didn't you go to college and play basketball instead of getting caught up in this crap?"

I looked at him and said, "Like I told you before, I didn't want to go to summer school. I was being stupid."

"Why didn't you go work for your stepdad; he owns a multimillion-dollar company."

"I did work for him part time when I was in the eighth grade."

"Yes, Travis, you were stupid. Remember, if you lie under oath on the stand while being questioned by the prosecutor or by your codefendant's lawyer, you will get charged with perjury. That carries, I think, seven years for each lie, and you may also jeopardize the case against the other codefendants you are testifying against. You and Ralph are the government's main witnesses."

We ended the meeting, and I said I would see them at the trial.

I left the federal courthouse and headed back to Naples, shaking my head and wondering what the hell I had got myself into. Why me? Why did I have to be the one to be involved with this drug ring? Those guys were being watched way before I got involved with them. I wondered if the feds knew about the money warehouse in Fort Lauderdale because at that moment I didn't know what the hell was going on. They might have had an agent or an informant wearing a mask in that warehouse. I wondered about other loads I had worked on with those guys and if the feds had posted an informant or an agent on those loads as well. Only the feds knew that and I hoped I was not caught in any more lies with them. I wondered if the well-dressed guy was the informant in Colombia or the one on the charter boat. I wouldn't know for sure. Either way, he was with the CIA out of Washington. I needed to go to Ralph's house to let him know what the hell I'd just found out and who these guys were he had hooked me up with. Hell, I didn't need to do that. I was sure Ralph had figured that out already. He had been playing this game long before I came along.

Yeah, I could've gone to college to play ball, but no, I wouldn't listen to my mom, and look at me now. This is what I deserve. Don't cry now, Travis. What's done is done. I can't change it now. So somehow I will have to try and deal with it just like I dealt with everything else in my short life. My high school coach always told me, "Life's a journey. Try to make the best of it."

Back in Ft. Myers, Florida, I sat in a private room in the federal courthouse, waiting to be called to testify against the Miami drug circle. The trial had been going on for a couple hours. I was the only one in this case who had a different judge from the rest of my codefendants, which I didn't understand. I testified in front of Judge Gagliardi, and I would be sentenced in front of Judge Kovachovich, a woman who was not afraid to hammer you with a long sentence. I was sure the feds were doing this for a reason, to benefit themselves, not me or the rest of my codefendants. The agents told me I couldn't win against the United States. It was their game, rules, and playing field.

The door opened and there stood Johnny, the shrimp-boat captain and his first mate, Skitter. I told the agent standing next to them, "I don't want those two in the room with me. I don't have anything to say to them."

The agent shut the door. Those two had screwed me over when they let the informant take them off the shrimp boat, leaving our load with the informant and the off-loaders. The door opened again and Agent Ryan walked in the room to debrief me on what was going on. He told me what I needed to say and not say. "It's show time," he said.

I stood up, took off my Rolex and handed it to my mom. I gave her a hug. She wanted to go in the courtroom with me. I said no, I didn't want anyone from the Miami gang seeing her face because I knew Juan had friends sitting in the courtroom watching everyone testifying against him, including family members. I told her I loved her and I would be fine.

"Stay in this room and I will come and get you when I'm done testifying," I said.

I also told the agents not to let anyone in the room with her.

I walked through the doors entering the courtroom. It was packed with family members. I walked up to the witness stand, raised my right hand and swore to tell the truth, the whole truth, and nothing but the truth.

I sat in the witness box, next to Judge Gagliardi. I looked over at Juan and Reuben and saw them sitting there in their custom three-piece suits. They gave me the evil eye. I knew they didn't want to see me sitting there pointing my finger at both of them. I bet Juan would love to have had me back in his warehouse, hanging out with his Asian friend for a little while. I was glad the two Colombians, Jesus and José, were on the run so I didn't have to testify against those two crazy bastards.

I was asked by the prosecutor to explain how I knew Juan and Reuben and to point them out. I did. They both looked at me, and I could see in their eyes they wanted to kill me. They both knew with Ralph's and my testimony they didn't have a chance. I explained to the jurors the inner workings of their smuggling operation and the load that we all were indicted on.

I will describe some of the questions that were directed at me by my codefendant's lawyer on cross-examination.

I was told by one of the lawyers that, based the amount of drugs I had brought into this country and the amount of drugs I had sold up north, he estimated I should have ten to twenty million dollars put away in another country. Perhaps I would use the money to go into hiding after this trial was over.

The lawyer asked, "Do you know where all the missing pot is?"

I said, "The off-loaders stole the pot."

That was what I was supposed to say if that question were asked and I was not to mention the extra 10,000 pounds of pot that was put on that load.

"No more questions," the lawyer said.

The next question from another of my codefendant's lawyers asked if I were a professional drug smuggler and a drug dealer. What was this question getting at?

"I don't know what you mean by that question, but if this answers it, I didn't sell drugs at stop signs on street corners, and I didn't sell drugs in school yards."

The lawyer said, "I think you, Mr. Waters, are a professional drug smuggler. That's what I think of you."

"If that's what you think of me that is fine by me."

The lawyer said, "I have no further questions."

The next question was from another lawyer. He understood that in addition to my smuggling business, I had a very profitable cocaine business on the side up north. "Is that true, Mr. Waters?"

"Yes, I did, but not anymore."

The lawyer said he understood I was also cooperating with the state authorities in Florida. "Is that true?"

"What does that have to do with this case?"

The judge said, "Answer the question."

I looked over at the prosecutor and said, "Yes, I am."

The lawyer said, "And I also understand you, Mr. Waters, failed a polygraph test six times regarding a question about a certain family member up north. Is this true, Mr. Waters?"

The fucking state had given this information to one of my codefendant's lawyers to get back at the feds for withholding information from the state. I was shocked to be asked this question. I looked over at the prosecutor and the agents and they looked as shocked as I was.

I said, "Yes, I did."

"Isn't it true, Mr. Waters, the state withdrew the plea deal that they were giving you if you passed your polygraph test and now the state wants to give you the maximum sentence of fifteen years on your state cocaine charge?"

"Yes."

The lawyer asked me if I would mind his reading the question out loud in the courtroom.

I said, "You might as well. You told the courtroom everything else," and the people in the courtroom laughed.

"Did you, Travis, ever have any narcotic transactions with Greg Jean Wilson in North Carolina?"

I was so shocked by the question I didn't answer right away.

The lawyer said, "Did you, Mr. Waters?"

Now I was fixing to lie under oath on a federal stand and I remembered the agent had said if I lied on the stand, I could get more time and jeopardize the case. It was okay for the feds to explain to me the things I should and should not say on the stand. It was okay because it benefited the government, but if I lied on a question to benefit me, I'd get more time added to my sentence. As the agent had said, it was their game and I couldn't win.

I said, "No, I never sold drugs to Greg."

The lawyer said, "Are you sure, Mr. Waters?"

"Yes, I'm sure."

The lawyer said, "I have no further questions, Your Honor."

I was asked to step down and was escorted by the agents back to the room where my mom was waiting for me. I was told not to leave. I hugged my mom and said it was over and she shouldn't cry. The agents came into the room and told us that with my testimony they finally had their conviction for the Miami drug gang. They acted as if they had just won the Super Bowl. I didn't feel that way. I had just signed a life sentence of fear, always looking over my shoulder and wondering if I would be thrown out of a plane or if I would meet the Asian guy again.

I said, "Mom, let's go home."

I told the agents I would see them at my sentencing.

My mom didn't like hearing the agent telling me that with my testimony the Miami drug gang would finally go to prison and that I was the star witness for the government. They added that I should receive an Academy Award for my testimony. Mom was scared and didn't trust them.

She thought the government had been using me all along and was worried I would still get a lot of prison time out of this mess. On the way home she kept telling me I could have gone to college to play ball and that I wouldn't listen to her.

"I know, Mom, you keep reminding me of that. You see Deion playing football on TV and I was as good as he was in basketball and I could've been on TV too."

My mom said, "I remember when you were in high school and were always on the local news channel playing sports and in the newspaper every week during basketball season. Now you have your mug shot all over the local news channels and the local newspapers. I wonder what your coach and all your other coaches and your sports friends think of you now. You were the number-one-rated quarterback in the state when you were young."

"Yes, I know, Mom, but remember you didn't want me to play football because I got hurt all the time. You wanted me to just play baseball and basketball. You took me out of football. I know all this. You don't have to keep reminding me. I wish I'd gone to college too, but now I'm getting a paid federal scholarship, and I don't know how long I will be there." I told my mom I'd plead guilty to one charge.

She asked me, "How much time is this plea deal?"

"You don't want to know, Mom."

She got mad and said, "You have to tell me, Travis."

"The judge can give me from one year up to a life sentence."

My mom said, "The judge can give you twenty to thirty years or a life sentence?"

"Yes, that's what I pled to, one count on the indictment."

She started crying and wouldn't stop. I told her because of my cooperation, I shouldn't get that much time and not to worry.

She said she didn't trust the government.

A few weeks passed and I was back in the federal courthouse in Fort Myers, Florida, waiting to be sentenced to federal prison. I hoped I could surrender myself to the prison I was ordered to. My mom was worried and wondered why I was to be sentenced by a different judge from everyone else in the case, especially because she wasn't the judge I had testified in front of.

I said, "I don't know, Mom. Only the feds know the answer to that question."

Judge Kovachovich entered the courtroom and everyone stood. Man I was really worried she was going to hammer me. This judge didn't like drug cases and wouldn't tolerate drug offenders in her courtroom. I wondered what the hell she was going to think when she saw the amount of drugs in my file.

I stood in front of her as she looked at my file. Her eyes opened up wide. She dropped my file on the desk and glared at me. I looked at the prosecutor and the agents, the ones who were supposed to be getting up and talking on my behalf. The judge picked my file up again and I really grew scared. She flipped through the pages and shook her head. She looked at the prosecutor and the agents, shaking her head, and asked the prosecutor if there was anything he wanted to say on my behalf.

The prosecutor stood up and said, "Travis' testimony against the Miami drug circle was the key to finally taking that drug ring down. He was one of our main witnesses."

The judge asked the agent sitting there if he had anything to say on my behalf.

The agent said, "No, your honor."

That mother fucker had lied to me. He said he would tell the judge my cooperation was what brought down the Miami drug gang and he didn't stand up and say shit. Now, I was really scared. I also faced a fine of up to four million dollars.

The judge looked at me and said, "Do you understand what you were doing and who these people you were involved with are?"

"Yes, I do."

She had read my file and it was a shame I had thrown my life away for drugs. I had it made before I got into the drug business. She asked me if I had anything to say. I told her no.

She said, "I see you were a big help to the government with your cooperation and I will take that into consideration. I'm sentencing you to eight years in federal prison. I hope you will take this time to think about what you did and turn your life around. After all is said and done, you will certainly find out who your friends really are, Travis."

I went over to the agent and said, "You were supposed to get up and talk on my behalf."

He said the prosecutor advised him not to get up and speak, and I shouldn't worry about my eight-year sentence. The prosecutor was going to file a Rule 35.

I said, "What's that?"

He said, "It's a sentence reduction appeal for defendants who cooperate with the government."

"I won't have an eight-year sentence?"

"No. It will be lowered to probably four years."

"Are you sure?"

"Yes. Don't worry about the eight-year sentence."

"Ok, thanks. I'll try not to."

I was fingerprinted and told I could self-surrender in thirty to forty-five days. I would be notified of which prison I would have to report to.

I left the federal courthouse not too happy with my eight-year sentence. My mom said she didn't trust the feds; they would not give me a sentence reduction to three or four years.

I said, "Mom, I know. I don't trust the feds either."

I figured that on this journey the feds played for keeps. They bent and broke the rules when it benefited them, that was for damn sure.

"Mom, you have no idea what the feds are capable of doing when they want the bigger fish in Miami and the biggest fish in Colombia."

My mom said, "I know they used you and put your life in jeopardy and now we have to worry about the Cubans and the Colombians killing you."

I said, "I know, Mom. Don't remind me."

My mom didn't know anything about the kidnapping and the nightmare I had already gone through because of this mess.

She said, "Now you have to get sentenced by the state this month."

"Yes, I know, Mom. Thank God they only busted one kilo of cocaine because the next buy I was going to make would have been for five to ten kilos and then more after that. I could have been sentenced to twenty years or life, so it could have been a lot worse." I didn't tell her I had perjured myself on the federal stand and I could get a lot more time.

My oldest sister was moving up north out of fear for her kids' lives since her Cuban ex-husband was also testifying in the federal case. The drug business I was involved in was tearing our family apart and now my sister, niece, and nephews had to leave town because of what we had done. It hurt me inside. My other sister also moved up north with her kids. So now, I was more alone than I'd ever been in my life. For what? Money! Was all this worth it? Tearing our families apart? Hadn't my family and I been through enough hell already, growing up with the nightmare my dad put us through? I had nobody to blame but myself for all this. No one had made me do it, but I hadn't realized I would be involved so heavily in the drug business so soon. I was around a lot of big fish, making all the right connections, and this was the outcome. I was glad it was all over with because the way I was moving up in this business meant I would have been killed eventually. My luck would have run out. There were millions of dollars changing hands all the time and all that did was lead to death or spending the rest of your life in prison. Now I had to live with the consequences and turn the page to the next chapter in my life. I had to try and survive in prison and I could only imagine what that would be like, locked in a cage. I had no idea how long I would be in prison for. I knew my mom would not be the same person because every day she would wonder if I were getting hurt or raped in prison. She would be free, but her mind and heart would be locked up until I came home. I would never forgive myself for what I'd done to her, the person I loved the most in my life, and I had let her down in the worst way.

I now stood in the Collier County Courthouse, waiting to plead guilty and face up to fifteen years in state prison. Why should I plead guilty to the maximum sentence and not take my chances going to trial? If I were to lose the trial, the most I would receive would be fifteen years. The state wanted to have my sentence run consecutively—after my federal sentence—which meant, once I'd finished my eight-year federal sentence, I would have to start serving my entire fifteen-year sentence in state prison. My lawyer explained to me that if I pleaded guilty, I could get my state sentence to run concurrently with my eight-year federal sentence. This meant while I was serving my federal sentence, I would also be serving my state sentence and receiving my state gain time while in federal custody. The state wanted to give me a five-year-minimum mandatory sentence along with a $250,000 fine. That was $4,250,000 worth of fines the state and the federal governments were trying to have hanging over my head. The feds dropped the fines. So I told my lawyer to have the state fine dropped or I would go to court.

I was sentenced to fifteen years with a five-year-minimum mandatory sentence, and my sentence was to run concurrently with my federal sentence. I stood there with a total sentence of twenty-three years after all that was over with. I still had the possibility of the perjury charges I could end up with, and the feds dropping another secret bomb on me because they knew I had brought in that 500-kilo load off the coast of Fort Lauderdale that I didn't tell them about. The feds had an informant working on the commercial charter boat the footballs had been loaded onto. All I could do was wonder and hope the twenty-three years was all I would receive because in the end it was still the feds' ball game.

They had all the power and that was just how it was. I couldn't win against the feds, and once I realized that, everything else would hopefully fall into place.

I was fingerprinted and photographed, and I walked out of the courthouse. I looked up at the sky and shook my head and wondered where I had gone wrong. I wished I'd gone to college and that I had listened to my mom.

Chapter 14

May 20, 1991 was the day I surrendered myself to the Federal Correctional Institute (FCI) in Tallahassee, Florida. I was to start serving my eight-year federal sentence for conspiracy and importation of 30,000 pounds of marijuana.

I remember this day so clearly, as if it were happening to me right now. I had on blue jeans with a gray dress shirt and topsider shoes. I wore my jewelry, a gold-rope necklace with an anchor charm that had three diamonds, and a gold submariner Rolex watch with a black face and black and gold bezel.

I had packed a bag with white socks, white boxer shorts (four pairs of each), cotton gym shorts (one gray and one blue) and a pair of tennis shoes. This was what the FCI allowed me to bring. My mom and stepdad took me to catch my flight to Tallahassee at Southwest Regional Airport in Ft. Myers, Florida. We had breakfast at the airport. It was to be my last meal as a free man. I remember I had ordered what seemed like a little of everything on the menu: eggs, pancakes, bacon, sausage, biscuits and gravy, and a Western omelet. My mom was sitting there with us, crying the whole time. She was so sad. It just killed me to see her like that, especially after all she and I had been through. How could I have been the one to hurt her like that? I was supposed to be the one with the storybook ending, the American dream, and college scholarships to play basketball and to get a good education. It hadn't worked out that way, had it?

It was time for me to board the plane for what I considered the longest flight of my life. I hugged my mom and stepdad good-bye one last time for what seemed to be an eternity before I would see them again. This flight wasn't going to be in first class and my personal pilot would not be flying me around.

It was a beautiful sunny day in Tallahassee when I arrived. I soaked in my last few moments of freedom.

I jumped into a taxi cab and the driver asked, "Where do you want me to take you?"

I said, "Back home to Naples."

He asked, "Excuse me?"

"Do you know where the federal prison is located?"

"Oh yeah!" He commented that he didn't want to go there to live.

"Me neither."

"Are you going there for a job interview? You look like you could be a federal agent."

I chuckled and said, "No, the United States of America classified me as drug kingpin out of South Florida, and I'm going there to start serving a twenty-three year sentence for smuggling marijuana and cocaine trafficking."

He said "You're kidding, right?"

"I wish I were."

Without another word he pulled into the prison parking lot. I didn't want to get out of the taxi. I handed him $50 and told him to keep the change. "The next time you're having a cocktail, have one on me," I said.

He said, "Thanks, and good luck."

I found myself standing in the parking lot, looking at the prison, imposing, intimidating, red-brick buildings with two, twenty-foot-high, perimeter fences that had rolls of razor wire on top. Barbed wire and rolls of razor wire were stacked up on top of each other, eight feet high, in between the perimeter fences and forty-foot gun towers. I was all alone now, no family, no friends. All the money and all the lawyers in the world couldn't help me now. I finally realized I had lost the war on drugs to the DEA, US Customs, and the CIA, which were calling all the shots from Washington, and to the federal informants and the snitches in the United States and Colombia, either dead or alive. I had moved millions of dollars' worth of drugs since I was fourteen—tons of cocaine and hundreds of tons of pot. This ride on the wild side was finally over. It was all over for the Westcoast Kid.

Should I leave the parking lot right now and walk away? What kind of life would I have looking over my shoulder every moment and never seeing my family again and never having another chance at a normal life?

I walked up the front steps and opened the front door. I told the guard I was Travis Waters and was there to surrender myself to federal custody.

"We've been expecting you Inmate Waters, welcome."

With all the fear running through my body, I could hear my mom's voice in the back of my head, telling me, "You will wish you had listened to me and gone to college to play basketball. You can't change the past, Travis. Once the past is gone, it's gone forever. Remember your mom telling you that?"

I heard it loud and clear. I followed the guard farther inside the prison, and he manually slid these large, steel and glass doors open. I stepped through and the doors slid shut behind me. Now I was officially federal property and most of my rights had gone.

On my way to being processed at Return and Departure (R and D), I had to walk out into the Courtyard. Since it was a weekday, some inmates were mowing the grass and planting colorful flowers around the flag pole and sitting areas. This place was kept up well. Inside, I was still scared, though, and felt like puking. I now walked out of the courtyard area and into the housing unit where the inmates lived. I went through a gate known as the rec yard. I looked to my left and saw an 18-hole putting course.

You have to be kidding me.

There was a field for softball, football, and soccer. There were volleyball and basketball courts with glass backboards, and two weight shacks, one with free weights and the other with cable machines. These were located on the lower rec yard. On the upper rec yard were four racquetball courts and a track.

Wow! They have everything here.

I walked into the R and D building and was locked into a holding tank with a couple of guys. I found out they were from the Everglades. Both of them had been caught stealing some bales of pot on a load that had gone bad. They had been hired to help with the off-loading and they had surrendered earlier that day. I asked them some questions about the load and what they knew about it. They told me what they knew, what month and year it happened.

I asked, "Did you know the name of the boat?"

They said, "No, the boat was sinking when we were called on the radio to go out and get what was left of the bales floating in the water." But by then the US Customs and the DEA were watching it with night-vision scopes from afar, and when they loaded some bales on their boat, a military helicopter hovered over them within minutes. Then their boat was boarded by US Customs and the DEA and they were arrested.

I asked, "Did you know whose load that was?"

"No, we were just off-loaders, hired by our cousin to help out if needed, but we heard the load was contracted out of Naples by some fat Cuban named Ralph, and an American guy the Cubans on the east coast refer to as the Westcoast Kid. At least that's what our lawyers and my cousin told us, but we don't know their real names."

They asked me where I was from and what I was in prison for.

I said, "I'm from Naples, and I'm here for smuggling pot on a load that went bad and was ripped off south of Marco."

They looked at each other with bewildered expressions. Then they asked me, "Are you the Westcoast Kid?"

Panic-stricken, they started telling me they were sorry and were just doing what they were told by their cousin.

I said, "Don't worry. I'm not the Westcoast Kid, but I've heard of him." I wanted to keep my identity a secret.

I found it amazing that I kept finding out more information about that load even when I was in prison with the guys who are were my codefendants and helped in some way to put me there. The feds didn't amaze me anymore. I could only imagine what they were up to at that point, especially with a case still hanging over my head.

I was taken out of the holding tank, told to strip, and handed a box in which to pack the clothes and jewelry I was wearing. It would be shipped home. I was instructed to open my mouth and stick out my tongue and cough. I had to run my fingers through my hair and was told to turn around, bend over, spread my cheeks open, and cough twice. I was photographed and fingerprinted while I was still naked. I was handed a pair of khaki pants, a shirt, a pair of white boxers, a pair of black brogans, and my photo ID with my federal inmate number. After being processed, I was locked back in the holding tank. It was four o'clock and count time. That was a nationwide count for all inmates in each federal prison. The inmate population there numbered 1400 to 1500. While waiting to be put in my new housing unit, I admired my clean and new-looking surroundings. The floors were waxed to a high gloss.

After the count was over, I was escorted to Charlie House. This dorm had two-man cells. It was old-looking and in need of paint. There was no air conditioning. This was where you were housed until your permanent housing unit was determined. When the four o'clock count was completed, it was chow time. Prison officials released one dorm at a time. The eating order of the dorms depended on an inspection each week. If your dorm was the cleanest, you ate first, and it went from there. My dorm ate third that week. I was walking down the sidewalk in the center of the Courtyard toward the chow hall when I heard my name called. It was one of my codefendants, my Cuban friend Ralph.

The commissary, or prison store, sold items you could keep in your locker. You could eat them whenever you wanted. You didn't have to eat in the chow hall if you didn't want to. Some evenings a group of us would have chow in our dorm. We would buy all our vegetables from inmates who would smuggle them out of the chow hall. You weren't allowed to have the vegetables in your locker, but 80 percent of the guards wouldn't take them. Some of the guards would eat out of our lockers, especially the night-shift guards. They would wake me up with "Waters, will you make me a peanut-butter sandwich?" or, "Can I have a can of tuna and some bread? My wife didn't pack my lunch."

I'd say, "No. You have a key to my locker. You make it or get what you want. I'm sleeping."

That was the relationship you'd have with the guards after you'd spent years together. They became your friends just like the other inmates. The guards would look out for you, and it went both ways. There were a lot of guys there from Naples. We were known as the Naples Gang. Some of the Naples Gang were my codefendants and some were from other smuggling rings in South Florida. There was a crew from the Everglades as well.

I started my first prison orientation and it lasted all day. Someone from each department of the prison came in, outlined the rules and regulations, and what the prison had to offer you to better your life when you were released. You were offered education, medical treatments, prison jobs, recreation, and an arts and craft department.

After orientation I was given my permanent-housing unit papers. I was assigned to North Dorm A. All the buildings were the same, red-brick with red shingles. It was an open-air dorm with two-man cubicles, bunk beds, and two lockers about five feet high with a desk in between the lockers and two folding chairs. No air conditioning at all. Two exhaust fans on the inside were mounted on top of the roof and sucked the hot air out of the dorm. The ceiling was made of planks of wood and painted white. Mounted on the walls were industrial metal fans blowing air down the aisles of the dorm. Windows lined each side of the dorm. They had bars on the outside, so you could open the windows in the summer. The TV room was about 30-by-30 feet with a window-shaker air-conditioning unit. You could hang out in there to beat the summer heat and watch a movie. We had a TV committee in our dorm. It was scheduled so we would watch sports during each season and inmates of various ethnicities would get to watch what they wanted. This was also done to stop some of the fights that broke out because a certain inmate didn't get to watch what he wanted to watch on TV.

My first roommate was a professional baseball player who had been drafted in the major league. He was in prison for dealing cocaine and was set up by friends of his. His name was Tom; he was married with one daughter.

The bathrooms and the showers were at the far end of the dorm. Showers lined the walls. The prison had installed shower curtains on each shower because inmates had grown tired of watching other inmates pleasuring themselves. So now they had privacy and everyone was happy. The toilets were separate and had dividers in between them, but stall doors weren't allowed because of the sex that would go on behind closed doors. Sexual intercourse wasn't allowed and if you were caught engaging in any sexual activity, you were sent to the hole. The sinks were in between the toilets, and the showers were divided by walls. Each dorm had counselors and a case manager to advise you of your gain time and any disciplinary problems you were having or complaints you had filed against the prison. You could ask any questions that you might have. Every three months you were up for a review of your progress, your behavior, transfers, and your requests for transfers to other prisons to be closer to your family. Also reviewed were prison gain time, visitation rights, and problems you had with inmates in the dorm.

My first job was in the woodworking department with my friend Hog Daddy. We worked in the tool shed, handing out tools for the inmates to learn a trade in woodworking. The inmates would build jewelry boxes, wooden trunks. You name it. They built it. These items would either be sent home or sold to other inmates for gifts for their families. Prison jobs ran from 7:30 a.m. to 3:30 p.m. Monday through Friday. My pay was twelve cents an hour. Some inmates made more. I chose to have my pay deposited into my commissary account. Others chose to send their money home.

I signed up to get my GED certificate. There was a black inmate who assisted the teacher. He was there to help you study and prepare for the GED exam. He went by the name of Barbeque. Barbeque kept trying to have me meet him in the evening for a one-on-one study group. I told him I didn't need his help and I had already passed my GED practice exam.

I told a friend that this guy was persisting in being alone with me. My friend informed me that Barbeque was gay and he was hitting on me. This was the first time I had been hit on in prison. The thought of having sex with any man, white or black, grossed me out. If sex had been forced on me, I would rather have died fighting than just being someone's bitch and being scared. I gave thanks to God that hadn't happened yet. I wouldn't really know until I crossed that bridge. That was how I felt at that point but my life wasn't in danger, and all those feelings can change when your life is on the line. I'd had near-death experiences. When you experience that life-or-death feeling, all your thoughts can change in an instant.

I passed my GED exam and received $25 from the federal government. It was deposited into my commissary account and the prison received a check for $2,500 to support the Education Department. I was given a maroon cap and gown to have my graduation picture taken, holding my diploma. I declined. I didn't want my graduation picture taken in prison. It didn't feel like a proud moment for me. They weren't my school colors, and it wasn't my graduation class, for that matter.

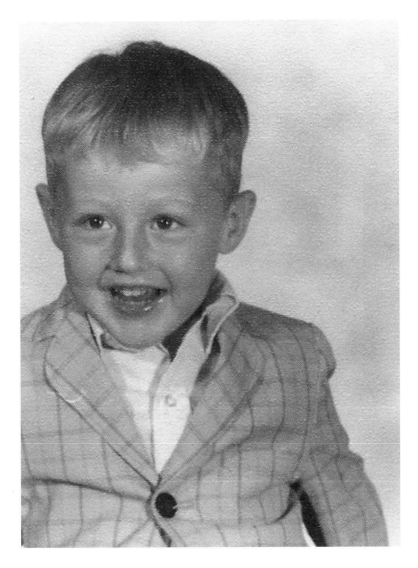

1971 – One of my first photos.

1974 – Palmetto Court, playing outside of our childhood home:
Tana, myself, my older sister, Ramona, and Gay.

Swimming with neighborhood friends in the second lake behind our house. Today, you can find the Naples Botanical Gardens here.

Family photo taken in our home on Palmetto Court:
Gay, my mother, father, and I.

1977 – My baseball picture.

1983-1984 – Team Trojan varsity basketball: Coach Don Stewart on the far right and I'm number 33. This was our first year playing together.

News-Press/Dan Fitzpatrick

THREE TROJANS GANG UP ON NORTH'S DION SANDERS
... but the Red Knights beat Lely 56-54 in district play

1985 – Deion Sanders and the Red Knights beat Lely
when I was on the team. We both scored 26 points that game.
Photo courtesy of Ft. Myers News Press, Don Fitzpatrick.

12 Grade 1985

Photo by Tom Rife

LELY'S TRAVIS WATERS LETS SHOT FLY
... during North-South All-Star game Tuesday night.

1985 – North-South All Star Game: Deion Sanders in center.
Photo courtesy of sports writer Tom Rife at Naples Daily News.

Coach Stewart presenting me with my All Star
plaque after our first All Star Game together.

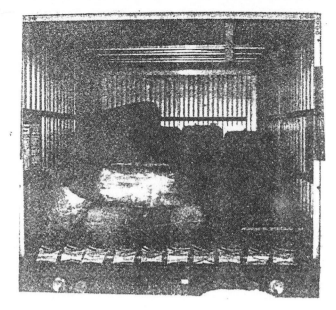

1987 – Bales of pot transported to a warehouse in Miami.
Picture taken by a federal informant. I was indicted for this load.

1987 – The shrimp boat used to carry the load of pot to off loaders.
Photo courtesy of US Customs. I was indicted for this load.

1987 – Unloading the bales of pot at a warehouse in Miami.
Photo taken by a federal informant. I was indicted for this load.

1992 – Me at the Federal Correctional Institution in Tallahassee, Florida.

2004 – My son, Travis Jr., and his favorite swampbuggy, Patriot.

July, 2008 – Travis Jr. and I with Don Stewart at his summer basketball camp.

June, 2009 – former 1983-1984 Lely High team with original jerseys. Coach Stewart and Shade Jones included in photo.

June, 2009 – Stacey Stewart, myself, Travis Jr., and Scott Stewart,
at Coach's retirement party.

2009 – Myself and Coach Stewart at the Annual Lely High Faculty Game.

2009 – Travis Jr.'s first grade class and I.

July, 2009 – Deion Sanders signing my newspaper article.

July, 2009 – Connie Knight (Deion Sanders' mom),
myself, and Travis Jr. at the TruthSelect football game.

December, 2009 – The first basketball team I ever coached; UCLA presenting me with a signed basketball. This was a dream come true for me.

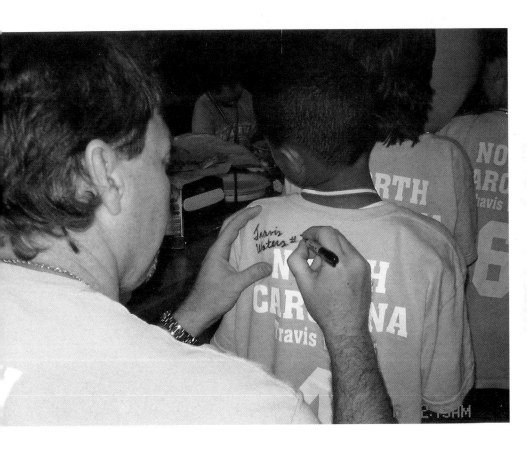

2010 – Autographing the Team North Carolina's jerseys.

2010 – Current photo of my grandparents' home in Palmetto Court. The house and concrete driveway have remained unchanged from my childhood.

2010 – Current photo of Dels Wholesale. I used to play games in this store. The store is listed in the Guinness Book of World of Records for remaining open for over 40 years.

2010 - Current photo of Bayview Park seawall. This is where I experienced my first load of pot. I was 10 years old.

2010 - Current photo of Bayview Park leading into Gordon's Pass. Across the bay is the wealthy section of Naples, known as Port Royal.

Travis Jr. and I on Grandfather Mountain in North Carolina.

June, 2012 – Team blue and me having fun at a pool party.

Chapter 15

It was 1991 and I had been in federal prison for three months. I was a twenty-four-year-old trying to adjust to prison life. The free world, as I knew it, was gone, and I didn't know when I would again feel what freedom was like. I just took my twenty-three-year sentence day by day. I felt it didn't matter how much gain time I earned for good behavior. I'd come to realize that I would spend the rest of my twenties in prison. It bothered me I could never have that part of my life back. It had gone forever. I started lifting weights once a day, walking and jogging five miles a day, getting in shape. This relieved the stress of being locked away from society.

I changed jobs and started working for the lieutenant as a CCS orderly. I worked on the main-entrance floor crew, waxing when needed. There were three inmates assigned to this job. The floor would be buffed every night with an electric floor buffer. It took about forty-five minutes. The three of us inmates would work a couple of nights each week. The only time we would work together was when we had to strip the wax off the floor and put new wax down. We did this every couple of months and it would take about eight hours to finish. This had to be done when a head prison official came from Washington to inspect the prison.

The privilege of working for the lieutenant revealed another aspect of my job. I was given permission to pour out hundreds of gallons of hooch. It was a mixture of fruit, yeast, and sugar, and after it set for a while, it would smell like rotten fruit. I didn't know how the inmates could drink it, but they did. It was sold on the compound just like the drugs that were sold there. However, even though I was allowed to pour out the hooch, I wasn't allowed to destroy drugs that were confiscated on the compound.

As for the perpetrators, the more drugs in their report, the more gain time they lost and the longer they stayed in the hole. I still made my twelve cents an hour for forty hours of work. I only worked a couple hours a week, so I had more time to work out.

I'd now been locked up for fifteen months, and I began focusing on my weight program. I started lifting weights twice a day. Working out released a lot of the stress of being locked up. My daily diet consisted of four to five eight-ounce cans of tuna, twelve egg whites—that I would buy from an inmate who worked in the kitchen and would smuggle them to my dorm— white rice, whole-wheat bread, salads, and fruit. I used the flavor pack from ramen noodle soup in my rice and tuna to give it flavor. I was in the best shape in my life. I played softball, racquetball, basketball, football, golf, and volleyball. The prison would hold sports tournaments at which you could win various prizes such as a Walkman or shoes. For the basketball tournaments, teams were put together. There were inmates from other states in federal prison, so each team represented the state it came from. I was chosen to be on Team Florida. We had some good tournaments. Because Team Florida had a lot of talent, we won most of the tournaments. There were guys just like me who had won scholarships to play ball and had thrown their lives away as I had. I wasn't the only dummy.

I had grown two inches since high school. I was now 6-foot-5. I was getting bigger, faster, and stronger. I squatted 450 pounds, benched 335 pounds, and dead-lifted 425 pounds. I bench-pressed 225 pounds, twenty-four times in a row and pretended I was in my own professional try-out camp for pros. My training went on six days a week. I ran a 4.36 forty-yard dash. My vertical jump had increased since high school to thirty-five inches. And now I was able to throw a football fifty-five yards in the air with one step. Hitting softballs 400 feet when I was practicing was routine. All these numbers I put up now that I was bigger, faster, and stronger didn't mean much. It just emphasized how much I had thrown away in my life for drugs and prison. I would have no fans on the football field, baseball field, or basketball court and I would never be able to see what I could have done.

Playing ball all your life with fans cheering for you and yelling out your name is the most thrilling thing that could ever happen. Unless you have experienced it, I can't explain it.

All I could do in prison was watch Deion on TV. A guy I used to play head-to-head with had achieved his dream. He became a superstar and earned millions of dollars legally doing something he loved. The only dream I had of that life was when I slept in my prison bunk. I'd wake up to the life and road I had chosen to go down, and I sat in prison thinking about how much I had fucked up my life.

I was now in my second year of being locked up and I was finally finding out who my real friends were. I began to understand what the judge had said to me during my sentencing: "You have no true friends in that kind of world."

They had been around only for the money, drugs, and toys. It was another part of life's journey. You learn as life goes on. I was still doing the same thing in prison. It didn't change. The only things that changed were the faces of the new arrivals and of the ones lucky enough to go home.

Chapter 16

———————————— /// ————————————

At four in the morning I was awakened by the night-shift guard telling me to pack all my belongings up and report to R and D. I asked what it was about, and he said he didn't know. I packed everything up and went to R and D. A US marshal was waiting for me. He had orders from the United States of America and the state of North Carolina to transport me to the federal office in Charlotte, North Carolina. I wondered if it was because of the cocaine case I had lied about on the stand. The case had been pending for years in the state of North Carolina. I was sure they hadn't given up trying to indict me and my family members. My cousin Greg was serving his federal smuggling sentence in Alabama. I wondered if he was also being sent to North Carolina, but I wouldn't know until I got there. The marshal threw me a pair of jeans and a red, short-sleeve shirt to put on. He put all the prison jewelry— handcuffs and shackles—on me and also put a black box over my handcuffs. I was escorted by two prison guards out the back gate. The gate guards, who weren't holding rifles, said, "Waters, whatever you did, the feds are going to give you some diesel therapy, so good luck."

We were outside the gate now, and the US marshal told me if I tried to run, he would shoot to kill and he wanted me to understand that.

I said, "I don't know how fast I could run with all these chains on me, but I understand."

It was just the marshal and me. I was locked into the back of a white van with bars on the windows, and I immediately got car sick. Only an hour went by before the marshal pulled into a county jail, opened up the van door and escorted me into the building. He informed me I would be held there for the weekend and he would get me sometime on Monday, maybe.

I was in a room with a jail guard, going through a strip search, normal protocol every time you enter a new jail. I was fingerprinted, photographed, and issued an orange jumpsuit. I went to a holding tank to wait to be put in a cell with a bed. The holding tank in this jail was where they held the town drunks. These people were throwing up everywhere. I had puke sprayed on me from every direction, and some of them were lying on the only bench in the holding tank. I stood in the corner, trying to get away from the spraying puke. The room was about 12-by-12 feet, and I was in there for about six hours. Ten people were in there with me. This trip was going to be a nightmare. I was on my way to North Carolina and I was still in Florida.

I was put in a cell ten hours later. My cellmate was an older, black, transsexual who was taking female hormone pills. I was tired. It had been a long day and this he/she started showing me his tits and wanted me to suck on them.

I said, "Listen here, freak, it's just you and me in this cell. If you try anything sexual with me, I will beat your fucking ass. I will be out of your cell in a few days, so don't fuck with me. All I want is to get some sleep."

I was getting more pissed at the feds and the North Carolina authorities for sending me up north and making me go through this bullshit. All this was punishment to make me rat out my family. But I wasn't going to give in. Two could play this game.

The dayroom guard came to my cell and unlocked my door. He said I was being transferred. I walked out of the cell and through all these winding hallways back to where I had been when I came in. I put my street clothes back on and I was put in the holding tank again, this time with a whole new group of drunks and puke everywhere again. It looked as if the mess had not been cleaned from when I was there a few days earlier, and the smell was indescribable, beyond belief. Back in the van, wearing my prison jewelry, I had some visitors, two black guys and a Mexican. The US marshal pulled in to a McDonald's. I thought he was getting himself something to eat. He opened a small door in the cage, separating us from the driver, and told us he was ordering us all Big Mac meals with Cokes. It had been a long time since I had eaten food from the outside world. The food was hard to eat because my hands were chained to a chain around my waist. After we ate, one of the inmates had to go to the bathroom because the food didn't agree with his stomach. The US marshal told him to hold it. Well, that didn't work; the inmate shit in his pants. We had no windows to open, and another inmate puked because of the smell. I wondered if this trip could get any fucking worse. I had thought the smell in the holding tank was bad, but this was the worst odor I'd ever smelled. My life seemed, for some reason, to get worse every time I thought it couldn't.

We finally made it to our next stop. This place had twenty-foot, concrete walls around it. It was the US Penitentiary, Atlanta. I never thought I would be glad to go into a prison. But as long as I could get out of the van and away from that smell, I didn't care where I was. The place was scary looking. It was old and the roofs were copper. I went through the same routine: strip search, bending over, coughing, fingerprinting, and having my photograph taken. I was put in the hole for my protection because I had codefendants at this prison. The hole was five-tiers high with cells that ran along each tier. The cells and walls had over sixty years of peeling paint on them. My cell was about 8-by-10 feet with two bunks bolted to the wall, a stainless-steel toilet, and a sink that didn't work. Water dripped out of it when you pushed the button. It was very noisy there because the inmates yelled back and forth from cell to cell and tier to tier.

It was evening when I finally got settled in, and I saw black inmates rolling food carts up and down my tier. I heard them handing trays of food to the cells nearby, but I couldn't see down the tier. I didn't have a plastic mirror to stick out my cell door to see what the hell was going on. One of the inmates walked by my cell.

I said, "Hey, I didn't get a tray of food."

The inmate looked at me and said, "Yes, you did."

I guessed I was not eating that night. All I had on was prison-issued flip-flops and a pair of boxers. I had nothing to read, so I did push-ups and calf raises. I also slept to pass the time. I started getting thirsty, so I would put my mouth under the sink faucet and push the button and the water would slowly drip into my mouth. The next morning I thought, *Good the food is here.* I saw the food cart roll past my cell and it left again. Still no food. I had been almost a full day there with no food and not much to drink. I decided not to exercise anymore because I had to conserve what energy I had. It was now day three and still no food. I was getting weak. At this point a black guard walked by my cell.

I said, "Hey, the inmates aren't giving me my food and I'm starving."

The guard was sure I was getting my food.

I said, "No, the black inmates are selling my trays of food to their friends."

The guard reassured me he would tell the morning-shift guards and to make sure I got my tray of food. It was the fourth day. No tray of food for breakfast or lunch. I now resorted to drinking out of the toilet with my two hands cupped together. The sink wasn't dripping at all now, and this was all I had for sustenance. I starting to get light headed. I didn't know when or if I would ever eat again. Day five and breakfast is served, but not to me. I was very weak at this point. I continued drinking a lot of water to stay hydrated. Every time I told a guard I wasn't getting my tray of food, they thought I was lying because the inmate delivering the food would place an empty tray in front of my cell. So the guard would see the tray and think I had received the food. I started wondering when the hell that

US marshal would come to pick me up because I might die there from starvation. I had to do something soon, but what? I was locked in a cell on the fourth-floor tier.

At lunchtime a guard happened to be walking by my cell, and I reached and grabbed him through my cell bars. I didn't give a fuck if I got charged with assault. I wasn't going to starve to death.

I said, "Listen here you, mother fucker. I'm starving to death. I haven't eaten in five days."

Then I fell to my knees because I was so weak. The guard unlocked my cell door and called for medical assistance. I was taken to a medical room and the nurse gave me fluids. She asked me what was wrong and said I was pale and looked weak.

I said, "I haven't eaten in five days, and I've been drinking out of my toilet. The black inmates bringing the food carts on the tiers sold my trays to their friends."

The nurse asked, "Why didn't you tell the guards on duty?"

"The guards didn't believe me. The inmates would place an empty tray in front of my cell and the guards thought I wanted more food."

Two more weeks went by. I sat in Buncombe County Jail in Asheville, North Carolina. This county jail was eighty-five years old. A guard at the end of the tier opened and closed the cell doors by raising and lowering a lever. I shared a cell with a guy who said he had killed four people with a hammer and a knife. He was on death row. After hearing his story, I began to wonder if I were in the right cell. Needless to say, I didn't sleep for the first three nights. On the fourth day, a guard came by and asked me what I was doing in inmate Johnson's cell. I wasn't supposed to be there because he was on death row.

I looked at the guard and said, "I didn't volunteer to come into this cell. Your guard put me here."

"The guard made a mistake, Inmate Waters."

He yelled down to the end of the tier and had my cell door opened. He told me to step outside on the walkway and asked if inmate Johnson had tried anything on me.

I said, "Like what?"

The guard said, "Did he try to hurt you?"

"No," but I didn't sleep for three days after he told me he was on death row.

I was transferred to a cell all by myself on the fifteenth floor of this county jail. I could hear something like gun fire or fireworks off in the distance.

I asked the guard, "What's all that noise I keep hearing off in the distance?"

The guard said, "They're filming scenes for the movie *The Last of the Mohicans* in the mountains."

I didn't sleep much in this cell either. Roaches raced up and down my stomach when the lights were turned off. There were times when I fell asleep and roaches would try to crawl in my mouth looking for food. It was disgusting. I couldn't wait to get back to my cell in the federal prison at Tallahassee. I was tired of being locked up in these cells twenty-four hours a day.

It was cold in Asheville and the heat in the county jail was dry. One night I could hardly breathe because of the dry heat. It made me feel claustrophobic. I would get out of my bunk and start banging my head against the wall. I thought I was starting to lose it. A few more days went by and I was escorted out of my cell and taken downstairs to where the North Carolina agents were waiting for me. Wearing my prison jewelry and my county jail jumpsuit, I was taken to a county courthouse in Asheville. I shuffled down the sidewalk, escorted by the agents while this guy took pictures of me. I walked past people who had kids on the sidewalk and they grabbed their children and took them off the sidewalk. They held their children close to them as I walked by. The fear on these kids' faces is an image I will never forget. That really upset me inside. I will never forget how I felt that day.

In a conference room the agents from North Carolina and Agent

Johns said, "We've been waiting for years to talk to you and now you're finally here. We know, Travis, that you are one of the major drug suppliers of cocaine and pot to North Carolina, Tennessee, and Ohio. A lot of people have been telling on you for years. You also lied on the federal stand, and they want to give you forty-three more years on top of the twenty-three years you already have. The state of North Carolina wants to also charge you with cocaine and marijuana trafficking. This is your chance to come clean. We will give you a good deal and run your new sentence from the state of North Carolina concurrently with the other sentences you already have. The federal government will not charge you with perjury and give you any more time. Travis, what are you going to do?"

I said, "It looks like you and the state of North Carolina already have me nailed to the wall. Why do you need me to talk?"

The agent said, "Because you are the main one and we need your cooperation to get a conviction against your family and some friends of yours here in North Carolina."

"It's all true. I sold kilos of cocaine every month and hundreds and hundreds of pounds of pot over the years in North Carolina and the other states you mentioned. I know from everything I've been through, you and the state of North Carolina aren't going to arrest me because if you were, you would've already done it. The way I see it, I'm going to finish the sentences I already have. The feds promised me a sentence reduction for my cooperation in bringing down the Miami drug gang and that never happened nor is it ever going to happen."

The agent said he would call and tell the feds I had refused to cooperate. That I had admitted to selling drugs in North Carolina, so I had perjured myself.

I said, "When you call the feds, be sure to tell them I said if they nail me with perjury, I will call the attorneys of all my codefendants, the ones I testified against. I will tell them everything I testified to in federal court I made up, and I lied about the Miami gang. I bet you didn't know my attorney received a letter from my codefendant's attorney demanding a new trial, since the star witness, myself, lied on the stand. So now I'm not a credible witness. I'm not going to testify against my family or any more friends for you or the feds. I'm done playing all these games, just take me back to my cell. All I want to do is finish serving out my sentence."

The agent said, "Are you sure you want to do that, Travis?"

"Yes, I'm very sure. I'm done being used and getting fucked."

The agents said, "Take him back to the county jail."

I went back to the jail and no sooner was I get settled in than one of the guards came to my cell and said, "Waters, you have a phone call from a federal agent in Washington and it's important."

Washington? Now what the fuck had I done? What was I going to be charged with now?

I picked up the phone. It was Agent Smith.

He said, "I got a call from the authorities in North Carolina telling me you refused to cooperate."

I said, "That's right."

The agent said, "Did you know your attorney and I received a letter from the Miami gang wanting a new trial?"

"Yes, I know. Didn't the agents here in North Carolina give you my message?"

"Yes, they did."

He asked me if I had called any of my codefendants' attorneys and told them anything about my lying on the stand about the Miami drug gang.

I said, "No, I haven't yet. I was waiting for a call from either you or the prosecutor, letting me know if I was going to get charged with perjury."

The agent said, "Travis, if you don't call the other attorneys, then we won't charge you with perjury."

"It's hard for me to trust you guys anymore, Agent Smith. Plus I never received my Rule 35 sentence reduction."

The agent said, "Since you lied on the stand, you are not able to receive that reduction. The federal prosecutor is pissed at me now because all the attorneys want a new trial for their clients."

"Oh well, that's the way these things work out. Remember you told me that in one of our meetings, Agent Smith."

Smith said, "You will not be charged with perjury. You have my word."

"Well then, Agent Smith, I want to be transferred back to Tallahassee. I want to be left alone. Please, no more games."

The Agent said, "Okay, Travis. I will have you sent back to Tallahassee."

I left it at that and hung up the phone.

Chapter 17

---///---

I was transferred out of Asheville and taken to Mecklenburg County jail in Charlotte, North Carolina, the very next day. This county jail was big. I was locked on a floor with twelve other inmates. I was able to go outside in the concrete jungle located on the fourth floor to finally get some fresh air and it felt good. The space seemed to be on the side of the building. There was one basketball goal and nothing else. Some black guys and a Mexican were playing a pickup game, and one of the black guys said, "Do you know anything about basketball, cracker?"

"You're a tall cracker," one of the other guys said.

I said, "Yeah, I've played before."

"Come on. We need another player. We're playing three-on-three, and we are the only ones here, so get your ass over here and play. Don't worry, us brothers will take it easy on you. Brothers know white boys can't play ball." This guy was starting to bother me.

We were playing for push-ups. The team that lost (each player) had to do fifty push-ups. My team consisted of me, the Mexican, and a short, older, black guy. Their team was young and they were all more than six feet tall. The tallest was 6-foot-3. They had the ball first and were up three to nothing. These two guys I had on my team barely knew how to dribble the ball. They sucked. The tall black guy on the other team kept talking trash to me, so I tied the game up, shooting from the outside. They were arguing with each other about the white boy who was scoring on them and how they had never lost to a white boy before. The tall guy came inside for an easy lay-up, and I jumped up and smacked the ball really hard. The others said, "Did you see that white boy?"

His teammates said, "He just blocked your shot!"

So the tall guy started pushing me.

I said, "It's only a game."

I turned to my two teammates and told them to stay out of the lane and go out on the wing. They both asked me what I was doing.

I said, "You'll see."

I had the ball on top of the key and I said to the tall guy who was pushing me, "Are you ready?"

He said, "You aren't going to do shit, cracker."

I faked to the left and he went for it. I blew by him on the right side and slammed the ball through the hoop. Now the three of them started fighting. Two guards come running out to break up the fight. One of the guards told me to turn around and put my hands behind my back. He put handcuffs on me and took me to the hole.

I said, "What did I do?'

The guard said, "You started a fight on the basketball court."

"I didn't start that fight."

He said, "Yes, you did when you dunked the basketball on those guys. I'm locking you up for your own protection. You dunk on them boys and make them look bad that creates fights because basketball is all they have in here."

I'm sitting in the hole shaking my head. I was pissed. I was stuck in the fucking hole again. This fucking trip I'd been on sucked. I just wanted to get back to Tallahassee. I started doing push-ups, calf raises, body squats and lunges to pass the time. There was nothing else to do. I looked back at my short life and wondered what the hell I had been thinking when I was free. Why did I let myself get in this situation to begin with? Why hadn't I gone to college as I had dreamed of doing while growing up?

Look at yourself, Travis, locked in a cage. Little kids on the sidewalk looked at you with fear on their faces. Was all that money and lifestyle worth it? Was it worth all of this?

I lay on my bunk and closed my eyes and considered killing myself. It would be the only way out of this nightmare. I already had twenty-three years and I didn't trust the feds. I wanted to have kids of mine own one day, to follow in my footsteps, and play sports as I had. I dreamed of coaching my son's team and of being the best father I could be to my kids. At that point my dream looked as if it would never happen. I just wanted to go to sleep because when you sleep and have dreams of the free world, it is the only time in your mind when you're really free. I started crying at the thought of what it would be like to have kids one day and to just be a normal person.

The next day I left Charlotte, North Carolina, and traveled south on a federal bus. It was basically a Greyhound bus with comfortable seats and lots of leg room. An armed guard was locked in a cage at the back of the bus and another guard was locked in the front of the bus. I was dropped off back at the Atlanta Penitentiary, the place where I had almost starved to death. I hoped I wouldn't go through that place again, but here I was, sitting in the hole again, this time on the top floor. I told the guards downstairs to make sure I got my trays of food. I was told I would be fed like all the other inmates in the hole and not to worry about not eating. This time my sink worked. I was alone and I was happy about it. I started doing push-ups, body squats, lunges, and dips off my lower bunk, along with calf raises. I did 500 a day of each exercise. It really helped me deal with all the stress of being locked up and not knowing where I would be in the next ten or fifteen years. It was something I had no control over. I got my trays of food, so it could have been a lot worse. I heard the inmates trading food for sex, shampoo, paper, books—you name it.

It was five a.m. I stood out in front of the prison with four other inmates and two US marshals. All the inmates were wearing prison jewelry except me and one other. I wondered why I didn't have any chains on, but I didn't say anything. I could have escaped and taken my chances of being shot by the marshal, but running wasn't on my mind. He started calling out our prison numbers and names. The other inmate not wearing prison jewelry was told to get into the van. He was going to a federal prison camp. A federal, military-style, prison camp doesn't have fences or gun towers. I thought I was also being transferred there since I didn't have any prison jewelry on. Great. The marshal stood in front of me and flipped through some papers. He started shaking his head as he looked at me. I wondered what the hell I'd done or hadn't done. He walked over to the other US marshal and one of them went to the van and started talking on the radio. I could hear him mention my name and the guy on the radio yelled out, "Secure Inmate Waters, now."

Suddenly the front doors of the prison opened up and three large prison guards ran in my direction. The marshals pulled their guns out and told the other inmates to lie on the ground. All their guns were pointed at me. I froze. I was gang-tackled by the guards and slammed down on the concrete. Three guards lay on top of me, pulling my arms to my back, and putting handcuffs on me. The marshals stood there with their guns still pointed at me. I lay on the ground, my arm and knee throbbing and bleeding.

I said, "What the fuck is going on? What the hell did I do?"

The guard stood me up. A woman counselor stood there watching what had just happened to me. I was taken back inside the prison to a room where a nurse was called in to clean up my scrapes. I didn't know what to think about what had just happened. I heard some men arguing outside the room. The nurse left the room as the marshal and woman counselor walked in. They asked if I was alright.

"Yes, I guess. What the hell is going on? The last time I came through here I almost starved to death, and now I'm gang-tackled to the ground in front of the prison. I don't understand."

The counselor apologized and said, "Someone here messed up your transfer papers and thought you were going to a prison camp. Since you were outside the prison, it was a security breech. That's why you were tackled and had the guns pointed at you."

"Couldn't you have just told me to go back inside the prison instead of tackling me and pointing guns at me? I wasn't going to run."

She said, "They have to follow procedure."

"Am I going back to Tallahassee?"

"Yes, you are."

The guard came in and cuffed me. I was escorted back out the front door and locked in a van. The other inmates being transferred had left, so it was just me. I began to wonder if I was really going back to Tallahassee or some other place I didn't know about. I knew the feds were pissed at me and so was the state of North Carolina, so I hoped I'd go back to Tallahassee.

I arrived back at club fed in Tallahassee, and was placed in Charlie House, waiting for a bunk to open up in A-Dorm. I was so happy to be back there. I made my rounds, visiting my friends and codefendants, sharing with them some of the nightmares I had gone through on my way to North Carolina. I was soon transferred out of Charlie House and put back in A-Dorm.

I unpacked my belongings and put them in my locker. My new bunk mate was a friend of mine. I called him the Colonel because he was a cocaine pilot who had flown coke loads out of Jamaica and into South Florida. His dad was a school teacher in Key Largo at Coral Shores High School, who had taught my stepbrother and stepsister when they lived there.

It's a small world. When you're in prison, it's a world of crime all put together in one place. Everyone plots and meets new connections so when you get out, the sky is the limit. Believe it or not, I had more drug connections in other states and other countries—a lot more—than before I went to prison. The temptation was still there even when I was locked up.

Drug smuggling is an addiction and it's hard to break. I was locked up and still thinking about doing one more load when I got out. I had all these new connections, Cubans, Colombians, Jamaicans, guys from all over the world. I had to keep telling myself, *What you are thinking, Travis, stay away from the drug business. You already have twenty-three years and possibly a lot more time is on the way.*

I was eating well again. I'd lost ten pounds on my trip to North Carolina. I started lifting weights and getting back into my old routine. It felt good.

I was approached by a white inmate named Calvin who had heard I had played basketball in high school against Deion Sanders.

I said, "Where did you hear that from?"

Calvin said, "Some black guys from Fort Myers, Florida, told me."

"Yes, I did."

Calvin arranged to play the supposedly two best black inmates in the prison yard in a game of two-on-two. He said there was a lot of money riding on the best of three games if he could convince me to play.

I asked, "Who are the two players?"

He told me, "Travis has seen both these guys playing on the rec yard."

Floyd was an all-round athlete. I played against him in kickball, softball, volleyball, and flag football. He was a good athlete, 6-foot-1. Albert—I'd just seen him play basketball and he was really good. He was 6-foot-4 and had also won scholarships to play basketball out of St. Petersburg, Florida but went down the drug road instead of going to college.

I asked Calvin, "Of the almost 1500 inmates here at this prison, why did you pick me?"

Calvin said he wanted to make some money. He said he had talked to other inmates who knew about me from high school. One particular inmate, named William, I played against in high school. He played for a Ft. Myers high school and was in prison with me.

William said all the brothers from our area were going to bet I could beat those two guys. The other prisoners said no white boy could beat Albert and Floyd. I asked William whom he was betting on to win.

William looked at me and said, "I know you, Travis, and I've played against you. I'm putting my money on you to win."

I said, "I will think about playing."

I decided to play against the two supposedly best basketball players at this prison. After a couple months of hype and egging me on, some of the brothers told me I was scared. The white inmates told me to go out there and show them I could win. In the prison yard it became black athlete versus white athlete. The white and black prison guards were also betting on this game. I would have white guards coming up to me and telling me, "I hope you beat their black asses on the court. I have a lot of money riding on you, Waters."

The black guards would tell me, "You can't beat those brothers, Waters. Basketball is their game. I'm going to win a lot of money betting against you."

It was the day of the match and I was out on the court, warming up. The basketball stands were filling up. There were at least 700 to 800 inmates waiting to watch us play, and more inmates were on their way to the court. I could only imagine how much money and bragging rights were riding on this game. I looked at the crowd and saw the guards standing all around the court. Wow! Talk about a black and white issue. I knew the black guys from the Fort Myers area had my back. Wayne and Michael were putting a lot of money on me.

It was decided that it would be the best out of three games. We'd shoot on top of the key. That shot would decide who got the ball first. Albert shot and missed. I shot. Swish! You could hear the black inmates in the stands already talking shit. It was our ball. The game started and I threw the ball to Calvin. Floyd was guarding him. Calvin shot the ball and missed. Floyd drove on Calvin and made it easily on him. They were up by four baskets and the black inmates in the stands yelled and counted their money, saying, "We told you crackers that white boy can't beat us in basketball." I looked over to see a couple of the black guards talking shit to the white guards and laughing. Albert and Floyd won the first of the three-game series. I knew if we were going to have any chance of winning this series, I'd have to do everything because Calvin couldn't play against these two guys.

The second game started, and I drove the basket and shot over Albert. Swish! The next play I blocked Albert's shot and the whites started jumping up and down. We won the second game and all the black inmates said it was a lucky win and they had let me win one. The third game was tied. Only three more baskets and that team would win. Arguments between the whites and blacks broke out in the stands. I shot the last shot, and we won the third game. Calvin jumped up and down and started hugging me as if he had won the lottery. The white guards and white inmates yelled and laughed and the black inmates were pissed and started leaving the stands. I could hear them saying the game wasn't fair. I had suckered the boys and all that crap. Michael and Wayne, the guys from Fort Myers, yelled to the black inmates, "I told you that white boy could play."

They then begin hollering for them to pay up. I got the hell out of there and headed to my dorm as fast as I could. On the way back everyone shook my hand and complimented me on winning the game. I took a shower and laid low. When I walked back to my bed from the shower, everyone in my dorm clapped except the black inmates. The white guard came to my bunk and said I would be the first go to the chow hall because he had won money off me. As I went through the chow line, the brother serving food said to me, "God damn white boy, you suckered them boys. Where did you play ball at and why are you in prison?"

The black inmates didn't play basketball for a couple weeks. The courts were empty. Wayne and Michael said the boys were embarrassed that the two best players lost to a white boy, and a white boy was the best basketball player in this prison. A group of black inmates came by my dorm to tell me not to get back on the basketball court or else something bad would happen.

I said, "Thanks for the information. I appreciate it."

Time passed and everyone went about their normal routines. Some left the prison to move on with a new chapter. Some were new faces trying to adjust as we had at some point in time.

I was awakened in the early morning by the night-shift guard. He instructed me to pack whatever items I wanted to take with me. I needed to pack the rest of my things that I wanted sent home. Afterward I was to report to R and D. The guard wished me good luck and said he was glad to have met me. I said the same to him. I made my rounds in A-Dorm to say my good-bye's to friends. I was a free man, sort of. I was released on parole by the federal government after serving forty months of my eight-year sentence for smuggling marijuana.

I was in R and D, looking through a pile of prison-issued street clothes. I asked the guard, "Why do I need street clothes?"

"State prison officials are coming to pick you up, so you can start serving your fifteen-year state sentence for cocaine trafficking."

The only clothes they had that would fit were, I think, blue polyester pants, a yellow short-sleeved shirt, and black socks, and the only pair of shoes in my size were white dress shoes. The clothes on my back were all I could take with me to state prison. I sent the rest of my items home and left some things with my former inmates. I was escorted under armed guard to the perimeter fence and then to the sally port that vehicles used to enter and leave the prison. Three large, black, state-prison guards met me, also under armed guard, to transfer me from federal custody to state custody. There were four guards with shot guns, two guards with automatic pistols, all pointing at me until I was secure. Two guards put shackles on my ankles and then a chain around my waist, both handcuffed together, and locked to the chain around my waist was a black box that prevented me from trying to unlock my handcuffs. The last chain went from my waist to my shackles. Since the guns weren't pointing at me, I was considered secure. Now I was finally ready to be transported to my new home, state prison.

A federal prison guard said to me, "Travis, you are now going to a real prison. Good luck."

I was escorted into the back of a white prison van. It had four bench seats and dark-tinted windows with bars on them. Two guards rode up front in the cab behind the driver and passenger seats, which was lined with diamond-mesh steel from the ceiling to the floor. This separated them from me. A third guard was locked in with me but had no gun. My destination was unknown to me. It was considered a security risk to tell me.

Twenty miles into the trip, I noticed we were heading northwest, and I started to get car sick. It had been a long time since I'd ridden in a vehicle. Being locked in the back and not knowing where I was going or what kind of hell I was going to face made me feel especially nauseous. The guard gave me a bag to throw up in and wasn't too happy with the idea of the smell of vomit since we had a long ride a head of us.

Chapter 18

———————————— /// ————————————

I finally reached my destination. It was Apalachicola State Prison. It was located in the panhandle of the state of Florida and was a maximum-security state penitentiary. It looked like something out of a horror flick. It was old, dingy, and in need of a paint job. There were three, deep, perimeter fences that had barbed wire and rolls of razor wire on top of each of them. Each of these fences was at least fifteen feet high. In between each perimeter fence were rolls of razor wire, stacked on top of each other, about eight feet high. The armed gun towers surrounding the prison were at least forty feet high and equipped with high-powered rifles. I couldn't believe what I was seeing. I was scared and feared for my life, especially since I was white. I wanted to go back to federal prison, where I felt safe. I knew that wasn't going to happen.

I got out of the van and was taken to the warden's office. While I sat there still chained and shackled, the warden argued with the guards who had picked me up. He wanted to know how the hell I had ended up at his prison. He called me a major drug kingpin, and thought I might have helicopters land in his prison to help me escape. I looked at him and couldn't believe what I was hearing.

Helicopters? Escape? You're kidding, right? I thought.

The guards informed the warden that the federal office had requested they picked me up. This made the warden angry since he hadn't been notified about my arrival. He started looking through the file that came with me. The more he read my file, the louder his voice became. He kept telling the guards, in his Southern accent, "He's got tons and tons of drugs in his file." The warden looked my way and told me he'd never had any one in his custody with as large an amount of drugs on file—ever. I sat there looking and listening to the warden going on about my file. He was a white man with brown hair, mustache, glasses, and a large stomach. His face turned red as he called the governor's office, demanding answers as to why Travis Waters was sitting in his office with DEA and US Customs reports in his file. He also saw in the file CIA reports of the marijuana and cocaine cartels from Colombia. He went berserk and hung up the phone because he had been put on hold by the governor's office.

He said, "Welcome, Travis Waters," and looked at me. "I will put you some where no one can find you or help you try to escape while in my custody."

And that he did.

I was taken out of his office still wearing all my prison-issued jewelry. As I shuffled down the outside sidewalk, I noticed at least 85 percent of the population was black, with the other 15 percent of the inmates being a mix of Mexicans, Latinos, Cubans, whites, and I couldn't make out what the others were. Here I was, the minority. It was obvious who ran the show and made the rules in this prison population. As we walked inside the prison, two black inmates walked in front of me and my guard escort. They kept looking back at me and making comments out loud. They said I didn't look like a killer. I couldn't figure out why they said this. It turned out the colors of the street clothes I still had on from my transfer from federal were considered death row colors. I thought that I looked like a pimp out of the 1970s, but without the hat. The guard escorting me went by the name of Bubba. He was 6-foot-6 and weighed about 325 pounds. I asked him why the two inmates ahead of us were yelling out that I didn't look like a killer. That was how I found out about the colors. Bubba informed me I was wearing death-row colors, a yellow shirt and blue pants, and I was also being escorted by a guard. I thought, just my luck, my first day in state prison and this happens.

This was my introduction to state prison.

My new home was "the hole." The hole was for inmates who couldn't live among the general population because, for example, they were violent, or rapists, or they were mentally ill and might cause harm to themselves or others. As I walked to my hole, or cell, all I could hear were screams of pain or fights going on. All I could do was think no matter how much money or how many attorneys or friends I had, nothing was going to help me out of there. I didn't want to be there.

I was inside now and the jewelry was coming off. I was taken downstairs by a different guard, named Luke. He was 6-foot-3 and weighed 275 pounds. He was smaller than Bubba. The cells were dark and had no windows. There was only a single light bulb hanging from a wire. That would be my only source of light while I was down there. There were seventy years of paint peeling off the walls from the leaking pipes that were hanging from the ceiling, not to mention the stench of mold, sweat, and sex that filtered through the air. I stood in front of my cell and was so scared I could feel my heart pounding in my chest and my knees starting to shake. Luke ordered me to take my clothes off, bend over and hold onto my ankles. He put on a glove and lubed it up with gel for my cavity search. As this was being done to me, I looked out of the corner of my eye and saw an old white man, who was skinny and bald, and his skin looked weather-beaten. I noticed he was smiling at me with the three or four teeth he had left in his mouth. His body and right arm were shaking, and I thought something was wrong with him, as if he were having a seizure. So I stood straight up.

The guard said, "What's wrong?"

I said, "There seems to be something wrong with that old man over there."

"Nothing is wrong with him. He's been locked up down here for such a long time that he's happy to see you. He's masturbating because he wants to have sex with you," Luke said. I looked over at the old man, and he stuck his dick in between the cell bars for me to see. Luke then ordered me to bend over again and hold my ankles so he could finish the cavity search. I wished this was over. I didn't know what he could possibly find. He finally finished his search and had me enter my cell. I was given a pair of white boxer shorts and flip-flop sandals. But I was never given a shirt to wear.

My 8-by-8 foot cell had two small beds that were bolted to the wall, a toilet made of stainless steel, and a ceramic sink with a rusty faucet. That was my drinking fountain. The only light in my cell was provided by a single, hanging, light bulb. It flickered quite a bit when it was on. I thanked God I was alone and I didn't have a cell mate to deal with. I soon learned you were lucky if you got a shower twice a week.

"Waters, put your back against the cell bars," the guard called out.

I put my hands behind my back and the handcuffs went on.

The guard unlocked the cell door, and I stepped out, naked. He shackled my legs together. After all of this, I shuffled down the hall to the shower. As I made my way, I figured out who and where the grunting and moaning noises were coming from after the lights went out. I was experiencing the worst freak show I'd ever seen. As I passed the cells going to the showers, these inmates yelled comments such as, "I can't wait to hit that ass, cracker" or "You're a fine-looking white boy with no tattoos."

They also showed their dicks to me as I walked by. Another yelled out to me, "He's a virgin."

"Not for long, white boy."

I finally got to the shower and prayed there were no freaks in there. The showers were empty, thank God. The chains and cuffs came off, courtesy of the guard. I was locked into the shower with a bar of soap and no shampoo. After I finished, the guard came back to chain and cuff me only to return me to my cell. Unfortunately, I had to endure more rude comments from those crazy inmates on the way back to my cell.

Four days passed and I hadn't been allowed my phone call. My family and my attorneys knew I had been transferred and they waited for my call. I knew my mom was at home worried to death about me, and that was killing me inside.

A couple of weeks went by and still no phone call. Now I was pissed. I had an idea no one would know where I was being held until the prison system found me a permanent home. While I served out my federal sentence in Tallahassee, I had hired two private attorneys to help me on some other ongoing cases, and I had hoped my new prison would be near their offices, but because this prison was in an unknown location and I could be a security risk, even my lawyers couldn't find me. Three weeks passed before a guard came to my cell to let me know I had a phone call from my attorney.

It's about damn time, I thought.

My attorney had to contact Tallahassee and demand to know my whereabouts. He had learned the warden of the prison didn't want me there, so he was working with the state on getting me transferred. I told him I didn't want to be there. After talking with my attorney I was able to make a phone call to my mom. She was worried and didn't understand why the attorney couldn't tell her where I was located. She thought the feds had taken me out of the country or I had been killed. So, to make her feel better and try to put her at ease, I told her I was fine and I was eating well, playing sports a lot, and lifting weights, and the reason I hadn't called was because I couldn't use the phone. After I talked with her, she sounded better.

I was awakened in the middle of the night by a flashlight shining in my face. I came to, and saw two guards standing in front of my cell door. I began to get excited. I started thinking I was finally getting out of this hell hole. But no such luck. There stood a white man, wearing all of his prison jewelry. He began asking me if I was the one who had arrived about a month earlier and if I was on death row. I asked why? He turned to the guards and pleaded with them not to put him in the same cell with me because he was scared. I hadn't told him that I wasn't on death row. The guards removed his chains and cuffs and put him in the cell.

He said his name was Jimmy, but he went by Gunner. He was twenty years old, 5-foot-8. His head was shaved and he was covered in tattoos. A gang banger. (I will not name any gangs in this autobiography.) Gunner was in there because he had gunned down three, rival, gang members in North Florida in a dispute over turf on the streets. Two victims were shot at point blank in the back of the head, and the third was shot eight times in the head and the chest. So Gunner was serving three life sentences. The reason he was down in the hole for six months was because he had stabbed a rival gang member in the yard over money. I looked at him, thinking, *And he's scared to be alone in a cell with me?*

To pass the time, Gunner and I would play tic-tac-toe and his favorite game, hangman, with our four-inch pencil.

I soon realized I was locked up in this cell twenty-four hours, seven days a week except for the occasional shower. The only exercise I would get were the 400 push-ups, 500 calf-raises, 300 squats, 300 sit-ups and 300 crunches I did a day. Sometimes I would do more. I missed seeing the sun and being able to get fresh air. When I left federal prison, I considered myself to be in the best shape ever. I had worked out twice a day with weights, walked or jogged five to seven miles a day, and worked my abs four times a week.

Chapter 19

It was my lucky day. I was able to take a shower. I felt I had won the lottery. In the shower I noticed something different this time. I had company. He was a good-sized, rough-looking, black man, six feet tall and weighing about 200 pounds. I recognized him from one of the cells I had to pass when I took a shower. He would always call out to me and say he couldn't wait to hit my "white ass" in the shower. I was locked in the shower with this crazy man and I realized I was in trouble. At that moment I started to remember back in federal prison I got hit on by a lot of gay men. That prison was considered minimum to medium security. Those men had committed mostly white-collar crimes. They didn't have life sentences, nor were they serving long sentences for their crimes. They were a whole different breed, so to speak. I remembered a guard at federal prison telling me I was now going to a real prison.

As I took my shower, I kept a watchful eye on this guy to make sure he didn't try to pull anything on me. He finished his shower and sat on the tile bench, waiting to go back to his cell. I hoped at that moment the guard would show up, but no such luck. I looked over at him and noticed he was smiling at me while masturbating. He was serving four life sentences for murder.

What the hell! Was everyone here serving life sentences for murder?

He said he'd been in there for twenty years and hadn't been with a woman in a long time and he loved men, especially young, white men. He said he'd completely given up on women. I listened to this man talk and all I could think of was he'd been locked up for twenty years at an all-male prison, so of course he'd given up on women. What a stupid motherfucker. He turned the conversation to how much he liked my body, especially my ass, and that I looked like I worked out. I told him I did. He said he was one of the best dick suckers in the prison and I should ask my roommate, Gunner. Apparently he sucked Gunner's dick sometimes.

This guy is in my cell! Great!

Can this prison get any worse than it already is? What a nightmare. I was convinced I was at the threshold of Hell. I now knew what being in Hell was like. I wondered if this was how courtships in prisons start. He kept telling me he was the best at sucking dick, and he wanted to suck mine. He said after he sucked my dick, he wanted me to fuck him in the ass and not to worry; we didn't have to kiss on the lips. It would be fun. I couldn't believe this man was saying these things to me. I was getting sick to my stomach. I thanked God there was no one else in the shower area to hear what he was saying. I told him no thanks. I didn't do that with men. I wasn't gay. He said he wasn't either. He just liked to have sex. I told myself he was not with it upstairs and he was a fucking nut case. I was trying to wash my hair while this guy continued with the sexual innuendos. I looked at him and told him to just shut the fuck up.

The next thing I knew, I felt an arm around my neck and a sharp pain in my lower back. He said we could do this the easy way or the hard way. He had a homemade shank and he would stab me in the kidney if I didn't cooperate. He didn't care. He had nothing to lose. He was serving four life sentences. So my choices, according to him, were to let him suck my dick or get stabbed. He also informed me there was no guard around to rescue me and no one would know about this little incident since it was just the two of us in there. I felt his dick, balls, and pubic hair rubbing against my ass and leg. It grossed me out.

I said, "I'll do it, but don't tell any of the other inmates. I don't want them to think I'm gay."

He said I didn't have anything to worry about. He took the shank out of my back and his arm from around my neck. I knew he had lots of practice in these situations. I wasn't his first. He wasn't stupid in the sense that this was his life. He'd been in there for twenty years. He was never getting out. He'd die there.

A million reactions ran through my head in a matter of seconds. My first was that of shock. Was this really happening to me? Was I really locked in a shower with this crazy black man, threatening to stab me with this shank he had made or even kill me if I didn't give in and let him suck my dick? My second reaction was fear, and my third was to rationalize the situation. Did I let him suck my dick and forget it ever happened? Or should I try to fight him and get that shank out of his hand? The thought of having sex with him just grossed me out.

I looked at him and asked, "What do you want to do first?"

He says, "I want to suck your dick."

I said. "No kissing."

He said, "Okay."

He said he'd been waiting for this moment to happen, and couldn't wait for the two of us to get locked in the shower together. I had my back to him as he was saying this to me. I asked if it was okay to turn around. He said yes. As soon as I turned, he grabbed my dick. I suggested if he got on his knees it would be easier for him to suck my dick since I was tall. He told me to relax. He grabbed my dick again and said I was going to enjoy this because he was the best dick sucker there. How could I relax? I was about to puke!

I waited for him to take his eyes off me and lower the hand holding the shank. When he did this, I brought my right arm up and back. Standing there flat-footed on the wet tile, I didn't want to slip and end up on the wet floor with him still holding his shank. I just wanted to end all of this by using a round-house punch with my shoulder and taking advantage of the adrenaline caused by fear. His head was waist high and at least two feet back while he held onto my dick with his right hand. The shank was in his left hand, his arm hanging down, ready to stab me. My fist came around in front of me and made contact with the left side of his head. I was hoping to hit him in the temple. I heard a loud cracking noise. He fell over onto the shower floor and didn't move. This seemed to be happening in slow motion. My wrist was throbbing from hitting him in the head. It was a lucky punch. I'm glad it was just him and me in there. I quickly grabbed the shank out of his hand. It was a toothbrush with tape wrapped around the handle to give it grip, and the other end was ground down to a point for stabbing. This weapon couldn't cut. I yelled for the guard, hoping he wouldn't wake up. Unfortunately he started to come to before the guard showed up and sat there against the shower wall, dazed and confused about what had just happened. He said he remembered being in the shower and getting down on his knees. Then everything went black.

I told him, "I hit you."

He asked, "With what?"

"My right fist,"

Finally the guard showed up. He asked me what was wrong with Williams, and then saw me holding the shank in my hand.

He said, "Waters, you're going to get another charge and lose your gain time. You just earned yourself a year in the hole."

The guard called the extraction team to have me removed from the shower by force since I was holding a weapon. The warden had informed the entire staff I was a drug kingpin and they were to keep a watchful eye on me.

I don't want to be stuck down here for a whole fucking year.

It just wasn't looking good for me, especially because it was for something I didn't do. The guard told me to throw the shank out on the walkway, and the extraction team showed up in their riot gear. There were a total of six guards on the team. The lead guard was holding a clear shield. I began to tell the team what had happened and the next thing I knew, the shower door opened up and I was slammed down to the ground. All of the guards were now on top of my naked body handcuffing me. My knees and elbows were bloody. The extraction team removed me from the hole into the yard where most of the inmates were. I was still naked. The sun was very bright and made it difficult for me to keep my eyes open because it had been a while since I been outside. I shuffled down the sidewalk and got nothing but cat calls from the inmates in the yard.

Once again, I found myself back where this nightmare had begun: the warden's office. The warden was shaking his head, smiling at me. I asked if it would be possible to get a blanket to cover me.

The warden looked at me and said, "Waters, this doesn't look good for you. This is your first time entering state prison. You've been here five to six weeks, and now you're facing an assault charge. This means more time on your sentence and the loss of earned gain time you received while you were in federal custody. You will serve one year in the hole and your transfer will be denied for disciplinary reasons. Officer Jones said he had found Williams dazed and confused in the shower and Williams had told him his head was throbbing and he was in need of medical attention. Officer Jones also told me that he found you had a handmade shank made out of a toothbrush in your hand. So, do you want to tell me what happened since you have a lot to lose?"

I said, "Would it really do me any good since you didn't want me here to begin with? Remember, you were scared I would escape because I'm a drug kingpin, so you put me in a place where no one could find me, not even my attorneys. Do you remember those comments to me, sir? Williams was trying to rape me with a shank in my back. He told me he wanted to suck my dick, and then I was to fuck him in the ass."

The warden looked at me and said, "This isn't the first time Williams has done this."

Apparently he tried to have sex with all the new inmates, especially the white ones. I stood up and showed the warden the mark on my lower back made by the shank. He asked how I had knocked out Williams, and I told him, "With my fist." I also let him know I wasn't a queer.

Inmate Williams entered the warden's office, still dazed, the left side of his face and head swollen.

The warden asked, "Williams, did you assault Inmate Waters in the shower with this shank? Officer Jones handed it to me as evidence, and Waters has a flesh wound on his lower back. By the looks of it, it came from the type of weapon that I have here in my possession. If you admit to this incident, I will drop the assault charge, which means you will have less time in the hole."

Williams admitted the assault and said the shank was his. He told the warden he had snuck the weapon into the shower by putting it up his rectum. I thanked God he admitted to all of it. The warden told Williams he had hoped he had learned a lesson from the incident and that he would think twice about sexually assaulting new arrivals again.

The warden turned to me and said, "Inmate Waters, you will not be charged with assault. You were acting out of self-defense."

And you, warden, are scared of me! This place is a fucking nut house.

"Your transfer papers have been signed, and you will be sent to a Florida processing center. From there you will be sent to your permanent home until you finish your fifteen-year sentence with the state. I had a chance to read your file—what was made available to me—and all I can ask is was all of it worth it? I wish you much luck, Inmate Waters."

I said, "Thank you," and was escorted out of his office to a cell for transfers. I was happy they hadn't put me back in my old cell with Gunner. I wasn't up for another altercation that day. It would only be a matter of time before he would start to hit on me.

I was by myself again and started thinking about what had just happened as I looked at my hand. The top of my hand and knuckles were swollen. Is that what I had to look forward to, for years to come, dealing with lifers, queers, fights, being gang–raped, and surviving prison gangs every day? Then it hit me. If I hadn't thrown away my college scholarships and sports, I wouldn't have been dealing with all that bullshit and could have made something good out of my life. Did I have no choice but to live in this nightmare? I started to cry.

Another week went by and still no transfer. I wondered just how much more of that nightmare I could take. I'd lost track of how long I'd been down there in my cell. I wondered if I'd ever be locked in the shower again with another lifer who would try to kill me or have sex with me. I couldn't stand the smells, the screams, and the noise of men having sex with willing and not-so-willing partners. Food was brought to my cell three times a day. I could only imagine what the inmates who delivered my food were doing to it since I'd knocked out their friend, inmate Williams. Anyway, the food there sucked. I missed federal prison more and more.

A guard came to my cell to take me to the showers, but I reluctantly declined.

Please, God, get me the fuck out of here!

Chapter 20

---///---

Finally, my transfer! I was handcuffed and put onto an old school bus.

As far as I knew, the Department of Corrections bought these buses from local school systems. They were painted white with a green stripe on each side and had the words "Department of Corrections" printed on them. The windows were covered with diamond wire that was bolted on the inside of each frame. There was no air conditioning, so the guard had to open the windows from the outside.

The bus was half full. The majority of the occupants were black. I wondered if the state of Florida sent mostly black people to prison. The bus made four stops to other prisons, picking up other inmates who were waiting for their transfers too, which could have been for reasons such as medical treatments, court appearances, change of custody and location, or new-inmate processing. Using the caged toilet in the back of the bus was a challenge, especially since we had to remain handcuffed. The smell was unbearable, not to mention the urine that was everywhere except in the toilet. Thank God the windows were open. The trip lasted about five hours. The bus finally pulled up to my next temporary home, Lake Butler.

This was the North Florida processing center. The fences were topped with the razor wire, and in the gun towers guards held high-powered rifles. We were taken off the bus and brought to a holding station. I sat on a concrete stoop against the wall. This prison looked newer than the one I had just come from. I hoped to God I wasn't thrown in the hole there too.

A guard walked in and welcomed us to the prison. He instructed us, "Stand up. Strip so you are naked, and stand shoulder to shoulder."

We waited for the guards to move down the line of inmates. They searched for contraband in our clothes and our bodies.

It was my turn. The guard told me to raise my arms up and out, run my hands through my hair, open my mouth, stick my tongue out, cough, turn around, bend over, spread my butt cheeks open, and cough. Inmates were randomly selected for cavity searches, and luckily, I wasn't chosen that time. After all the searches were complete, the guard said to leave our clothes in front of us and sit down. Our names were going to be called out in alphabetical order, so I instantly knew I would be sitting there for a while.

A big, fat, white guard with chew in his mouth walked up and down where we sat. He told us how to address the prison guards and all the staff. "When inmates are spoken to at this prison, inmates are to reply, "Yes, sir," and "No, sir," "Yes, ma'am" and "No, ma'am." He continued yelling and the chew in his mouth flew out every time he yelled, "We run this prison military style. We walk in military lines. When an officer is talking, you listen."

I sat on the cold concrete with my head down, not paying attention to this fat-ass, red-faced redneck screaming and looking as if he would have a heart attack. There was silence for a few seconds. Footsteps came closer to where I was sitting. My head was still down, my chin resting on my chest. All of a sudden I felt a sharp pain on my lower leg. The fat-ass redneck had kicked me.

He screamed at me, "On your feet, convict! Bend down so I can be face-to-face with you, you low-life motherfucker. When I'm addressing you, you will give me the courtesy of listening to me. I didn't put you in prison, you white piece of shit."

I stood there while his spit and chew hit me in the face, wishing I could meet this fat-ass redneck on the street one day when I was released.

"Do you understand me, convict?" he snarled.

I said, "Yeah."

He went off on me some more. "It's 'Yes, sir,' and 'No, sir.' Do you understand me, convict?"

I yelled, "Yes, sir. I understand you loud and clear, sir."

He backed away. "What's your name, convict?"

I replied loudly, "Convict Waters, sir."

"Where are you transferring from?"

"Federal prison, sir."

He yelled out, "This ain't a country club, boy. This is prison."

I yelled, "Permission to wipe the spit and chew off my face, sir."

The other inmates laughed. He turned and said something to them.

Fat-ass looked back at me. "Permission granted, Waters, and you may be seated."

What a difference a five hour trip could make. I had gone from a nut house in the basement to a military-style prison. I could only imagine what I'd have to look forward to in the coming years.

I wish I was in college playing basketball, but I wouldn't listen to Mom.

My name was called over the loudspeaker. My first stop was to the barber chair for my state-prison haircut. There were two pictures on the wall of two men with buzzed heads. The white inmate holding the clippers told me to look at the pictures and asked me which haircut I wanted.

I said, "Does it really matter?"

After my buzz cut, I was sent to be photographed. I got my picture taken and went to another counter to pick up my photo ID and be fingerprinted. My first state-issued prison number started with a zero. The zero let the guard and staff know, without looking in my file, how many times I had been in prison. The zero rating indicated it was my first time in prison. The letter *A* indicated an inmate's second time in prison. The farther down the alphabet the letters went, the more "professional" the convict. I looked around to see if there were any first-timers besides me. The closest rating was the letter C.

We were issued our clothes: a pair of blue pants with a white stripe running along the length of the pant leg on each leg; a blue-collar, button shirt with short sleeves; and a white T-shirt. We were always to wear our photo ID on our left shirt pocket. The photo ID was our prison "Social Security card." You used your ID when you shopped at the prison canteen.

I stood in a single-file, military-style line outside, waiting for the drill sergeant to give us the command to walk to our housing units.

I can't wait to get out of this prison.

I felt sorry for the black guys there with all those white, redneck guards. I'd already seen one incident in which three white guards kicked a black inmate on the floor in the bathroom. When I walked in, the guards stopped and told me to get the fuck out, or I'd be next. I backed out of the bathroom and shut the door. I was told by other inmates waiting to be processed that the guards there would jump you, hit you in the back of the head, and kick you all over your body. They didn't hit you in the face because it was hard to cover bruises and cuts on that part of your body. A guard would then lock the inmate in the hole. The CO filled out an incident report, stating the inmate fell out in the yard or he had been fighting. The inmate would be locked in the hole for thirty days until he healed up, when he would be let back out into population in the yard.

In the units where the transients were housed there was no phone for them to call their attorney, family, or anyone. Now I knew why the inmates called this place the Wild Wild West.

I marched to my new home. The prison yard consisted of grass and concrete sidewalks. The open-air dorms were painted white with windows and no air conditioning, only fans to cool you off in the summer months. The prison was a controlled-movement environment. Inmates could only move to certain areas when instructed by the guards. You were locked in one area until moved to another location. That way the prison could keep order and escapes to a minimum. Everyone was always accounted for no matter where he was in the prison compound.

In the rec yard, I sprinted with some of the inmates. We ran the forty-yard dash and timed ourselves with my wrist watch. It had a built-in stopwatch. I knew I was in the upper 4.3 because I was timed at federal prison when I trained there. Some black guy challenged me to run against him for five soups from the canteen. I told him no thanks. I thought if I outran that guy, he'd be pissed and embarrassed in front of his friends.

The inmate kept egging me on. "Come on, white boy, I'll take it easy on you!"

Now a crowd was watching. Whites, blacks, guys of every ethnicity you could think of, placed bets on us. It was all about money in prison—anything the inmates could do to make a dollar. I mean anything, they'd do it, especially the prison gangs.

I was stretching when a black inmate walked up to me and said, "I saw you playing basketball by yourself on the court earlier, and I couldn't believe how good you were." He saw my name tag and said, "I thought that was you, Travis. I've seen you play in the Dr. Pepper tournament in Immokalee. You made the all-tournament team and were the high scorer in the tournament."

He asked me how many points and rebounds I had. "You dominated that game," he said.

"I had twenty-four points and twenty-three rebounds."

"What the hell are you doing in prison? What happened? I thought you went to college," he said. "Look at Deion. You used to play against that superstar. You look bigger and stronger. It's a shame you wasted your life for this place."

"I worked out at federal prison and I grew two inches to 6-foot-5."

He said, "Between you and me, the brothers were watching you on the basketball court and couldn't believe how good you are for being white. They see you as a money-making machine for them, playing against the others."

"Did you tell them about seeing me play in high school and about me and Deion?"

"No, not yet, Travis, but some of the others here thought you were Travis Waters from Lely, and now we know."

"Don't tell any of the others I told you this. The prison gangs will jump me and beat the hell out of me."

"I won't."

He wished me good luck wherever I ended up and told me to watch my back. I had known it was only a matter of time before someone would recognize me from my basketball days. I didn't tell him I beat the supposedly best two players at federal prison and was never paid for the bet I won, and how the brothers were embarrassed. A lot of money had been lost and they were pissed.

A huge black man walked up to me and said, "I was watching you work out and train yesterday on the rec yard. They call me Bad Dog."

I thought the name fitted him. He was 6-foot-4 and weighed 300 pounds. He and his posse were betting a lot of money on the race.

I'm not racing this guy.

I said, "What do you want me to do? Let him win?"

He said, "No, me and my gang are putting all of our money on you. All the other brothers and whites are betting on him to win. Do you understand how this works, we and the gangs run the show? It's our world in here, Travis. Get used to it. You will have your world back on the streets one day if you make it out of state prison."

I said, "What if I don't want to race?"

He told me to look over at his posse. They were standing there pounding their fists into their open hands.

I said, "What if I don't beat this guy?"

He pointed back over at his posse and they pounded their fists again.

"Those aren't very good options. What's going to happen if I beat this guy, and the other gangs might want to jump me?"

He said he would talk to the other guys, and they would agree that, win or lose, no one would jump the white boy except his gang if I were to lose.

I'm taking the word of all these convicts? That's not good.

The black inmate and I lined up on the starting line. It was time for the race. One of his gang members held the stopwatch at the finish line. The brother said not to worry; he wouldn't make me look that bad.

Don't worry, shit.

Big dog raised his hand and when it dropped, we took off. He got me out of the hole. He was smaller than me, and once I got going and up to speed, I passed him and barely beat him. He was fucking fast. I heard the black inmate yelling out that the white boy ran a 4.35 in the forty. Some of the gang members started arguing among themselves and a fight broke out. I got the hell out of there and ran over by the fence, right under the gun tower for some kind of protection in case I got jumped by the guys who had lost money on the race. The rec yard was closed and everyone lined up in single file on the basketball court, waiting for the command to walk back to their housing units, one line at a time. I was locked in the dorm and ready for count time at dinner when black guys came up to tell me I was fast for a white boy.

Every day I had to leave my dorm so the inmates assigned to the cleaning crew could clean the dorms. That meant the inmates were locked in the rec yard all day long. I stopped running sprints in the yard and stuck with lifting weights.

I waited for my money from home to be processed and put into my account so I could eat something besides the food that was served there, which sucked.

I missed everything about federal prison. I wished I'd never been to the federal parole board but had been paroled to state custody. I had my stupid-ass attorneys to thank for that move. I found out I could've served most of my sentence in federal prison. My state sentence ran concurrently with my federal sentence, and I also received state gain time while in federal prison. That was the only smart thing my attorneys did for me.

I ran through my basketball drills, the same drills Coach Stewart had taught me. I thought about him often and wondered how he was doing and what he would think of me being in prison. I felt I'd let him down in the worst way. He believed in me. I wondered what he would have thought of me running a 4.35 forty with a thirty-five-inch vertical, hitting softballs 400 feet and throwing a football fifty-five yards in the air with one step. I thought he would be thinking the same thing I was: *What a waste of talent, and life!*

When I made it out of there, I'd tell him how I felt and I was sorry for letting him down. This was just another chapter in my life I couldn't go back and do over.

Bad Dog approached me. He wanted me to play against this black convict who was 6-foot-3 and skinny.

I said, "No, I don't want any part of that bullshit."

He said, "Do this for me, and I won't ask you again. I need some money. I lost on the rec yard, and if I don't pay this gang, they will stab me."

I said, "What about your posse? Can't they help you?"

The bet was between him and the gang, and he alone was responsible for the debt.

I said, "Why me? Can't you make some money off the others? I'm the white guy in your world. Remember, you told me that the other day when you won money from my race."

"I know you're white, but you're the best athlete in this prison," he said.

I said, "I'll only do it for you this one time, and you'll owe me."

"Whatever you want, Travis, name it."

"Does this inmate know who I am, and that I played sports in high school?"

Bad dog said, "Yes, and he knows about you playing against Deion in high school. This inmate was bragging in the dorm last night that he didn't care you played against Deion. He thinks Deion is overrated, and that he plays pro football and baseball, not basketball. He didn't think Deion couldn't make it in the NBA."

"This guy really said that?" I said.

Bad Dog said, "Yeah. He's in the dorm with me. I heard it out of his mouth. He also said no white boy will beat him one-on-one, and if he lost to a white, he would never play basketball again. I'm counting on you, Travis. I'm putting all the money I have left in my prison account on you. All the white boys are going to bet against you. That's the word on the yard if I can talk you into playing him. This guy's good, Travis. He can jump. The talk on the yard is he's the best right now until new arrivals come in and beat him. He played ball in high school in Tampa. He had scholarships, but he got hooked on crack and started dealing to support his habit and got busted."

"Is there anything else I should know?"

"Yes, he doesn't like to lose, especially to a white boy, and his reputation is on the line, and he likes to fight."

I said, "Okay, you go get him and let me run some drills, and I'll be here waiting."

I saw this large group of inmates walking toward me. It was pretty much the same thing that had happened to me on the basketball court at federal prison. I saw white guys in that crowd. There weren't a whole lot of them there, but they weren't on my side at all. That bothered me. I felt alone and betrayed by my own race. The only one on my side was Bad Dog. The inmate I was to play against was named Jesse D. He was about twenty years old. I told him to warm up and take some shots.

As he was warming up, I saw more inmates heading to the court.

Word spread through the prison rec yard. There were at least 300 inmates watching the game along with a few guards. I thought about what Coach Stewart told me when we played Cypress Lake, North Ft. Myers, Riverdale, and Ft. Myers High, mostly all-black teams. We had one black player on our high school team.

Before the game started in high school, Coach would pull me to the side and tell me, "Travis, you have the talent and the ability to play with these guys. Don't let them intimidate you. You play your game and you'll be fine." That kept running through my head the whole time Jesse D was warming up.

It was time to start the game. It was one-on-one: first player to make five points won the game. Each basket was one point. Jesse D had the ball first because I was white and it was his world. He started talking trash, telling me I was no Deion Sanders, and Deion was in the pros and I was in prison. Jesse D shot from the outside, and swish!

He said, "One up, cracker. This is going to be the easiest money I ever won."

Now I had the ball at the top of the court. I dribbled toward him, stopped, and shot. Swish!

I said, "One up."

Jesse D didn't shut up. He still talked shit. He shot from the outside again, off the back board. This time it went in. He said Deion and I sucked. I shot. Swish!

"Two up," I said.

I hoped he'd try to bring the ball inside on me. He was outside, dribbling the ball around, talking shit and telling me he was going to drive to the basket and white boys couldn't jump and I couldn't stop him. He drove on me and tried to lay the ball up on the backboard, but I jumped with him and I slammed the ball off the back board. The crowd yelled and screamed, "Did you see that white boy jump?"

Jesse D pushed me.

I said, "I don't hear you talking shit now about me and Deion."

I dribbled around and took him inside for a lay-up.

"I'm up three to your ball."

"It was a lucky block," he said.

"If you think its luck, bring it inside again, and see what happens."

He shot from the outside. Swish!

"Three up, white boy."

I got the ball and shot. Swish! It was now four, three.

He dribbled around, faked to the left and went right, a close-in shot, but he missed. Everyone yelled at him, telling him he was losing to a white boy.

He yelled back to the crowd, "This cracker isn't going to beat me!"

"One more point, Jesse D, and you've lost to a cracker."

The score was four–three. I dribbled around on top of the key. Jessie D took up his defensive stance. The game was on the line, and I heard this fucker telling me throughout the game I sucked and Deion had never made it to the NBA. I was going to embarrass this loud mouth.

I said, "Jessie D, I've been thinking about what you've been telling me the whole game."

He said, "What's that, white boy?"

"You told me I'm not Prime Time, and I heard you telling guys in your dorm Deion's overrated, and he doesn't tackle on the football field, and you won't lose to a cracker."

I thought about my coach one last time. I could hear him telling me, "You can play with these guys."

"Jesse D, are you ready?"

He said, "Waiting on you, white boy!"

I was on top of the key, dribbling. I took off toward Jesse D, and I faked him to the right. I brought the ball around my back with my right hand and into my left hand, and I passed him with the ball back in my right hand. I took off into the air a couple feet inside the free-throw line with my arm and the ball extended back behind my head. I slammed the ball through the basket and everyone went crazy. The backboard shook back and forth.

I told Jesse D, "You're right. I'm not Deion Sanders. I'm Travis Waters, and I played for Lely under Coach Stewart, and you just lost to a cracker."

He came over to me and threw the first punch. I moved and he missed. I threw a left jab, nailing him in the cheek. He threw a right, hitting me on the side of my face. He and I exchanged blows toe-to-toe, and I was finally tackled by three guards on the court. I was handcuffed. The guards took me back to my dorm and put me in the office. I sat there, my knees and elbows bleeding again from another tackle by the state guards. I swore some of those guards in state prison had to have played football in high school. They tackled you like a linebacker. The right side of my face hurt and was beginning to swell. The top of my eye was hurt too. One of the black guards told the dorm house man to go to the chow hall and get a bag of ice. I waited for the sergeant to come to our dorm so I and the guards could explain what had happened. One of the black guards asked me where I had gone to school and why I was in prison. He had watched the game. "What a waste of talent," he said, "and why is this inmate talking shit about Deion Sanders to you?"

I said, "He was my main rival my senior year of high school, and I chased the South Florida scoring title."

The sergeant showed up. The guard said, "Inmate Waters beat the black inmate on the basketball court, and he was embarrassed, so he threw the first punch at Waters. Inmate Waters defended himself, and me and two other guards broke up the fight."

The sergeant said if I was this good in sports, it would be a good idea to stay off the basketball court, especially since I was white and I was beating the black guys. He added, "I'm sure there was money on this game, and we wouldn't want a riot to break out. It's their world in here, and that's just the way it is. Sit tight, Waters. You'll be transferred soon to your permanent prison."

Then the sergeant told the guards I was free to go. He ruled the fight self-defense, and Jesse D was to be taken to the hole.

My knees, elbows, and face finally healed up, and I was back on the rec yard, lifting weights and jogging on the track. I was pretty much ordered to stay away from the basketball court. It was the sergeants' easiest way of warning me, and I wasn't happy about it. I wanted to play basketball. I could only jog and work out for so long. I couldn't wait to get the fuck out of there.

During the night a guard came to my dorm and handed me some paper work. It was my state-prison papers informing me where my new home would be, the Holmes Correctional facility in the panhandle, which is even further than Tallahassee. I had filed a request to be sent closer to my home in Naples, Florida, so my mom and family wouldn't have to drive so far to visit me. It was a six- to seven-hour drive from Naples to Tallahassee, and my mom tried to see me every month at the weekend. I wasn't happy to see my request had been denied. Rumor had it the state prison system didn't like sending inmates close to their homes for security reasons. There were fewer temptations to escape when inmates were not in their own localities with friends and family close by to help them. But the prison staff told inmates they placed them wherever beds were available, based on the length of their prison sentence, custody level, and behavior in prison.

I hadn't seen my mom in months. I had talked to her once when I was in the nut house at Apalachicola Prison. I knew she was worried to death. She probably thought I was being beaten up or raped, or had been killed. I hoped she was eating. My sisters said she wouldn't celebrate holidays or put up a Christmas tree because I wasn't home. I wished I could tell my mom she didn't need to serve this sentence with me. It was my fault I was in prison, and she shouldn't have to suffer too.

Chapter 21

It was early on a Thursday morning when I was told to get up and report to the R and D building for my transfer. I was so happy to get out of that military-style prison that I didn't care what time of day it was. I wore all the state-issued prison jewelry again, and the bus was full of inmates also waiting for their new homes. About 80 percent were black and the others were of different ethnicities. The bus headed north. It had made two stops that morning. Our third stop was in Starke, Florida, at Raiford Penitentiary. That place looked scarier than the nut house at Apalachicola. The inmates were talking, and I heard them say this prison was the Rock.

No shit.

I'd heard of this prison growing up and was glad I wasn't going there. Other inmates also said they were glad they weren't being dropped off there. This was the worst prison in the state. Ninety percent of the inmates there would never get out.

The bus pulled into the prison entrance and the gate closed behind us. I'd never seen so much razor wire and security before. I could see guards in the gun towers, sticking out the window, holding their high-powered rifles and watching the bus. A big black guard from Raiford entered the bus with papers in his hand. He looked at everyone and smiled. He knew nobody on this bus wanted to get off. I was glad I wasn't, especially being white. The whispering stopped among the inmates so we could see who the hell was getting off the bus. The guard called out names in alphabetical order and inmate numbers. You could see the fear in the inmates' faces as they walked down the aisle to get off the bus. I was glad the guard was getting to the end of the alphabet, but he flipped to another page and called out, "Travis Waters." I was in total shock. Had he just called my name? I hoped there was another Travis Waters on that bus. The guard called out my inmate number. It was my number! I didn't move. I had to let the shock of hearing my name sink in. He called my name and inmate number again. A million thoughts went through my mind right at that moment. The first was I hoped it was a mistake. The second was the thought of rape and the third was the thought of being killed. I finally got the strength and courage to stand up.

I said, "There must be a mistake in the paper work. The papers I received said Holmes Correctional."

The bus was so quiet you could hear a pin drop.

The guard said, "I know, Inmate Waters. This transfer order came down this morning from Tallahassee. I don't know what the hell's going on with you, but someone high up wants you here."

The fucking feds. It was payback time because I had lied under oath in my federal trial and jeopardized the feds' whole case. Agent Smith said the federal prosecutor was pissed at me.

The guard said, "Inmate Waters, are you getting off or do I need to call the extraction team to have you removed from the bus?"

I said, "No. I'm getting off."

I and four other inmates shuffled through a part of the prison called Old Rock. It was where inmates used to live and die. It was four stories high. We came to an area called the Courtyard. We sat at a table, locked in the courtyard with four stories of concrete on all sides. We were still wearing our prison jewelry. The only way out of there was to scale up the walls like Spiderman. There were two solid steel doors that we would use to come in and out of the Courtyard. They were unlocked by the guard so you could come inside to an office to meet your new prison counselor. The Courtyard was fucking scary looking. If only these walls could have talked. I could only imagine the horror stories. Some of the windows were busted out and the bars on them were rusty. Parts of the concrete were busted off the walls. I was the last inmate sitting in the Courtyard, all alone, and scared to death.

I don't care how tough you think you are, or who you were on the streets, this fucking place will kill you. The majority of the inmates are there for murder. Florida State Prison is right across the street. That's where they house the inmates on death row. When a death-row inmate wins his appeal, and his sentence is reduced to two to five life sentences without parole, he's transferred across the street to the prison I was sitting in at that moment.

The steel doors opened up and this big white guard, 6-foot-3 and weighing an easy 280 pounds, said, "Inmate Waters, you're next."

I was convinced every state-prison guard was an offensive lineman in football before becoming a prison guard. It had to have been a requirement in order to work in prison. You had to be huge. I got up and could only imagine what the counselors would say to explain why I was there. There were two counselors, one black and one white. Both men dressed in street clothes and were of average size.

Mr. Dean, the black man, said, "Welcome to Raiford, the Rock. You may be seated."

The other counselor, Mr. Jones, asked, "How are you doing today, Inmate Waters? You're probably wondering what the hell you are doing here in a supermax penitentiary."

"Yes, I am. Did I get three or four life sentences added to the twenty-three years I already had on the bus ride here from Lake Butler?"

They both laughed.

I said, "I know I brought in tons of drugs, but my custody level is low to medium security."

Mr. Jones said, "Yes it is, but I must say you have the largest amount of drugs in your file that has ever come across my desk. You have stuff in your file we aren't even allowed to see. It's blocked out. You lead a very interesting life."

"Yes, that's what everyone in state prison seems to be telling me. This is now my third stop in a matter of months."

"Well, this will be your last stop because this is where you will finish your fifteen-year state sentence. Once your debt is paid to the state of Florida you will be released."

I said, "You are kidding, right?"

They both said no at the same time.

"Just tell me the truth. Why am I here? Is it because the federal government wants to punish me? The guard on the bus told me the order came down this morning from Tallahassee because someone high up changed my transfer papers from Holmes Correctional to here at the Rock."

Mr. Dean said, "No, Travis."

Now I'm being addressed by my first name.

"But I did find out some interesting things about you when my phone call to Tallahassee was transferred to a US Customs office in Washington. I spoke to an agent named Smith. Do you know him?"

"Yes, I do. He's the lead agent in South Florida. He was based out of Miami. Is Mr. Smith now in Washington?"

Mr. Dean said, "It appears so. He tells me you and your partner Ralph were bringing in loads for the cartel, and you were one of the government's main witnesses."

"Mr. Smith told you that?"

"How else would I know this information? It's blocked out in your file. He also informed me you were known as the Westcoast Kid to the Cubans in Miami and to the Colombians in the cartel. You played a big part for the government in their eyes in helping take this smuggling operation down."

"Mr. Smith told you all of this?"

"Here's your file. Look at it. All this information I'm telling you is blocked out."

I said, "I was promised that this information and the Westcoast Kid, the name I went by in the federal government's operation, would never be disclosed to any agencies here in the States or other countries." So much for any deals I had with the government and the confidentiality agreement."

Mr. Dean said, "I can't control what you and the government have worked out with your case. You are the property of the state now. The main reason why you are here at the Rock is that you owned a lawn service and you also owned an auto detailing business when you were a free man, right?"

"Yes, I did, and what does that have to do with why I'm sitting here in a maximum-security penitentiary?"

"You're here because they need you to work outside the prison, cutting grass with the outside maintenance crew when needed and washing the prison trucks."

I said, "Outside the fence? Where am I going to live?"

"Here's where it gets complicated. Travis, we have an outside living facility with inmates that are allowed and have the custody to live outside, but with your resources and ties to the cartel, we feel you can't live outside this prison. You might escape or just walk away at night. You're white and you have the knowledge in your file to run the maintenance crew during the day. You will be supervised by an armed guard watching over the maintenance crew. When the workday is over, you will be escorted back here to live among the inmates. I'm sure you are aware most of the inmates at this prison will never get out and will die here."

I was now in total fucking shock. Could this nightmare really and truly get worse than what I'd already been through? For the first time I seriously thought about killing myself.

I said, "Let me get this straight. You want me to go outside this fence every day Monday through Friday, come back inside to live, and let these inmates see me doing this every day? It's like letting a rabbit out of his cage during the day and then bringing the rabbit back inside the cage at night with the lions."

"Yes," Mr. Dean said. "That's a good way of putting it."

"What do you think these lifers are going to do to me, knowing that I will go home one day? I wouldn't even go outside the fence. Not to mention I'm a white man in a black world here."

I took a breath. I was almost raped at shank point at Apalachicola Prison. What was I supposed to do when the inmates tried to gang-rape me or kill me if I didn't let them fuck me? Or did I just let them fuck me in the ass and be my boyfriends. Or should I try to kill them and then end up with a life sentence? I didn't know.

"Mr. Dean, what would you do if you were white and these were your options?"

"I don't know what I would do, Travis, if these were my circumstances. First of all, I wouldn't smuggle drugs."

I said, "Don't give me that bullshit story. I'm asking you what you would do."

He said, "You're a big guy. You can handle yourself. You handled yourself at Apalachicola."

"That was one old man. What happened to the other crew leader? Did he go home?"

Mr. Dean didn't say anything.

Mr. Jones said, "No, Travis, he's in the hospital. He was coming in and out of the fence and he was gang-raped and stabbed."

I said, "You mother fuckers want me to do the same thing knowing I can be raped and killed."

"Travis, we're just doing our job."

"You both might as well walk me across the street and put me in the electric chair and get it over with fast. You both might sleep better at night doing it that way instead of waiting for me to die slowly. You still didn't answer the question, Mr. Dean."

He said, "Travis, you seem like you will have a productive life when you are released. It says in your file you have a loving family at home. But to answer your question, I wouldn't go anywhere near that outside fence. I would stay inside this prison and tell the inmates I have three or four life sentences for murder and stick to myself and have my attorneys get me the hell out of here because I shouldn't be here in the first place."

"I appreciate your honesty. I wouldn't want your job."

"Travis, it's not all the state's fault. Whatever you did to the government, they have it out for you. We will write in our file you refused to go outside the fence. We will assign you to woodworking. That's in your federal file."

"That's good because I'll never go outside that fucking fence.

They wished me luck.

I was escorted to my new housing unit, still wearing my prison jewelry. This place got more frightening on the inside. I saw inmates walking around wearing helmets, so I asked the guard escorting me, "Why are those guys wearing helmets?"

He told me they were mental patients. "This prison is a mental reception center for the entire state. This is where the mental patients end up when the other prisons in the state can no longer control them."

This can't be happening. This just has to be a bad dream and I will wake up.

I asked, "Where do these inmates live?"

The guard said, "Right here with you and the other inmates. Also, a bit of advice, avoid the mental patients as much as possible. The prison here gives them a lot of medication to try and settle their violent behavior down."

I shook my head. I was even more scared, if that was possible. I saw women staff and women guards walking in between the male guards.

I asked the guard, "What's that all about?"

He said the female staff and guards weren't permitted to walk in the prison compound alone because it was too dangerous.

"You need to get transferred out of here, Travis."

I said, "Thanks for the advice."

Chapter 22

I arrived at my housing unit. It was a concrete two-story building, painted a light-brown color. The guard removed my chains and unlocked the door. We walked in together and he took me to the dorm control center where the guard was locked inside the dorm. He assigned me to my room. This prison didn't mix different ethnicities together. There were too many stabbings and fights. I was escorted to my room on the first floor. I saw an inmate standing next to a wall, wearing a helmet and hitting his head over and over, not really hard, just continuously. I saw another black inmate standing next to a TV, flailing his arms about and yelling at the TV.

I asked the guard, "What the hell is he doing?"

"He's arguing with the TV. He's another one of our mental inmates."

I thought Apalachicola was the nut house. Boy was I wrong.

I was put in my room and the door knob locked automatically when shut. You could only open the door up from the inside, or the guard could open it from the control center or with a key. My roommate and I got a key as well. My roommate was at work. I hoped he was not a nut. I had the top bunk. I looked around to see posters on the wall of girls wearing bikinis. That might be a good sign, but it didn't mean he wasn't queer.

There was a shower right outside my room that was shared with other inmates on the first floor. I heard a knock on my door. Who the fuck could that be? A guard would have announced himself. I wondered if I should open it. I couldn't hide in the room. I opened the door and a black inmate stood there. He was about 5-foot-10 and he wore eye glasses.

He said, "Hi, I'm your neighbor next door, and I want to welcome you home here at the Rock." He asked me my name and said I looked like an army guy or something, clean cut and no visible tattoos. I stood up and shut the door so it would be just him and me in the room. Inmates there would knock on your door while two or three others stood outside. They would rush in and shut the door, and no one would see anything as they gang-raped you. He tried to give me candy bars and chips.

I said, "No, thanks. I don't need it."

He pulled out an eight-inch shank from his pants and two steel bearings, about an inch in diameter. They could be put in a sock and used to beat the hell out of someone. He said his name was Wilson and anything I wanted he'd get for me. He said, "I'll be your man and will protect you."

I said, "No thanks. I can take care of myself."

I'd learned if you took gifts from inmates you'd owe them sexual favors and become their bitch.

He said, "You don't want to be my friend because I'm black?"

I said, "Don't let that get you down. I don't want to be your friend or your buddies' friend. As a matter of fact, I want you out of my fucking room and don't come back."

I opened the door and pushed him out. Shit! I'd only been there twenty minutes and they were already hitting on me.

My roommate arrived. He was in his thirties, white, balding, six feet tall and weighing about 170 pounds. He told me he had ninety-five years for kidnapping a politician's daughter and holding her for ransom. He filled me in about prison etiquette and what I could and could not do at that prison, and he told me to be careful in the chow hall. "Riots breakout, and the guards lock the doors, and you can't get out."

He asked me if the black inmate had approached me from next door.

I said, "Yes, he did."

He said, "He's trying to draw you in with his queer buddies."

"I pushed him out of the room. He was offering me gifts."

"Don't take anything from anyone who is offering you gifts. You can borrow, but don't take offerings."

For now my roommate seemed to be okay, but I didn't trust any of these mother fuckers. They all worked together in their little cliques to get what they wanted. I told my roommate I had a life sentence for drugs and was charged with murder.

I just couldn't believe I had been sent there just to work outside the fence. As soon as I could get to a phone, I'd ask my mom call my attorneys in Tallahassee and have them start trying to get me out of there.

I finally got on the phone with my mom. She asked, "Where are you at? I haven't heard from you in weeks. I couldn't sleep or eat. I didn't know what happened to you!"

I said, "I'm at Raiford."

She said, "Where's that? Are they mean there?"

"I'm at the Rock, Mom."

She said, "Where they kill the inmates?"

"No, I'm across the street where the death-row inmates end up when they win their appeal."

She started to cry and wanted to know why I had been sent there. I explained to her what I had been told, and she just kept crying.

I said, "Call my attorneys in Tallahassee and tell them to start getting me transferred out of here." I told my mom I had to get off the phone, and I loved her and would call her in a few days.

I finally got to leave the dorm. Every movement there was controlled. You couldn't move around on the prison compound freely as you could at the federal prison. This was my permanent home now.

I noticed that groups of inmates entered the chow hall at the same time. You sat down to eat as fast as you could and get out before the next group of inmates entered. It wasn't club fed. That was for sure.

After my dining experience, I decided to check out the rec yard. I started kicking a ball around with other guys and, by mistake, it rolled over to the fence, so I ran after it. All of sudden the guard in the gun tower yelled at me to back away from the fence, or he would shoot to kill. I looked up to see a high-power rifle pointed right at me, so I took his advice. I backed up and left the fucking ball there, against the fence.

My roommate looked at me and said, "I forgot to tell you. Don't ever run over by the fence, or you will be shot and killed. The guards in the towers think you are trying to escape."

I went over to the basketball court and started shooting around with my roommate. A couple of black inmates walked up and wanted to play two-on-two. The black inmate named Earl wanted to place a bet on the game. My roommate asked me if that was okay, and if I was any good.

I said, "I've played before."

I didn't tell them anything about playing ball in high school. The bet was for two candy bars. I wondered if my roommate could play. The game started and the black guys were up on us. My roommate sucked, so I told him to take the guy he was guarding and get him out of the way and give me the ball. I dribbled to the basket and went around my guy and scored.

Earl said, "That white boy can play."

I took the game over and we won. The black guys were pissed. My roommate said, "I didn't know you could play basketball. There are some good guys here that play basketball and they take basketball seriously. They make big money doing it. That's how they survive."

Sunday morning, after breakfast, I lifted weights in the rec yard. I had a new weight-lifting partner who went by the name of Psycho. He was white and about 5-foot-6. I asked him why he was there. He said he had just got off death row from across the street at Florida State Prison. He had four life sentences for killing four people he hadn't liked. That explained where his nickname came from. He was also in my dorm. He walked the track barefooted.

I asked him, "Why do you always walk the track barefooted?"

"I want to toughen up the bottom of my feet because I don't plan on dying in prison. You can't climb a fence real fast with shoes on and I have some unfinished business on the streets."

"Yes, I guess you're right."

I hope you never get out and kill more people again.

I was approached on the track by a couple of black inmates with a business proposition.

One said, "How would you like to make some money?"

I said, "No thanks. I don't need any money. I'm fine."

The bigger of the two said, "You don't understand. This is our world in here, and we've seen you play basketball yesterday, and a brother from Lake Butler, who transferred with you last week, told us you beat the best brother on the court at Butler. You blew by him and slammed the ball, finishing him off on the last point. He really got embarrassed. The one from Butler said he heard you used to play against Prime Time in high school, and you both were the top players in South Florida. One of the guys at Butler told the Butler brother he seen you play in high school."

I asked, "Why? Did that guy from Butler tell you all this?"

"Are you telling me all this about Prime Time and high school didn't happen, and the Butler brother is lying to us?"

I said, "No, it's all true."

"Then we have a deal?"

"What if I don't play?"

"If you don't play and contribute financially to my gang, I'm going to order you to be gang-raped, which won't be hard to have done. There are rumors going around already with the brothers wanting to be the first one to hit that cracker ass. Then I'm going to personally stab you myself when you are out here on the rec yard."

I said, "Can I think about it?"

He said I had until Monday evening to give him an answer.

"I will be on the rec yard after chow waiting for your answer."

I asked, "What's your name?"

"They call me Big D."

"I'll think about it, Big D."

There was a big gathering of inmates over at the entrance gate leading into the rec yard. They couldn't get out because we were locked in. I heard screaming and I ran to see what was going on. All the inmates were cheering. Across from the rec yard was the chow hall, where this huge black inmate was beating the hell out of this white guard. The white guard didn't have a chance. He was on the ground, not moving, already knocked out. The black inmate grabbed a fifty-five-gallon trash barrel, lifted it over his head, and slammed the barrel down on the guard, trying to kill him. The inmates yelled, "Kill the fucking cracker guard!" Just then a white van pulled up, and eight or ten guards jumped out in full riot gear. You couldn't see their faces, but there was only one black riot guard. They beat the shit out of the inmate with night sticks to get him to stop. They got the inmate on the ground and strapped his feet to his hands behind his back. They lifted him up and tossed him in the van, and the guard who was beaten was put on a stretcher. The black inmates in the rec yard shook the fence and turned on the white inmates locked in the rec yard. The black inmates were pissed the white guards had beat the black inmate. I feared for my life. All the white guys in the rec yard were way outnumbered by the blacks, and there were all kinds of weapons, especially on the weight pile. The prison was automatically put on lockdown. The riot guards marched in two single files and shot smoke bombs over the fence to break up the large crowd. I was so fucking happy to see those guards coming to the rescue. We were all ordered to lie face down on the ground and put our hands behind our head. The gun towers that had a view of the rec yard had their guns pointed at all of us. We were ordered back to our dorms.

Every day there was a wake-up call. You always looked over your shoulder, wondering what was going to happen to you that day and if you would make it through the day. I decided I couldn't play basketball there. The inmates were in a wholly different world than the rest of the planet. It was basically kill or be killed. Only the strong or being a member of a gang gave you your best chance of survival. I decided I wasn't going to be part of any gang. Once you became a part of a gang you were everyone's bitch and considered at the bottom. Part of being at the bottom meant you had to perform sexual acts on guys whenever they wanted. You were also gang-banged to earn gang members' respect. I would rather have died first than have to earn someone's respect by getting fucked in the ass. This was the most bizarre place I'd been in, with its rules and etiquette. If I hadn't been there to see and hear all of it, I wouldn't have believed it was real. A part of me kept wondering if I would become that kind of person, if I had four or five life sentences or even one life sentence.

You're not getting out and will die here.

I wondered if I would ever be the same person I was before I came into this bizarre environment. I hoped I'd make it out of there without getting another charge for protecting myself, which would mean I'd end up there for longer than my original sentence. The place started playing tricks on my mind. This wasn't me. This wasn't the way life was. But in reality I was only kidding myself because that was the way life was in there and that didn't change. I would find myself staring in the mirror for long periods of time to see who was looking back at me, wondering if it was me in the mirror. I did this to reassure myself that it was really me staring back and not one of those animals.

It was Monday morning, and I was waiting with about twenty-five inmates for orientation to start. A female counselor, escorted by two male guards, talked about the effects that being locked up there could have on you. "Most of you will die here and if you need to talk to someone about your feelings or any issues you have about adjusting to this environment, I'm available. If you want an appointment, fill out your request, and turn it in to your dorm officer. That's all I have to say and have a great day."

Next, this psychiatric nurse came in. "How's everyone doing today? I hope everyone is having a great day. It's a beautiful sunshiny day outside."

I began to think she must be swiping some of the medication to help her cope with this world.

She said, "You guys are probably wondering why some of these inmates are walking around wearing helmets. The reason is they are mentally disturbed, and this prison is the mental reception center for the entire state of Florida. We have the best facility to treat these mental inmates, but we heavily medicate them to keep them calm. I advise all of you to stay clear of them. They will harm you or even try to kill you without cause. That's the state their mind is in, especially when their medication starts wearing off and they need to take more." She asked if anyone had any questions she could answer. One guy in the back raised his hand. She said, "Yes, go ahead."

The inmate said, "There are a couple of these mental inmates in my dorm. I don't like one of them. He bothers me. Do they feel pain because I know you said they are heavily medicated?"

She said, "Why would you ask that?"

"I want to stab him and I want him to feel the pain."

No one laughed. That was a normal conversation there.

She replied, "Of course he feels pain. I wouldn't recommend your stabbing him. You will go to the hole, and you might lose some gain time."

He replied, "I just got off death row. I have five life sentences. I don't get gain time. Most of the inmates here don't get gain time. Besides, I like the hole."

She said, "Okay, I think that's about it. Remember, keep your head up, and tomorrow is a new day."

The fat redneck sergeant came in with his mouth full of chew. He tugged at his pants, trying to keep them from falling down. He sat in the chair, looked at everyone, and said, "You inmates fucked up. Now I look around at some of you, this prison is the worst of the worst, the bottom of the barrel. The other prisons couldn't tolerate your behavior so you ended up here. I see some of you jitter bugs [young inmates] in this group. You fucked up. Now, you play your games here, I'll find you in your dorm dead … Billy, how long have you been locked up now?"

"Going on twenty-six years, Sarge."

The sergeant said, "Jimmy, you won your appeal on death row. How many life sentences did you end up with?"

"Six, Sarge," the inmate said.

The sergeant said, "I'll make this brief. If you want to do drugs, you go to the north tower. If you want to drink, go to the south tower, and if you want to stab each other, try to do it outside. It's less of a mess to clean up. Any questions?"

One inmate asked, "Where is the best place to have sex with my bitch?"

The sergeant said, "That would probably be best in your dorm. Good luck to you all."

This was the most bizarre orientation I'd ever been to.

Afterward, I ate in the chow hall and went back to my dorm. I didn't go to meet Big D on the rec yard. I decided I was not playing basketball for him and his gang. I would take my chances if he wanted to have me gang-raped, or he tried to stab me. I grabbed my belongings for my evening shower. My roommate was at the library. That was where he spent most of his evenings. He was working on his appeal, trying to get his ninety-five-year sentence reduced. I opened up the shower curtain to find a prison orgy going on. There were three black guys and the white dorm bitch, all fucking and sucking each other's dicks.

The white bitch said, "Do you mind? We're making love. Can you give us some privacy? Or would you like to join us?"

I shut the curtain quickly and decided that I didn't need a shower that badly that night. I was too disgusted by what I had just seen and smelled. I didn't ever want to take a shower in there again. I went to bed early that night. I was glad the door locked. I was safe in my room for that night anyway. I'd seen and heard enough crazy shit for one day.

I had seen a lot of crazy shit growing up, but my life's journey still shocked me from time to time. Just when I thought I'd seen it all, there was always something more. It seemed as if it would never end. When I was dead and laid to rest, it would all stop for me, and at that moment I figured death wouldn't be a bad thing. I didn't want to die at the hands of those animals. I kept trying every day to not become one of them. I had to get out of bed and look in the mirror to make sure it was still me in the mirror before I could go to sleep.

Good night, sweet dreams.

I didn't believe in sweet dreams anymore.

Chapter 23

Tuesday arrived and I waited to start my job in woodworking. I would never go outside that gate as long as I was there. I hung out in my dorm room, waiting to receive my money from home and have it put into my account so I could buy food from the canteen. I could eat in my room and stay out of the chow hall as much as possible. I hadn't been in the yard since my deadline to play basketball on Monday evening. I was lying low hoping Big D would forget about his business proposition to me out in the rec yard. I couldn't hide in my dorm forever, and I wouldn't. I didn't want to be stabbed, but I'd rather be stabbed than raped. I went to the chow hall to eat dinner. I had to eat. I saw Big D in the line and we made eye contact. He and his gang friends were talking, laughing, and pointing at me while thrusting their hips forward and backward as if they were having sex. I didn't say or do anything. I just stared at them and thought, *You fuckers will have to kill me first.*

One of the gang members came up to me while I was sitting at the table and said, "I can't wait to hit your white ass. I've had my eye on you since you first came in."

I said, "Why don't you go fuck one of your friends and leave me alone."

I hurried up to eat and get the hell out of there. I went back to my room and thought about what had just happened.

It was Tuesday evening and pretty quiet there in the dorm. A lot of the inmates were in the rec yard or doing their own thing. I got my things together to take a shower. It was a two-man shower with two showerheads. I was in the shower getting my head wet when suddenly I was grabbed around the neck by a large black arm and another black inmate held my arms. The third one said they were going to rape my cracker ass and there was nothing I could do about it.

I said, "You will have to kill me first."

One of them said, "Welcome to the Rock."

I was scared to death. There were three of them. They tied a sock around my head and stuffed one into my mouth so I couldn't scream for help. I tried to get out of their grip, but they kept squeezing me tighter, especially around my neck. I started blacking out because they were cutting off my air supply. I became weaker, and that's what the inmates wanted. They tied my hands behind my back, and one of the inmates already had his dick out and was getting it hard. He rubbed some kind of cream on himself. They covered my eyes with my towel, and an inmate stood behind me. There were four of them now. I could hear another voice as one of them rubbed cream on my asshole and stuck his fingers in my ass. I felt something hit me in the head, and I blacked out. I woke up with a stabbing pain in my ass. I didn't know how long I had been knocked out. As I came to, I looked down at the floor to find an inmate sucking my dick. I heard another inmate warn the guys in the shower the guard was out of his office, and they all scattered.

I found myself sitting in a pool of blood. My head and ass were throbbing. I untied myself and took the sock out of my mouth. I turned on the shower and washed the blood down the drain. I took my washcloth and stuck it in the crack of my ass to keep the blood from getting my shorts bloody. I didn't want anyone to know what had just happened, so I grabbed the rope and the sock that had been tied around my hands and mouth and threw it in the dorm trash can. I went to my room and cried. I was so pissed, but what could I do? I was going to get that mother fucker next door. The inmates had wanted me to become an animal, so an animal I would become. I would stalk his schedule, find out when he came and went from his dorm room and plan my attack. I had to get word to Big D. I would have to play basketball for his gang. I didn't have any other choice. I definitely didn't want this to happen to me again and have him come and personally stab me out in the rec yard just because I wouldn't play basketball for his gang. First, I had to heal up. I was glad I was not working yet because I couldn't sit down or walk. It hurt too much. I wouldn't be able to eat for a couple days because I didn't have any money in my account, and I couldn't stand in line or sit on the metal stools in the chow hall.

I removed the blood-soaked washcloth from my ass, flushed it down the toilet, and grabbed a clean one. I was still bleeding. The thought of contracting AIDS hit me like a ton of bricks. I started to panic and began to cry really hard. If I got AIDS from that mother fucker next door, I would kill him. I started crying again. I was really scared now. If I died from AIDS in prison, everyone in Naples would think I was a queer and somebody's bitch. My head throbbed but I wasn't going to the prison doctor to file a report. I was too embarrassed to tell the medical staff what had just happened. Besides, snitching on someone there was sure to be a death sentence. But did it really matter now? I told myself I had just received my death sentence in the shower and I began to cry again.

It was Friday evening and I was still sore as hell, but I hadn't eaten since Tuesday. I was getting weak. The only thing good about not eating was I hadn't been going to the bathroom as much because when I sat on the toilet, it hurt like hell. I thought my insides were coming out my ass. I didn't see Big D in the chow hall. I started to feel better after I ate. I was getting my strength back. I just couldn't stand the thought of sitting on the toilet again. The back of my head was sore and I had a large knot there. I couldn't lie on it at night. It sucked not having any pain medicine, or even an aspirin, or anything. I received the job paperwork. I was to start on Tuesday, so that would give me three more days to heal up.

I'd been writing down on a piece of paper the times when the asshole next door left his room and returned, and when he took his shower. Luckily for me the shower was right by his room. He walked by the shower to get to his room, and his back was to the shower when he unlocked his door. I calculated the average times of his departure and return. The return times were pretty consistent. I figured out that I had to attack him when his back was to the shower. I didn't want him to see it coming or even know it was me. Not knowing who or what had happened would bother him. That asshole and his clique hustled so many inmates there, his attacker could be anyone he had raped or ripped off. After he recovered, he might walk around the prison wondering what gang had tried to take him out. I hoped if he didn't know who had done it, he'd get into a blame game with other gangs. That should lead to his getting his ass beaten again for accusing other gangs of putting a hit on him. The main reason I didn't want him to know I was his attacker was I could be charged with assault and lose all the gain time I'd earned. I had twenty days a month knocked off my sentence for every month I served with good behavior. An assault charge could erase all my gain time and add more years to my sentence. The way the prison was there, I was lucky to still be alive. I'd only been there a few weeks and I'd already been through hell. Most of those guys could act any way they wanted. They had nothing to lose since they were never getting out. This made it hard on the few who did get gain time. I wanted to go home and start my life over. I didn't know if that would happen.

A couple of weeks went by, and I started playing basketball for the gangs on two-on-two and one-on-one teams. I won money for the gangs, and Big D was happy. The other gangs weren't happy with a white boy beating them all the time. My partners and I would lose games sometimes, but not the ones that big money was riding on. We would lose on purpose the games that had small bets. This was the scam Big D would pull on the other gangs. They would see us lose and bet big money against us in the next game, which we then played to win. This went on for a while. My partners and I always won the big games. The gangs began to catch on to Big D's scam.

I was out on the court in a one-on-one game, beating one of the best black guys in the prison. It was a best-of-three game. The third game of the series was tied. We had one game apiece. In the stands a black inmate told one of the other gang leaders that Big D and I were running a scam on everyone, so the gangs stopped the third game, when I was ahead by two points. The other gang leader told Big D he had just found out from the brother who had come in with me from Butler I had played high school basketball against Deion Sanders and I was chasing the South Florida scoring title. The inmate from Butler had promised us he wouldn't tell anyone, and we had paid him to keep his mouth shut, but he told the gangs everything. The news spread like wildfire among the gangs sitting there, watching us play. They yelled at me and Big D that we had cheated and ripped them off. They told Big D if I had been good enough to play against Deion, I shouldn't have been allowed to play against the other inmates in the yard. It wasn't fair. Big D's gang yelled back at the other gangs and fights broke out. For the first time in my life I realized how much talent I had wasted for this shit.

My talent started a riot. Three gang members jumped on me and choked me. They said I had played against Prime Time and hadn't told them. They kicked me in the back and stomach until the wind was knocked out of me. The last thing I remembered was being kicked in the head really hard and everything turning black.

When I gained consciousness, I saw other inmates lying in the yard, knocked out, and guards were handcuffing everyone. The yard was ordered locked down. I got on my feet and a guard took me in for questioning. I said I had been playing basketball and beating a black inmate in a friendly game of one-on-one. Fights broke out and I was jumped and knocked out. The guards told me they had heard I was running a scam with Big D, beating everyone for money and ripping guys off.

I said, "I'm not doing that. They're lying."

The guards said, "You're ordered off the basketball courts, and if you're caught on the courts again, you're going to the hole, and if you have any gain time you will lose it. Do you understand, Inmate Waters? A goddamn riot was developing out on the rec yard today. Leave the basketball courts to the black inmates. Do you understand that, Inmate Waters?"

I said yes, but I was thinking, *Thank God the basketball games are over. No more threats on my life. Hopefully no more beatings or getting raped.*

I wanted to forget it had ever happened. I was still planning my attack. I had not thought I could love something so much in all my life as the sport of basketball. Yet it could bring me such harm and almost cost me my life.

I was told I needed to see a nurse because I was having trouble breathing. I was escorted to the nurse, who wrapped an ACE bandage around my waist up to my chest. My ribs were badly bruised. She thought I might have a couple of cracked ribs. I also had a concussion. I was given Tylenol for the pain and ordered to rest in bed. I walked back to my dorm on my own.

I lay in bed, unable to move and barely able to breath. I was in intense pain. I told myself if there was one thing I could do when I got out of there, it would be to try to make sure no child threw his life away as I had. I wanted to share my story to spare children from the hell I was going through. I had to do something. I wanted to let them know this was what would happen if they gave up their dreams for fast drug money. This was the price they would pay, lying in bed, beaten up, raped, and alone with nothing. Every day there was a struggle to survive.

A couple more weeks went by. I couldn't cough or sneeze because it hurt like hell. Inmates there didn't forget about losing money, especially to a white boy. I watched a football game on the dorm TV, and when a commercial of Deion came on, several black inmates who had lost money and felt I had cheated them turned around in their chairs and looked at me. "Yeah, cracker, you ripped us off, and we're going to beat your ass again."

I'd got up, grabbed my folding chair and locked myself in my room. I hoped Deion realized what a superstar he had become since high school because I had found out the hard way with the beatings. I wanted to tell Deion, when I was released, I truly appreciated what a superstar he had become.

I'd been collecting rocks in the yard and smuggling them in my pants back to my dorm room. The rocks were an inch to two inches in diameter. I'd collected ten rocks and they weighed a couple pounds. I also had three, heavy, master key locks too. I put the rocks and locks into a double sock. I made the sock into a ball larger than a softball. I wrapped tape around it several times to make it as tight as I could. It was not the kind of sock weapon in which you put whatever you wanted and continuously swung it to hit a guy

It was Wednesday evening and everyone was doing his own thing, another normal prison evening. I'd decided that night would be the night of my attack. The asshole next door was pretty much still on his same schedule. He came back to his room around six o' clock. When no one was in the shower, the curtain was open and the light was off. I hid there, wearing a pillowcase over my head, which had two eye holes cut out of it. I waited for him to walk by. The TV was loud, as always. The TV room door was open so the noise would help muffle the sound I made when I came up from behind him. He might have heard me at the last second before impact and turned his head, catching a glimpse of me. I couldn't take that chance. All I needed was about ten seconds. I heard the dorm door slam closed. I was nervous, and my breathing became faster. He walked by. I stepped out of the shower, barefoot to mute the sound of my approach. He put the key in his door. I raised my right arm up, and with all my strength, I slammed my arm down, holding my hand-made weapon tightly. It landed right on top of his head. He instantly dropped, and his whole body went limp. His face also slammed on the concrete floor. The blood pooled on the ground around his head. I was going to kick him, but I couldn't do it. I couldn't be like those other guys. I threw the weapon and pillowcase in the dorm trash can before going back into my room. I felt sorry for him, the man who had gang-raped me and knocked me out. I lay on my bed, trying to calm my breathing so I could pretend to be asleep when I was questioned. I heard some guys talking in the hallway outside my dorm, his friends. They found the asshole lying there. About twenty minutes went by before I heard a key unlocking my door. I put my head phones on and lay on my side, pretending to be asleep. My bed shook, so I rolled over and removed my headphones. Two black guards stood there.

One said, "We just found Inmate Wilson lying on the floor, unconscious in front of his room door, with his head split open and blood all over."

I said, "What happened?"

The guard said, "We have no idea."

I said, "Is he alright?"

"He's alive, but he doesn't know what happened."

One of the guards asked me if I had heard or seen anything. I said no, I had my head phones on listening to music, and I must have fallen asleep.

The guard said, "Okay. You can go back to sleep."

My plan had worked. Asshole didn't know what had happened, and he was alive.

A week went by before I saw Wilson at the chow hall. I'd been wondering how he had been doing since I'd hit him in the head. He had been transferred out of our dorm for his own protection. I saw him sitting there in the chow hall with the left side of his face black and blue, and his head wrapped in a gauze bandage, and no matter how hard I tried to tell myself that was what he deserved for knocking me out and raping me, I still felt sorry for him. I actually felt bad for what I had done. He was simply a product of that environment. We made eye contact, and he made a gesture with his head to let me know he saw me there. I ate and headed out to the rec yard.

I was working out with my partner Psycho when realized I was not out in the rec yard at Raiford. I was in a public hospital bed, naked, covered in blood from head to toe, chained to the bed, not knowing who I was. I saw armed, uniformed men in the room. I asked them who I was and why I was there. I was scared.

"Where are my clothes? What are you guys doing to me?"

I didn't know why I was chained and handcuffed to the bed.

I thought I was in a bad dream. My head was throbbing and I was vomiting nonstop. I was told I couldn't have any medication because the doctor had said my brain was swelling. I didn't know anything. A nurse tried to comfort me. She and a guard had brought me my prison ID and a mirror to show me who I was. I stared in the mirror with a blank face.

The guard said I was Travis Waters and I was a drug kingpin from South Florida. I had been transported from a federal prison in Tallahassee to a maximum state prison at Raiford. "All we know at this time is you were lifting weights and the inmates notified the rec yard guard a white inmate was attacked and there was a lot of blood. The inmates thought you were dead. A guard also thought you might be dead or close to it with the amount of blood you lost. He called an ambulance and you were transferred here to the public hospital and the medics tried to bring you back to life. None of the inmates would tell the guard how long you had been lying there bleeding. A mentally ill inmate was ordered by one of the prison gangs to try and take you out—and something about how you wouldn't hang out or have sex with him."

I said, "Are you sure you have the right guy? I don't believe any of this."

The doctors said they were hoping I would regain my memory in time. I screamed as loud and as much as I could at the guards for the doctor and the nurse to unchain me. "I'm getting the fuck out of here and you're not performing any fucked up experiments on me," and then everything went black.

Chapter 24

I woke up in a room that looked like a hospital room. I wore a hospital gown and the blood and chains were gone. My head throbbed. It was wrapped up with gauze bandages all the way down to my eyes. I looked down at my arms and saw IVs connected to them. I looked around and saw about ten men in the room with me. They too were lying in bed, wearing hospital gowns. Some of them had IVs in their arms. I noticed one man was making moaning sounds as if he were in a lot of pain. I started to remember the armed guards talking to me before I blacked out. I began to think I was part of some kind of experiment and I was fucking scared about what was happening to me.

I yelled, "Get me the fuck out of this place."

I tried to get out of the bed and fell on the floor. I couldn't move my legs very well. I became even more scared. Two nurses and a uniformed guard stood at the entrance to the room. They came in and said they were glad I had woken up. They offered to help get me back in bed.

I said, "I'm getting out of here."

My speech wasn't right, and I didn't have much control over my limbs. "What are you people doing to me? What are you people doing to the rest of these men?"

The nurse said, "We are trying to help you to not hurt yourself."

I said, "Where am I?"

She said, "You're in a prison hospital at Lake Butler," and when she said "Lake Butler," something clicked in my head. My memory started coming back.

I said, "I was at a maximum-security prison at Raiford, lifting weights."

She asked me, "Are you remembering where you were?"

I said, "Yes."

She asked another nurse to hurry and get the doctor. The female doctor came in the room. They all stood around me while the doctor took out her flashlight and looked into my eyes. She asked me my name.

"Travis Waters."

"Do you know you're in prison and what you are in prison for?"

"Yes. I was smuggling drugs."

"Do you remember where you were smuggling drugs and who it was with?'

"I was smuggling drugs with Cubans in Miami for The Colombian cartel."

"Do you know where your hometown is?"

"Naples, Florida."

The doctor told me she and the other doctors hoped after the swelling in my brain had gone down, I would regain my memory. She tested my senses by putting something under my nose. I couldn't smell it. She put some kind of liquid on my tongue, and I couldn't taste it.

I said, "Why is it hard for me to speak clearly. Am I going to speak this way for the rest of my life?"

She said, "First, let me run some more tests. Then I will try to explain everything to you so you understand."

Two nurses helped me out of the bed and onto my feet, still holding me up.

The doctor said, "Can you take a step?"

I tried moving my leg forward. It wasn't responding to my command. I could barely move it forward.

She said, "Sit on the bed and stick your left arm straight out."

I could stick it out, but it would fall back down to my lap. The same happened with my right arm. I couldn't hold it up long. I started getting scared. "Am I going to be in a wheelchair the rest of my life? I barely have any movement in my limbs. My body isn't responding to my commands."

She looked at me and paused. "First of all, you're lucky to be alive. I will let the guard here explain what happened to you."

The guard said, "After you were attacked, the black gang held your weight-lifting partner down so he couldn't go get help."

This was the guy who had killed four people on the streets and he wanted to save my life?

"Another white inmate saw what was going on and started yelling for the guard. He was jumped by more members of the gang that wanted you to bleed to death. The guard in the gun tower saw the scuffle going on at the weight shed and called a guard on the ground. The gang of inmates left you there to bleed to death. They wanted you to die. The paramedics said you were almost dead when they found you on the weight pile due to the amount of blood you lost. From what I was told, the gangs were losing a lot of money betting against you on the basketball court and they felt they were cheated when they found out you were playing against Deion Sanders in high school."

I said, "The other guard told me when I was at the public hospital that a mental inmate tried to kill me because I wouldn't hang out with him or have sex with him."

"Yes," the guard said, "it was a mental inmate that did this to you. The gang told the mental inmate you didn't like him, you wouldn't have sex with him, and you wanted to kill him. After the gang told the inmate this, they suggested to him he should kill you, and if he did kill you, the prison gang would give him a candy bar. This is what the mental inmate said during questioning after the incident. The gang lied to him so he would try to kill you. Do you have any questions?"

I said, "Yes. What did he try to kill me with?"

"He used a thirty-five-pound dumbbell. You were sitting on the bench doing preacher arm curls when he came up and hit you in the head from behind. The prison gang told the inmate to keep hitting you to try and crush your skull. He hit you twice and your weight-lifting partner told him to stop because you looked like you were already dead with all the blood coming out of your head. Then the mental inmate dropped the dumbbell and started walking on the track like nothing ever happened. You have your workout partner to thank for you being alive."

I looked at the guard and said, "I don't have any more questions."

The doctor said, "Travis, your brain is badly bruised, and you have a lot of blood in between your brain and your skull that we had to drain. One more hit from the dumbbell in that same area of your head, and you would've died just from the impact. It would have mattered how much blood you'd lost. Your brain is badly swollen."

"How long have I been here, knocked out?"

I had been in a semicoma for four days. The doctors had not known when or if I would wake up.

"It all depended on how the swelling in your brain reacted. We didn't know the extent of the damage to your brain until the swelling went down."

"You haven't answered my question. Am I going to be in a wheelchair the rest of my life?"

She said, "I know all of this is a lot for you to understand right now."

"Just tell me the truth. You have no idea what I have already been through in my life. I would rather leave this prison in a box than go through the hell I'm going through to go home in a wheelchair."

The doctor said, "I can't answer that, Travis. Your memory has come back, so this is a positive sign. All of your motor skills and senses might also come back. But we, as doctors, can't give you any timeframe or guarantee you anything."

I lay in bed thinking about my life.

All the money, toys, girls, and the fun I had from the drug business—is any of it worth it? Everything I've been through in my short life with my near-death experiences—and now I might be in a wheelchair for the rest of my life, all because of a sport I grew up loving, a sport that took me away from my childhood nightmare, gave me peace and something to live for when I was young, something that has brought me so much happiness and now has turned into my worst enemy. This sport has almost cost me my life and got me gang-raped by black men. My whole life I was a white kid trying to compete in a black-dominated sport, and now I'm doing it all over again in a black-dominated prison. Only, now, I'm not playing for fun; I'm playing for my life so I don't get gang-raped again. Was my entire God-given talent supposed to end up this way? Is someone up above trying to punish me and teach me a lesson because I didn't go to college and use my talent in a positive way? I wish the talent I have wasted was never given to me. All the sports I loved growing up I now hate.

The nurse came into my room and said she had to put me in a wheelchair. I had visitors. I didn't want to see anyone in my condition. She said my mother and stepfather were waiting downstairs.

"Your mother went to Raiford to visit you and the guards told her you were alive and had been transferred to a public hospital, and now you are in the prison hospital here in Lake Butler. She is downstairs, crying. You need to see her and let her know you're alive."

I started to cry. I knew this was killing my mom. I kept putting her through so much hell. She didn't deserve this. She'd been through enough hell already in her life and now this shit.

I said, "You bring her to this room. I can't have her see me in a wheelchair."

The nurse said, "Your mom isn't allowed to come in this room. There are other unrestrained inmates here and it's against prison policy."

I said, "Tallahassee sent me to Raiford to work outside the fucking fence. The counselors told me I shouldn't be there, so fuck your prison policy. The state is going to bend the prison policy rules. That's what got me gang raped, beaten, and almost killed, and now I can't walk, so you go and tell the warden what I said and have two guards escort my mom and stepdad to this room, right now, and don't fuck with me. I know your fucking name. You make it happen. The state owes me that much."

The nurse looked at me in disbelief and said, "I'll go talk to the warden immediately."

I lay in the hospital bed, and my mom and stepdad entered the room. My mom grabbed my hand and started to cry. She was scared to death at Raiford when they told her I had been taken to a public hospital. She said she almost fainted because she thought I had been killed. She wondered why I was mumbling. It was the medication I was taking. I didn't tell her what the doctors had told me. The truth was I was never given any pain medicine. I couldn't take it because of my brain swelling. She had cried all the way from Raiford to Lake Butler and was worried I wouldn't be alive, and she wished I had gone to college and played ball so none of this would have happened.

I said, "I know, Mom. Me too."

I asked her if she'd talked to the attorneys. She had told them what had happened and they were working on getting me transferred out of Raiford. She and the attorneys had worried something like this would happen to me before I could get my transfer.

"It's over with now, Mom. I'm not at Raiford anymore. You don't have to worry. I'm alive."

The nurse told my mom she and my stepdad would have to leave. I told my mom I loved her and I would be in the prison hospital for a few weeks. I would call as soon as I could. She asked if I would be sent back to Raiford. I said I didn't know, but if I was, I would kill myself before giving the inmates the chance to finish the job of killing me.

I was finally released from the hospital. My motor skills were improving. Sometimes I would get really dizzy and have to sit down. I sat in the captain's office, where the doctor tried to determine if I needed any more medical attention. The doctor told the captain all my motor skills were working, but I still couldn't smell or taste anything and I had dizzy spells from time to time. The captain said he was going to send me back to Raiford and let the state and Raiford decide what other facility I should be sent to.

The doctor said, "What are you thinking? Travis is lucky to be alive. They tried to kill him and the prison gang let him lie on the weight-room floor, bleeding to death. They wouldn't let other inmates tell the rec yard guard to get help. I'm going to write in my report that Travis Waters almost lost his life because he was sent to the worst state prison in Florida to work outside the fence and then had to live inside with inmates who were never getting out. Travis is classified as a minimum- to low-custody inmate. I'm sending my report directly to Tallahassee and I will tell the Department of Corrections that you, Captain, want to send Inmate Waters back into that environment where the inmates can have another chance at killing him, all because he was forced to play basketball so the prison gangs could win money off him. It almost cost him his life."

I couldn't believe what I was hearing. The captain was going to send me back to Raiford. Neither one of them knew that I'd been gang-raped nor did they know about the hell I'd gone through. Thank God the doctor was going off on the captain.

The captain looked at me and said, "How do you feel about going back to Raiford?"

I said, "If you knew the rest of the hell I went through there, you wouldn't send me back. I do know if you send me back, I'm going to buy the biggest shank I can get my hands on, and when the prison gangs try to make me play basketball for them under threat of death or rape, I will try to kill as many of those fucking queers as I can before they try to kill me again."

The captain said, "You sound angry."

The doctor said, "How do you expect him to feel? The Raiford counselors told him because he was white and had a low custody level, he shouldn't be there."

The captain said, "Don't worry, Waters, I will see to it that you will not ever be sent back there."

The captain told the doctor to send her report to Tallahassee so that, before an incident like this happened again, they would stop sending low-security inmates to Raiford to work outside the fence and then allow them to be exploited and threatened by the lifers.

The captain looked at me. "Son, you're lucky to be alive."

"Yes, I know that, Captain. Thanks for not sending me back to Raiford. I do want to go home one day."

I was put in the population at Lake Butler and waited to be transferred to another prison, hopefully not to another nut house like Raiford. I promised myself I wouldn't set foot on another basketball court again.

The inmates at Lake Butler would stare at me and ask what had happened to the side of my head because you could see where my stitches had been. My head was basically shaved, and the hair wouldn't grow in the spot that had been split open. I stayed at the military-style prison for about six weeks.

I was transferred to Columbia Correctional in Lake City, Florida. I had been hoping to get closer to Naples, but it seemed that wasn't going to happen. I stayed at the main prison and was transferred to the prison camp located next door. I couldn't have been happier. Finally I was in a minimum-security prison where I didn't have to worry about getting gang-raped or having the hell beaten out of me by a mental patient or a desperate lifer.

The prison camp had one perimeter fence with no gun towers or high-powered rifles. I was placed in a dorm with seventy inmates. Sixty-four were black, six were of different ethnicities and three were white guys. The inmates there were going home or to a work-release program in a couple years or less. I was assigned to work on a chain gang. That was what the inmates called the outside work squad. The old chain gangs had to wear leg irons and the guards carried a gun. That isn't done in today's world.

I was glad to be out in the free world and working in the public arena.

It gave me a taste of freedom and the hope that I'd be going home soon. I was still thinking, though, of the perjury charges and the North Carolina indictment. But for now I would enjoy the relative freedom.

Our job consisted of picking up trash on the sides of the roads, building playgrounds, and mowing the grass at parks in Lake City. When the clean-up crew was out on the road, people in cars would throw joints out their windows for inmates to pick up. Some people would hide beer up the road so the inmates could have a drink before going back to the prison. On occasion, our guard would bring us food from home.

Finally I was sent to a work release center in Ft. Myers, Florida, to finish out the remainder of my sentence. Unlike the other prisons that had been a six- to seven-hour drive from Naples, this place was close to home.

Chapter 25

May 30, 1997, Fort Myers, Florida: I'd been locked up in federal and state custody for a total of six years and ten days. After being locked up for that long, it was hard for me to realize I was actually walking out into the free world. I'd become so institutionalized for so long that I questioned the reality of my release. Would I walk out the front door only to be handcuffed and sent back in custody because of perjury or an indictment in North Carolina? I was worried the feds would try something again. I'd been through so much with them. They ended up winning all the time. They had beaten me at their game. That was for sure. I was a pawn in their court.

I began to reminisce about my life during the past six years. I'd met a lot of good people and made a lot of good friends along the way. On the other hand, I'd met a lot of crazy people and seen a lot of crazy shit, things I hoped to never ever see again for the rest of my life.

I heard my name called, so I walked into the staff office. The counselor there asked if I was ready for the big day.

"Yes, I am. It's been a hard, long journey for me."

She said I had no restitution or any fines from the state or federal government, but I did have three years of federal parole. After signing papers that released me from the custody of the state of Florida, my sentence was complete, and I finally became a free man.

I walked out the front door, looked up at the blue sky, and took a deep breath of fresh, free air. I told myself it was finally over. The Westcoast Kid had survived. I saw my mom and stepdad waiting to pick me up. I took a look around to make sure the feds weren't there. I didn't see them, just my mom standing there, crying. Now she too was finally free. I walked over to my parents and gave them a hug. I told my mother it was all over, and she didn't have to worry anymore.

We headed south on I-75 to Naples, and I mentioned I wanted some country food, so we stopped at Cracker Barrel to eat. I ate all I could. After eating, we arrived at my mom's house, and I went into my old bedroom. I sat there on my bed, looking at my trophies still sitting on the shelf, and I thought about all the joy I had playing sports while growing up. I saw a scrapbook of mine and opened it up. I saw letters I had received from colleges. I couldn't open them up and read them again. That would have been too hard since I had thrown that part of my life away. I would never forgive myself, especially because of what I now knew.

I lay back on my bed and cried. I looked up at the ceiling and saw the air-conditioning vent where I used to hide my drug money. I had also hidden money in my closet. That had been the beginning of my living nightmare. I started thinking about all the beatings and the hell I had gone through in prison because of my talent in sports.

My mom walked into my room. She saw me lying there, crying. She looked around and saw the scrapbook lying next to me, open. She asked if I was alright. I was. She turned and looked at me and said, "I bet you wished you had listened to me back then. You could've gone to college."

"Mom, you have no idea how much I wished I had gone to college. I'm thirty years old now. I spent most of my twenties in prison."

Adjusting to freedom was hard for me. I had friends who wanted to come and see me, but I was scared. I had trouble sleeping. I would wake up sweating from dreaming I was on the run from prison and being chased by the cops. I went as far as telling my mom she needed to take me back to work release or prison. I felt I was doing something wrong all the time. I had become so institutionalized that when I went to the mall with my mom, I had to go and sit in the car. I was scared and felt out of place. These were things I was told I would have to work on as time passed. It was not an easy adjustment.

One thing I had to trudge through was going back to my own home. One day I decided to have my mom take me out to my house. I hadn't seen the place for six years. I wanted to see what kind of shape it was in before I moved back in. I looked around from room to room, remembering all the parties and good times I used to have. I couldn't believe I still had some of my toys in the garage. I noticed some of the garbage cans I used to fill with millions of dollars after a load from the Cubans was sold. Now they sat empty. I looked over at another corner, and I noticed PVC pipes sitting there that used to serve as money and cocaine caches. I discovered one of them was missing. I wondered where it could be.

After checking everything over, I decided it was time to come back home, back to *my* home. Since I'd been gone for six years, my house needed a lot of work before I could live in it again. I had to cut everything back that was overgrown on the property, removing all the dead trees and brush. I had to pressure-clean the house. I couldn't believe how much had changed over the years. I then had to put in a new air-conditioner unit as well as a water heater, dishwasher, stove, washer, dryer, and refrigerator. All of the old appliances were rusted because they hadn't been used in all those years. I had the carpets cleaned too. I was really excited about getting back in my house and starting to live a somewhat normal life.

Friends I made in federal prison started to call me from other countries, wanting me to bring in drug loads for them. I would say to them, "I just came home and already you want me to start smuggling?"

I'd tell them I was on parole and not going to have anything to do with drugs.

Welcome home, Travis.

After getting settled in my house, I had to report to my federal parole officer. He acted as if my life didn't matter. He began to tell me I had to attend a drug treatment center there in Naples and that the feds were footing the bill for this.

I looked at him and said, "I'm not an addict. I'm a drug smuggler."

He told me I either attended these classes or be sent back to prison. Those were my options. I let him know I had a job at Naples Lumber. He was required to go out on job checks. Also my urine would be tested on a monthly basis and he could come out to my home at any time and do random urine tests as well. After all this had been explained to me, I signed his paperwork and left.

My probation required my having a steady job, so I started working at my stepdad's company, Naples Lumber. I found it had grown since I had last worked there part-time when I was in the eighth grade.

My work duties included loading up trucks for deliveries, sweeping out warehouses, and mowing ditches around the company property. I helped out wherever I was needed at the time. Some of the other employees told me they had been warned the owner's stepson would be working at the lumber yard. They were also told to watch what they said and to look busy when I was around. A few of the employees said they thought my stepdad didn't like me because my supervisor had me sweeping or mowing the ditches, doing all the bullshit work no one else wanted to do.

One afternoon my parole officer arrived at the lumber yard to have a meeting with my warehouse boss and one of the division managers. He was checking on my job performance and verifying I actually had a job there. He walked into the cabinet shop where I was working and commented he hadn't realized how big the business was—so many employees. He asked me how I was doing in my new job and if I were adjusting to working around the public and being free. I said I was doing well, and I was very glad to be free. Then he asked me if I had any second thoughts about smuggling drugs again since I was free. I looked at him. Did he really think I would tell him I was thinking about bringing in a load of coke or pot?

"What kind of stupid question is that? And you really expect me to answer it?" I said to him.

He looked at me and asked, "Was that an exciting life? I'm curious to know all about the money and the girls that I read about in your file."

"Here's an idea. Why don't you fly to Colombia and set up your own load, and that way you can find out how exciting it is for yourself."

He didn't like my answer and stormed out of the cabinet shop to his meeting with my bosses.

I was in the lounge eating lunch along with the other employees when my parole officer came to the door and asked to talk to me in private.

He looked at me and said, "You didn't tell me your stepdad owns this entire company. How did you ever get involved with drugs and why didn't you come to work for your stepdad instead?"

"It's a long story," I said.

"I understand you had basketball scholarships to play ball? What happened, Travis?"

I wondered if I had to hear about how I had thrown away my life—again! I thought I had that figured out. I just wondered how much this parole officer was going to like me now that he'd found out exactly who my stepdad was. In his eyes, I was no longer just this low life with no family. He was looking at me from a whole new perspective. I agreed I had thrown my life away for drugs and prison.

I said, "Is there anything else we have to talk about because I have to finish my lunch and get back to work. So do you need me to piss in a bottle for your?"

"That won't be necessary. I think from this point on, you and I will be getting along just fine, Travis," he replied.

"Okay. I'll see you later," I told him.

Great! Just what I needed: my parole officer wanting to be buddies with me. Before he had come to my stepdad's company and found out who my family was, he treated me as if I were some kind of low life.

Soon after my first meeting with my parole officer at work, I got a call from my stepdad. He informed me he had found out from his insurance company my license had been suspended and my identity had been stolen. When I got home, I didn't have a vehicle to drive, courtesy of the federal government. He gave me one. It was suggested that I didn't drive until we had cleared the problem up. If I were to get caught driving with a suspended license, I would be arrested and sent back to federal prison for the remainder of my parole, which happened to be three years.

I was in touch with a detective and the state's attorney and found out an old friend of mine had used my name while I was serving time in prison. Apparently he had created quite a file. He had committed crimes from 1989 to 1997. There were arrest records, a mug shot with my name and numbers under his chin, several pictures of him getting arrested for numerous things such as stolen property, drugs, violation of probation, and finally driving with a suspended license. I couldn't believe what I was hearing. I was in total shock. It was going to take at least three months to clear up this horrible mess; so much for driving anywhere on my own. I asked the state's attorney how something like this could have happened. He explained to me the local system treated me as if I were dead because I had been away, serving time. However, the booking department should have had this information. They would have to look into the problem further so this kind of mistake would never happen again.

It turned out the friend who stole my identity was wanted in Texas under my name as well. I was advised not to go there and I should be okay.

My friend was never arrested for doing this to me, and I had to become somewhat of a prisoner again for three months. It just didn't make sense to me.

Chapter 26

A year passed and I no longer worked at the lumber yard. I'd started my own lawn-maintenance company. I had previous experience in this type of work and had always wanted to do something on my own. I started to build a prosperous clientele and became really proud of achieving a goal I had set for myself when I got out of prison. I wasn't playing pro basketball, but my business represented something positive in my life.

On the Sunday evening of Labor Day weekend one of my friends, Abby, called and asked me if I wanted to go to the Naples Beach Club to have some drinks. There would be a lot of people there because it was a long weekend. At the time I didn't realize it was Labor Day weekend, so I said no thanks. I didn't really feel like going, seeing people from the past, explaining to them where I'd been for years, and answering all their questions, but after thinking about it I realized I couldn't run from the past anymore. I had to move on with my life sooner or later. I called Abby back and told him to come and pick me up.

He was right. The Beach Club was packed full of girls. I was nervous until my first drink started kicking in. Then I checked out the crowd to see if I recognized anyone. I walked by a crowd of girls and saw this girl watching me. I wondered why. I noticed she was talking with my friend Abby. So I approached them, and Abby said, "You remember Travis."

I reached out and shook Michele's hand and she shook mine and said, "That's your name! I knew it started with a T, but I would never have guessed it was Travis."

I had been out on Friday night with Abby and had briefly met Michele at another establishment, the Sports Page.

I looked at her and said, "So where are you and your friends going after here?"

I wanted to go out with her. I was glad she was there at the Beach Club. We started talking. She was Italian and reminded me a lot of my high school girlfriend, Pietra. She was the all-American girl. Michele said she had graduated from Barron Collier High School in 1984 and gone to college at the University of Nebraska.

After learning that, I wasn't about to tell her I had served time in both federal and state prisons for six years on drug smuggling charges. I didn't want to chance scaring her off as soon as I had met her. I damn sure wasn't going to tell her about the things that had happened to me in the drug business and especially in prison.

Abby and I met up with Michele and her friends at the Ridge Port Pub. We had a good time, and I saw a lot of old friends I hadn't seen in years. Some were from my high school days. They asked me a lot questions such as, "Did you move? Where did you go to college and play ball?"

"I didn't play college ball," I replied, "but I did move to Tallahassee for a short time and now I'm living back in Naples."

Michele asked, "Are you from Naples because I haven't seen you around?"

I said I had grown up there and graduated in 1985 from Lely High School.

She asked, "Where have you been lately?"

"I was in college in Tallahassee."

"How long were you in college?"

"Six years," I told her.

Michele looked at me and said, "Hum … six years in Tallahassee. I'm going to go out on a limb and guess you were in prison and I'm also going to guess it was for drugs."

Oh great, my chances with her are probably slim to none now that she's figured out where I've been.

I looked at her and said, "Yes, I was. Are you okay with knowing that I was in prison?"

I hoped she would say yes and stay with me. She looked at me and said, "Yes, I am." And the rest is history.

After three years of dating, Michele became pregnant with our first child, so she started to work for me in the office of my lawn-maintenance company. I was working on expanding my business with a landscaping division. I would jokingly say it was as close as I would ever get back into the grass business without going to prison. The business's name was West Coast Lawn Service and Landscaping. A part of me wanted to keep my name from the past, and since we lived on the West Coast of Florida, I thought it was a perfect name.

We both were so excited about Michele's pregnancy. I wanted my first child to be a boy, have my name, carry on in my footsteps and play sports. About halfway through Michele's pregnancy she had an ultrasound exam. She didn't want to know the sex of the baby, but I did. So the doctor wrote it down on a piece of paper and sealed it in an envelope and told us to do what we wanted with it. It was decided on our way home that I would go over to my mother's house and my mom would let me know what the baby's sex was. I dropped Michele off at home and headed over to my mom's house and handed the envelope to her as soon as I got there. She read it to herself first and then looked at me and said, "You got your son."

We both started to cry. My dream was finally starting to come true.

On August 10, 2001. Michele and I were at North Collier Hospital awaiting the arrival of our first-born son, Travis Jr. Michele was in quite some pain, and I felt sick to my stomach. I didn't like to see her in pain, especially when there was nothing I could do about it. Our room number was ten. The significance of the number ten was my grandmother, whom I loved very much, had unfortunately died of cancer on January 10, when I was ten years old. Now our room number was ten and our first child was being born on the 10th of August. Travis Jr. arrived around 5 p.m. that afternoon. Michele's father had filmed the whole birthing process of our son and my mother was there to experience it with us too. It was the first time she had gotten to see one of her grandchildren being born. I was really happy for her. All I really remember is when Travis Jr. was born, I had to sit on a chair. I had seen a lot, but nothing compared to seeing the birth of my own child.

Holding Travis Jr. in my arms was the happiest day of my life. I finally had my son.

Four years went by and Michele found out she was pregnant again. After a few months into her pregnancy, the doctor decided to do an ultrasound test to make sure everything was going well. During the ultrasound test, Michele discovered she was carrying twins, a boy and a girl. The ultrasound tech took pictures of each baby and gave them to her to take home. On the way home from her appointment, Michele called me right away, and I don't know how she did it, but she kept her cool and didn't let me in on what was going on. After what seemed like the longest drive home, Michele arrived and told me to sit down.

I asked, "What's wrong?"

She didn't say anything. She just handed me a photo from the ultrasound test and asked, "What do you think?"

I sat there and looked at this ultrasound photo for a while, and then it hit me. I saw twin A and twin B on the bottom of the photo. I looked at her and the photo again just to make sure I was looking at it correctly and said, "Twins? Are we having twins?"

She said, "Yes, but it gets better."

"What is it?"

Michele said, "We are having the best of both worlds. We're having a boy and a girl."

Michele was so excited, especially about having her girl. She looked at me and said her name was going to be Olivia. I was stunned, excited, and scared all at the same time. My dreams were coming true again, another boy to carry on my name and play sports along with Travis Jr.

After spreading the word to all of our family and friends we were having twins, life went very well for both of us. More time marched on, and Michele and I went see the doctor for a routine visit. He decided to have another ultrasound test done since carrying twins was considered a high risk. During the ultrasound test, the technician saw something that didn't look right. She sent the readings to the doctor, who informed us we needed to go to a facility that specialized in high-tech ultrasounds.

A few days later, I found myself, with Michele, looking at another ultrasound test of our babies. This time the doctor who was performing the ultrasound said Olivia was fine and was head down, ready to go, but our son, whom we decided to name Nicholas, was not doing so well. She explained to us his DNA was not connected like Olivia's and he had Down Syndrome so severely he would have many physical and mental complications when he was born. I couldn't believe what I was hearing. I thought I was in a nightmare all over again. Why me? Was God making me suffer for all the wrong I had done? The doctor told us we shouldn't blame each other for this tragedy; it wasn't mine or Michele's fault. She told us to look at it as if it were a bad train wreck. I just couldn't accept what I was hearing. Michele was so upset I felt sorry for her. Here we were, so excited we were expecting twins, especially a boy and a girl, and now this. No amount of money or doctors in the world could change the fact that our son had a severe birth defect and probably wouldn't survive.

Several ultrasound tests later, Nicholas's health started to decline. He hadn't responded very well to stimulation during an ultrasound exam. The next week, Michele was scheduled to see her regular doctor and start taking steroid shots. She took Travis Jr. to daycare and went to see her doctor. The maternal-fetal doctor told Michele's doctor she should have another ultrasound test.

During that test, technician turned on the machine and looked at Olivia.

"Everything is good there," she said.

She looked at Nicholas and turned the machine off immediately.

Michele looked over and said, "Now what?"

The technician turned it back on and showed her Nicholas' heart had stopped and he had died. They believed it had happened sometime during the night. Michele called me from the doctor's office to let me know what had happened and said she was going in for an emergency C-section.

This was one the worst days of my life.

When I received the call about Nicholas's death, I started to yell and cry. I punched a hole in our bedroom wall. All these emotions began to run through my head. Was I being punished by God because of my past? Was it because of the families I had probably destroyed, families I didn't even know? We had smuggled tons of drugs throughout the country. Was it payback time? Was it because of all the cocaine I had snorted and my body wasn't right? Was it Michele's fault since she was the one who had the babies in her uterus? I needed to know why my son had died.

I arrived at the labor and delivery ward and found Michele being prepared for her emergency C-Section. She was really upset. As I was watching Michele getting ready for surgery, I began to wonder if Olivia would survive and be normal. A childhood friend of mine, Jesus, his brother Jorgé, my mother, and my sister Nancy were with us for support. The nurse gave me a pair of scrubs and a mask to put on before going into the operating room with Michele. I went into the bathroom to change and all I could do was cry. Jesus walked in and saw me all upset. I didn't think I could go through with seeing Nicholas being delivered and not moving, breathing, or crying. Jesus said I had to be strong and go in there for Michele.

We were in the delivery room and I was sitting behind Michele. She was hooked up to a machine with all of these tubes transferring blood. I couldn't believe what I was looking at. The doctors delivered Olivia first, and we heard her cry. I was so happy. It was music to our ears. They brought her to us so we could see her and talk to her. It was a precious moment. Then it was time for the inevitable: the delivery of our son Nicholas. The doctors took him next, and all you could hear was the roaring of the machines being used. No crying, no nothing. I couldn't see him. It was too hard at the time. The nurses took Nicholas out of the delivery room immediately. Olivia was taken to the neonatal nursery because she was six weeks premature. Michele was moved to the recovery room, and family and friends who had come to support us, were also there. I went into the room to let them know if they wanted to, they could go and view Olivia in the nursery, or see Nicholas if they so chose.

After some time, the nurse asked me if I wanted to go and see Olivia. I couldn't at that moment. After everything that had happened, I was afraid of getting too close to her. I wasn't sure if she was going to survive. I wanted to make sure she would be healthy and normal. I wanted every test known to man to be run on her. The doctor gave me a bewildered look and said, "Okay, we will start running tests on her as soon as possible."

After finally settling into our room at the hospital, the nurse came in to check on Michele and asked us if we were ready to see Nicholas. Michele wasn't ready, but I was. I didn't tell her that. I just agreed to see Nicholas whenever Michele was ready. The nurse talked to us for some time and was somewhat persistent about us viewing Nicholas. Michele finally agreed, so she brought him into the room. I knew I had to see Nicholas before he went forever. Believe me when I say I have seen a lot of crazy shit in my life, but I had never seen a dead baby before, especially one that was mine.

The hospital had Nicholas dressed in a blue outfit. I held him first. He had blonde hair and looked like Travis Jr. and me. I put him up to my face and began to cry. I couldn't comprehend I was actually holding my son, my dead son. I gave him a kiss on the cheek and handed him over to Michele. She cradled him in her arms and began to kiss him and tell him how much she had loved him. While Michele was holding Nicholas, I saw some blood and fluid dripping out of his nose. I got excited and hoped for a brief moment he might be alive. I took a tissue and gently wiped Nicholas's nose and told him I loved him with all my heart, and I was so sorry he hadn't lived. I also let him know it wasn't his fault; it was mine. I told him about all the fun we would have had with Travis Jr.

The nurse returned so she could take Nicholas back to the nursery. I lay on my pull-out bed, put my face in the pillow, and began sobbing. I started to blame myself for Nicholas's dead. It was a rough night, but somehow we got through it.

After a couple days went by, the doctor let us know Olivia was perfect and would live a healthy, normal life. Michele and I were both very happy to hear the news. I started to believe there was a God out there. All I wanted to do was hold my new baby girl for the first time. Olivia was beautiful and tiny. I really believed Nicholas survived as long as he did so his sister Olivia could be born without any complications. I told Olivia we needed to thank him for that.

Travis Jr. came to visit us while we were in the hospital. As we were walking to the nursery, Travis Jr. turned to me and said, "Daddy, I thought we were having twins. I was supposed to have a brother and a sister. What happened?"

I told him God had made a mistake and given us a baby girl, his sister Olivia. "Let's be thankful we have her and that she is healthy." I showed him his new baby sister through the window of the nursery.

A lot of friends and family let me know Nicholas didn't die because of my past, but I still thought most of it was because of my past, and that was something that I'd have to deal with. I came to realize, I couldn't change the past, no matter how hard I tried.

In honor of our son Nicholas, we had a children's book drive during the months of February and March. It was called Nicholas's Angels. We collected books, new and used, for ages 0 months to 18 years. They were donated to the playroom at the hospital for others to enjoy. The donation was made in our son's name. This was our way of keeping Nicholas's spirit alive when we celebrated our daughter Olivia's birthday.

Chapter 27

Ever since Travis Jr. had been born, I'd been waiting for him to reach the age when he could attend the summer basketball camp that my former high school coach conducted. We went to the complex center where the basketball camp was being held, and as I filled out the paperwork for Travis Jr. to attend the camp, I wondered if Coach Stewart would recognize the name on the signup sheet.

On the first day of camp, Travis Jr. and I walked on the sidewalk leading up to the complex where the gym was located. I couldn't wait for him to meet my former high school basketball coach, nor could I wait to see the coach myself. I considered this man my mentor. Some of my best times as a kid were spent with him. Suddenly I heard someone behind me yell out my name. I knew that voice. It sounded like the voice I used to hear during basketball practices and games. It was tattooed on my brain. To this day I can still hear it in my dreams. I stopped and turned around. As I scanned the sidewalk, there, smiling from ear to ear was my former coach, Don Stewart. I smiled back and said I was very glad to see him after all those years. We walked into the gym together, and Coach Stewart began to tell me about other former and current players he had coached, and he told me that I still held the Lely rebound record. I couldn't believe it.

I looked at him and said, "Are you serious? I still hold the rebound record after all these years?"

He said, "Yes, you do."

I still couldn't believe it, especially with all the great teams he'd had after I had been long out of high school. I was in complete awe. I looked up to Coach Stewart, so much that sometimes I couldn't talk to him.

I had done the same thing when I'd seen my hero, Larry Bird, at the Golden Gate Ace hardware store.

In the store I saw this guy at the checkout counter. He was tall and when he turned to the side, I thought he looked like Larry Bird, but I didn't believe it could be him. Then the girl behind the counter told the other cashier that he was Larry Bird. He walked right past me out the exit doors, and I turned around and followed him out the door. I couldn't believe it was him. I wanted to cry. I followed him out into the parking lot and was in shock. I noticed the way he walked and the big shoes he had on. I was so petrified that I couldn't talk to him. He was parked right beside my truck. He drove a gold, 250 Ford with an extended cab. He looked at me and probably wondered if I were going to ask him for his autograph. I still couldn't talk. I pretended to look in my truck tool box, and I stared at him at the same time. He pulled out of the parking space and drove away with me staring at his truck the whole time. I had to get in my truck and turn the air conditioning on. My legs were getting weak. I had idolized Larry Bird when I was growing up. I wanted to play just like him.

It had been a very long time since I'd seen my old coach. After speaking with him, I began to wonder what he thought about me going down the wrong road and serving time in prison. I bet he also wanted to know why I hadn't gone to college instead. For twenty-five years I believed that I had let him down. I'd always looked up to my stepdad and Coach Stewart as the most positive role models I'd ever had in my life. And I went to prison instead of completing my dream of playing basketball. I would never forgive myself for letting down so many people who believed in me, especially my mother, who had driven me to every one of my practices and attended every game that I ever played.

I was on Coach Stewart's first basketball team at Lely when he moved from Michigan to Naples, Florida. I remember the first day I met him. I was so excited. He made me believe in myself. I couldn't wait for school to be out that day so I could go home and tell my mom about our new coach. In prison I would keep up with what Coach had accomplished over the years through the newspaper, and I learned that he had become legendary. I had known he was going to be special. I would also watch Coach's son Scott play on TV when he played point guard for the Florida Gators. He went to the Final Four in 1994 with the Gators. I remember watching that game in prison. I was so proud of Scott. He was the best point guard to ever come out of Collier County. Scott also held records at Lely. He was the basketball team's little brother.

I'd often wondered if my record of rebounds in a single game would hold when I left Lely. I put up twenty-three rebounds against Moore Haven high school in a tournament. We didn't have a three-point line back then in high school. I thought the twenty-three-rebound record would stand, but I broke my own record with a twenty-seven-rebound game in the same year, playing against Immokalee High School. For twenty-five years I wondered if I still held the rebound record. Coach Stewart had trained number-one-ranked teams in the state of Florida. I thought for sure my twenty-seven-rebound record would fall.

Coach Stewart told me that a newspaper article was going to be written about him.

I asked, "What's the article going to be about?"

Coach Stewart said, "It's going to be about our first year together and having Travis Jr. attend my camp for the first time."

I'd waited twenty-five years to tell my former coach and everyone in Naples just how I felt about him, and now I finally had the chance to do that. I owed a lot to Coach Stewart, especially for teaching me the game of basketball. He didn't know it, but he saved my ass a lot in state prison. I wouldn't have held the rebound record in his program at Lely if it hadn't been for him.

You can have all the God-given talent in the world, but if your coach doesn't make you believe in yourself and believe that you can do anything, if he doesn't help bring out the best in you, your talent will not show to its full potential. That is what Coach Stewart did for me.

"Lely's Stewart Brought Full Circle at Camp." This headline appeared on the front page of the sports section in the Sunday edition of the *Naples Daily News*, courtesy of writer Adam Fisher. The following quotes are from the article.

"Stewart called Waters 'one of the school's first great players. Waters still owns the Trojan's record for the most rebounds in a game—twenty-seven in a game against Immokalee.'"

Stewart still credited Waters with helping shape who the Trojans were a quarter-century later. "When I first got here, he was one of the key kids; we were able to get the program up and running."

"Waters going head-to-head with another South Florida prep that went on to fame and fortune in two other sports. Deion Sanders, the eight-times, NFL, pro bowler and his North Fort Myers High team got the best of Lely that night, but Waters matched the twenty-six points put up by the future two-sport star."

"Out of all the coaches I ever had—baseball, football, basketball—he was the best ever I had," Waters said. "He cares about the community and he cares about the kids a lot. That's who he is.

After all these years my questions were finally answered. While I was reading the article, I began to cry because I was happy. I read the article on several occasions so the words, "the school's first great player," would sink in. Reading that comment made about me by the legendary coach, Don Stewart, made me realize just how much talent I had actually thrown away.

Every award I have ever won—MVPs, Junior Olympics, McDonald's Player of the Week, All-Star Games, All-Tournament Teams, my rebound record, scholarships, even being in the same sentence with Deion Sanders—doesn't compare to having my former coach calling me the "school's first great player." It is the greatest compliment any athlete could ever want to hear from a coach after their career is over or nearing the end.

I began thinking about how much bigger, faster, and stronger I had become in prison and what could've been. If I had just listened to my mother.

It's something that has bothered me my whole life. No matter how hard I've tried to put it behind me and accept I made a huge mistake, it never goes away. I wish it would, though. Every time I see Deion on TV, or when I watch my favorite college team or pro team, I am reminded. I don't try anymore to put it behind me because that doesn't work.

Chapter 28

After much contemplation about what Coach had said about me, I thought of the perfect opportunity to finally give something back to him. I decided to have a basketball signed by his first basketball team at Lely High School, the 1983 team. I also decided to have a second basketball signed by the coaches and the best players we had played against at high schools in Naples and Fort Myers in the 1983 season. I had to track down players and coaches. What former players I could find in Naples would lead me to other players who had moved away from our hometown. They were located around the United States. I used the phone book and called directory assistance so many times I began to think that I had become a private investigator.

I worked on getting players to sign the ball and realized the player I worried most about was Deion "Prime Time" Sanders. I knew he lived in Crawford, Texas, worked for the NFL network as a sports analyst, and had a reality show on TV. I started my quest to reach Deion. My first stop was the NFL network. I was unsuccessful. I was sure the network got a lot of calls from fans of Deion. I needed to find a way. I knew Deion's former high school basketball coach, Levon Simms. He had coached at North

Fort Myers, so when I met him in Ft. Myers to get his signature for the ball, I had Coach Simms sign the North/South Senior All-Star Game program and my original all-star shirt. Coach Simms coached the North squad. Coach Stewart coached the South squad only after his second year of coaching.

As I continued getting signatures, I had all the players and coaches sign both basketballs and I had a picture taken of them holding the ball for a scrapbook that I was putting together for Coach Stewart. I had to go to Fort Myers to find one player and get his signature. He had played for the legendary Coach Tremont at Cypress Lake. His name was Riley. I told him I was having trouble getting through to Deion. He advised me to give Deion's mom a call. She could get through to him. So Riley gave me her phone number, and I contacted Deion's mom and explained to her who I was and what I was doing for Coach Stewart. She gave all of Deion's information to me and said she would call Deion to let him know that several items were being sent to him to be signed. If it weren't for Deion's mom, I would never have been able get his signature. I owe her a lot of gratitude for helping me out.

After the ball came back from Deion, it began to make its way around the state of Florida. Then it began its journey through the United States. This ball went to Texas, New York, Michigan, Georgia, and Minnesota. Knowing that Deion's signature was on the ball and the fact that it was going out of state gave me many sleepless nights. I knew one thing: this basketball I was giving Coach Stewart held the record for the most miles traveled. The best part of this project for me was getting a chance to catch up with the players, coaches, and former teammates I hadn't seen since 1984. I always wondered how all of these guys were doing in their lives and what they looked like after all those years.

I got a call from Scott Stewart telling me his dad wanted to let me know he was hanging up his whistle after twenty-six years of coaching the Lely Trojans basketball team. Scott wanted me to know before he made a public statement announcing his retirement. He wanted to spend more time with his family. I didn't know how he would be able to handle stepping down from something he loved so much. The gym and basketball was his second life and home. I received a call from Adam Fisher from the *Naples Daily News*. He was doing one of many retirement stories on Coach Stewart and asked me what I thought about Coach's retirement, and what he'd done for me as a player and Collier County. On March 23, the *Naples Daily News* front-page headline read: "Lely's Don Stewart Retires after 26 Years."

I quote what I said in Adam Fisher's article about Coach Stewart: "I knew he was going to be special. It's a sad day for all the kids in Collier County who ever got to play under him and for those who will never get to be on the same court with him. He brought the best out of me. They should put a statue of him in front of the school for what he's done for thousands of kids."

"For putting Lely and Naples on the basketball map throughout the state of Florida I hope the school names the gym after Coach Stewart for all he's done for basketball in the area."

I was glad to have Scott and his older brother, Stacey, signed the basketball I was giving to Coach. I learned from Scott that his dad was going to do his last coaching gig at the student/faculty game. This was the last game of the school year and it was a tradition at Lely High School. He thought that it would be a perfect time to present his dad with the first team's ball. Scott was also going to present his dad with his last team's ball, which had the current players' signatures on it. As a surprise for Coach, I took my first MVP trophy from the 1983–84 season and had two new inscriptions added to it. The first inscription read, "Coach Don Stewart, Most Valuable Player of All Time, 1983 through 2009." The second inscription read: "Working Hard to Be Champions."

Along with the first team's ball, I presented a trophy to Coach. This was the very first MVP trophy that he had handed out his first year of coaching. I had looked at the trophy on my shelf all these years, and I thought that this gesture would show him how much I cared about what he'd done for me. It was a great moment for both of us.

Scott and I decided to throw a retirement party in honor of his dad. We wanted to celebrate his career with players and coaches, past and present. I got the last of the signatures of the players and coaches on the basketball and finished the final touches to the scrapbook that I planned to surprise Coach with.

I'd waited twenty-six years to do something special for Coach. He had believed in me and I wanted to let him know that I knew I had let him down. The party was perfect. I presented the ball and the scrapbook to Coach Stewart. He was completely surprised by the gifts. He sat in total awe looking through the scrapbook, reliving those memories. It was very touching. Seven members from our first team showed up, and one of coach's special guests was the legendary Coach Elmer Tremont, who had coached Cypress Lake High School.

Out of all the coaches who signed the ball, Coach Tremont has coached the longest—fifty-four years. The respect that these coaches showed for my former coach blew me away. I had the coaches tell me what they thought about Coach Stewart, and I included their quote in the scrapbook under their picture.

The following are two of these quotes:

"Coach Stewart is the best coach to ever come out of Collier County no one has done it better. He put Naples and Lely on the basketball map" (Elmer Tremont).

"Coach Stewart made me a better coach. I knew if I could compete with Lely I would have a good season" (Deion Sanders's North Fort Myers high school coach, Levon Simms).

Getting to meet all the former players was pretty cool. Coach looked as if he were enjoying himself. He spoke about basketball, his career, and life.

I left the party with a lot of emotions running through my head, hoping Coach would remember for the rest of his life what I had done. All of us who stepped on a court with him had the lasting impression that no matter what road we might have traveled down after t leaving high school, we all still loved him. To a lot of us he was our second father. I hoped that when he was sitting in his rocking chair thinking about his life and what he'd accomplished, he would realize we felt that way about him and would understood the impact he had on young men's lives. I hoped he would hold his head high because he had made a huge difference in this world to thousands and thousands of kids.

I couldn't sleep that night, knowing that newspaper article was coming out in the morning, and I wondered what everyone would think of me. Would I lose a lot of old friends because of it? What would they all think about the school's first great player after all that would be said and written about me? Whatever the outcome, I would deal with it as I'd done with everything else I had faced in life. I knew that on Sunday morning, when that article about what I had gone through and how I had thrown away my dream for drugs was going to be in the paper, everyone would know, and I didn't have to run and hide from it anymore. I could finally move on with my life.

As I stared at the morning paper, the headlines read: "I was out of control. Sometimes I'd look in the mirror and I didn't know what was happening to me. I threw everything away, threw all my dreams away for that" (Adam Fisher, *Naples Daily News*). Those words ran across the top of the page. I couldn't believe that I was actually reading this and it was about me. Under that quote, was a picture of me holding one of the signed basketballs I had given to Coach Stewart. The rest of the article was my life story. The article also included a picture of me playing against Deion in high school.

As promised, I called Deion's mother. She'd wanted a copy of the article, and I wanted to let her know that I had sent a copy to her and Deion. A few days later, she called to tell me she thought it was one of the most beautiful stories she'd ever read. She said she had chills reading it and knew how my mother had felt when she tried to keep me from going down the wrong road. She knew all about that. She told me I wasn't the only one going down the wrong road, and my story could make a difference in other kids' lives.

When I talked to Deion's mom about my article, she said he was coming to Naples for a football tournament. She invited me, Michele, and Travis Jr. to go and meet him. He coached a youth football team, Truth Select, in Texas, and they were coming to Naples to play the Naples Gators at Fleishman Park in August. Deion's mom hadn't seen me since I had been on the court playing against Deion many years earlier. I was nervous about meeting Deion again. When I saw him walking around, with people following him and wanting his autograph, and when I saw what he had become in person, it blew me away. I knew firsthand what a superstar athlete he was. I hadn't seen him personally since we had walked off the court in the Senior All-Star Game in 1985 at Edison Community College in Fort Myers.

I had him sign the June article about my life. I thought his signature was appropriate for that article.

I couldn't really talk to him. I guess I thought about everything I'd been through in prison, and when I was finally face-to-face with him, I froze up as I had with Larry Bird. I told Deion's mom I had frozen, and she laughed and reminded me that he was "just like you and me." At the end of the day's events, I thanked her for inviting me and for everything that she had done.

It truly was a memorable day for me and my family.

Chapter 29

As I wrote this book, I began reliving some of the events in my life. Sometimes I'd have to stop writing temporarily. I know I deserved what I got, but I never imagined I would experience the things that I went through. Even though I'm free, I have nightmares of the past. They never stop. My goal today is to keep kids from throwing their lives away, and with the help of this book, I hope they will fully understand in detail what prison is all about. Maybe they will listen to their parents and not make the mistake of thinking their moneyed friends, girls, and fancy cars are worth throwing away their dreams for. Then I'll know I've done something positive with my life. I hope this book gives me the opportunity to speak to kids about wrong choices in life. I don't want anyone, regardless of race, to go through what I did. There are no guarantees in life. All I can do is try to let kids know the dangers of drugs and what they lead to.

In conclusion, after twenty-six years of dreaming about it, I've finally been given the chance to coach youth basketball. I coach the basketball team of my son, Travis Jr., the UCLA Bruins, and the North Carolina Tar Heels. I've always tried to imagine playing for them, but will settle for coaching eight- to nine-year-olds under the same names. So far, one of many dreams that have come true for me is giving back to my community by sponsoring community teams. This is an experience that I will treasure forever.